DOING
BUSINESS
ON
THE
INTERNET

How the

Electronic Highway

is Transforming

American

Companies

DOING
BUSINESS
ON
THE
INTERNET

How the
Electronic Highway
is Transforming
American
Companies

MARY J. CRONIN

 VAN NOSTRAND REINHOLD
_____ New York

Library of Congress Catalog Card Number 93-37806
ISBN 0-442-01770-7

I(T)P Van Nostrand Reinhold is an International Thomson Publishing Company. ITP
logo is a trademark under license.

Printed in the United States of America.

Van Nostrand Reinhold   International Thomson Publishing Germany
115 Fifth Avenue   Königswinterer Str. 418
New York, New York 10003   53227 Bonn
                                             Germany
International Thomson Publishing
Berkshire House, 168-173   International Thomson Publishing Asia
High Holborn   221 Henderson Building #05-10
London WC1V 7AA   Singapore 0315
England
                                             International Thomson Publishing Japan
Thomas Nelson Australia   Kyowa Building, 3F
102 Dodds Street   2-2-1 Hirakawacho
South Melbourne 3205   Chiyoda-Ku, Tokyo 102
Victoria, Australia   Japan

Nelson Canada
1120 Birchmount Road
Scarborough, Ontario
M1K 5G4, Canada

ARCFF 16 15 14 13 12 11 10 9 8 7 6 5

Library of Congress Cataloging-in-Publication Data

Cronin, Mary J.
    Doing business on the Internet : how the electronic highway is
transforming American companies / Mary J. Cronin.
        p.   cm.
    Includes bibliographical references and index.
    ISBN 0-442-01770-7
    1. Business enterprises—United States—Communication systems.
    2. Internet (Computer network) 3. Information networks.
    4. Communication, International.   I. Title.
HD30.335.C76   1993
650′.0285467—dc20   93-37806
                                                        CIP

To Jim, Rebecca, and Johanna

Contents

Preface

The impetus for this book came from teaching a course on International Information Management in the Carroll School of Management at Boston College. Introducing business graduate students to the importance of global networking, and specifically the Internet, I found a lot of material explaining how to use the network at a "hands-on" level, but very little discussion of its strategic value for business. A research leave in 1993 provided the time to investigate in some depth how and why different types of companies use the Internet, and what impact the global network has on corporate information management.

Starting with a sample of a hundred corporate Internet users, drawn from a cross-section of large, medium, and small American companies, I developed an Internet use survey form. After gathering preliminary information on this sample with the help of a number of Internet service providers, sixty-five companies were selected for follow-up visits and interviews. Contact people in each company provided information on the motivation for connecting to the Internet, the type and level of network use throughout the organization, problems and desired enhancements, training programs, evaluation mechanisms, and future plans. Information from respondents was organized into several major categories of use: communications and current awareness, marketing and information distribution, research and development, sales and product distribution, and customer and product support services.

In the course of this research, it became clear that despite an impressive array of Internet business applications in many types of companies, a large number of employees and managers were not familiar with the network and its potential as a business resource. The number of commercial Internet connections continued to rise, and it seemed there was a need for a non-technical, strategic consideration of the Internet from a management perspective. I undertook *Doing Business on the Internet* to help to fill that need.

This work owes a great deal to the incredible vitality and intellectual generosity of the Internet community—where busy people really do take time to answer their e-mail, discuss issues, and share their insights with information seekers. I deeply appreciate all the time and information provided by the hundreds of people I contacted during the course of this project. I especially want to thank the respondents at the companies I surveyed about Internet applications; their insights and experiences form the book's core. In many cases they spent significant amounts of time providing, reviewing, and updating information about the use of the Internet in their organizations. While every effort has been made to verify their observations and quotes, it should be noted that the interpretations and any mistakes are my responsibility. I hope they enjoy the final product as much as I enjoyed the process of learning from them.

The assistance of Internet service providers around the country was invaluable in selecting companies and establishing contacts. Sincere thanks to John Rugo and John Curran of NEARnet, Paul Baer of BARRNet, John Hankins of CICnet, Robert Collet of Sprint, Dennis Fazio of MRnet, Ed Vielmetti of MSEN, Jim Luckett of NYSERnet, and Thomas Bajzek of PREPnet for their early help and advice. I am also indebted to Barry Shein and Mary Reindieu of Software Tool and Die, Susan Calcari at the InterNIC, Daniel Dern at *Internet World* and Bill Washburn at CIX for enlightening me on various aspects of the Internet community.

Without outstanding institutional support, many books would never see the light of day—and mine is certainly among them. My appreciation goes first to J. Donald Monan, S.J., president of Boston College, and Academic Vice President William B. Neenan, S.J., for their support in all things administrative and in particular for their approval of my research leave. I am also tremendously grateful to everyone at the Boston College Libraries for their help and interest in my project, and especially to Tyrone Cannon for taking over during my sabbatical. Special thanks to Susan Bellers, the best research assistant in cyberspace or anywhere else, to Barbara Thornton, for her constant support, and to Rebecca Cronin for her database searching help.

There are no words that measure up to the thanks due to my family. Jim Cronin's scholarly achievements have been an inspiration, and his unfailing willingness to discuss, critique, and simply listen have been a source of energy and insight throughout this project. Rebecca and Johanna have contributed understanding and enthusiasm through long stretches of research and writing. I salute them.

CHAPTER *1*

The World of
Networked
Information

> *Call it the first great business showdown of the 21st
> century. The giants of American communications are
> locked in a struggle to build and control a vast web of
> electronic networks. These so-called information
> highways will be of glass fiber and will deliver an
> abundance of services to offices and houses—video
> images, phone calls, helpful data in many guises. They
> promise to change the way people work and play.*
> —**Andrew Kupfer,** Fortune

Networks have already changed the way
America communicates. Each day, millions of transactions zip
across tens of thousands of high-speed connections among
computers spread all over the world. It takes only seconds to
transmit hundreds of pages across the United States. Requests
reach England, Japan, or Australia with a flicker of the computer
screen and answers arrive well before a telephone call or fax
transmission could be completed. Software stored on a mainframe in California can be downloaded instantly to a desktop
in New York using a few simple commands. Researchers from
universities and corporate development labs who have never met

face to face collaborate on-line to develop and test a new product, saving months or even years in the process.

For the millions of individuals already connected to global networks, traditional limitations of time and distance no longer apply. The computer in Sweden or Hong Kong is as close as the office next door. Messages can be sent to thousands of interested readers simultaneously with one keystroke. Network users today answer customer questions, keep abreast of rapidly changing technology, debate the merits of new products, debug software programs, search and exchange giant data files without ever leaving their workstations.

These networkers will testify that the information revolution, long awaited and much debated, is actually well underway. Popular attention is just catching up, as futuristic predictions about interactive television systems merging with video telephones and full-service home computers connected to the world are rapidly turning into demonstration projects around the country. Feature stories from *Time* to the Tallahassee Free-Net highlight the potential of a new "information highway" connecting homes and offices, offering health care, education, and recreation on demand (Elmer-Dewitt 1993). Meanwhile, the flow of information over existing networks continues to circle the globe every minute and every hour, in quantities that would have sounded like science fiction a few years ago.

The ultimate shape and ownership of the future information super highway is still hotly contested, with cable and telecommunications companies jockeying for ascendancy in the race to supply individual homes with connections capable of handling the full spectrum of products and services envisioned. But the terms of the discussion have already shifted from whether and why consumers need high-speed networks to when and how they will get them. The proliferation of announcements of pilot and demonstration projects that involve installing interactive networks in numerous communities over the next two years make a new era of universal connectivity seem virtually around the corner.

The federal government, which earlier played a key role in the development of high-speed networking for research and defense, has made the information highway a feature of its economic and technology planning. Only three months after taking office, President Clinton announced a plan to stimulate development of an advanced electronic infrastructure through a combination of government and private efforts. While federal dollars will be directed primarily toward promoting a National Research and Education Network (NREN) program, an infusion of government funding for high-speed networking will have a major impact on business as well. Clinton's trip to Silicon Valley in February 1993, highlighted by the announcement of a new federal technology policy, reaffirmed the government's interest in partnerships with high-technology companies to improve American competitiveness (Clinton and Gore 1993).

As proposals for a National Information Infrastructure (NII) wend their way through Congress, the prospect of constructing a high-performance electronic highway has attracted the attention of corporate executives and policymakers. In a rare show of unanimity, telecommunications executives issued a statement in the spring of 1993 supporting the Clinton-Gore technology initiative while emphasizing the advantages of private development of the "production section" of the information superhighway (Weiss et al. 1993). But the response of CEOs in other industries is far from uniform. Although a cluster of high-tech executives joined John Scully of Apple in expressing strong support for the Clinton plan, other Silicon Valley CEO's are lobbying hard against any federal funding of the new infrastructure. They point to the many privately funded projects already underway, and stress the importance of open competition to ensure broad business participation in developing the best technology (Rogers 1993). The particular balance of government and private funding for the information highway is likely to be debated for some time (Cook 1992); nevertheless, the consensus seems almost universal that network connections to the home and office will soon transform American life and work.

ENTER THE INTERNET

In the meantime, millions of people will not wait for the superhighway of the future. They have business to do and messages to send right now. Around the world, computer networks have emerged to serve today's communication needs. Sometimes described collectively as the Matrix (Quarterman 1990), these networks interconnect in ways that are largely invisible to the individual user to transmit electronic traffic to the most remote corners of the globe. Dominating the world of high-speed networking, defining it in terms of sheer size and reach, is the largest, best-known, most-used network of all—the Internet.

The Internet today is the premier network of networks, characterized by an incredible diversity of users and applications combined with an even more dazzling rate of growth. Although it cannot be measured precisely, estimates of its size in mid-1993 included more than 1.5 million host computers attached to more than thirteen thousand separate networks linking more than a hundred countries (Styx 1993). Traffic on the Internet gets heavier and more diverse with each new connection. The number of transactions on the National Science Foundation segment of the network has increased at the rate of approximately 10 percent each month for the past three years (Catlett 1993). If this overall growth rate continues, some experts predict the Internet will connect over a hundred million users in the foreseeable future (Cerf 1993). The impact of such a super-communication resource will be enormous. As Tony Rutkowski, vice president of the Internet Society and director of technology assessment for Sprint International, observes in a message posted to an Internet discussion group, "It [the Internet] not only constitutes a national information infrastructure on a par with the telephone and broadcast systems, but a global information infrastructure as well. There is nothing quite like it in human communications history"! (1993)

The Internet and its predecessors served splendidly but rather inconspicuously as federally funded research networks for almost two decades before catching the attention of the general public and the business community. A high-speed network "backbone" connecting research universities and supercomputer centers around the United States is still dedicated to supporting advanced research. With the opening of nongovernment sections of the network to commercial traffic in the early 1990s and a proliferation of connection options ranging from individual access at a low monthly cost to full-feature, privacy-enhanced connections for corporations, the Internet has burst into public view. Internet references may be spotted in *New Yorker* cartoons, daily newspapers, and radio talk shows, as well as on the front page of the *Wall Street Journal.* The White House accepts e-mail over the Internet (the address is: PRESIDENT@WHITEHOUSE.GOV) and so do newspaper editors, travel agents, real estate companies, and millions of others who want to improve their connections to the world at large.

The connectivity and resources offered by the Internet represent an unprecedented opportunity for American business. Even the smallest company can use the network to exchange data with customers or suppliers on the other side of the world. Communication with development partners can flow over standard, widely implemented network protocols. International, federal, and statistical resources previously available only to firms with their own information centers can be accessed easily on the network. New, fee-based information services and electronic publications designed to add value to Internet connections have become a growth industry in themselves.

Commercial connections are the fastest growing component of the Internet today, as more and more companies move to establish closer links with customers, business partners, vendors and information resources via the network (Gerber 1993). Not only has the rate of growth for commercial Internet connections exceeded academic and research growth for the first time, but the largest absolute number of Internet users is beginning to come from outside higher education. Researchers and scientists, whose work provided the original impetus for the Internet, now comprise only about one third of its users. This shift is bringing about a massive change in the culture of the network and the needs of its users (Anderson 1993).

So far, the external characteristics of the Internet have captured the lion's share of attention. Its rapid spread into companies and organizations around the world, the exponential growth of the traffic it carries, and the overflowing reservoirs of its information and data resources have been noted frequently in the past few years (Churbuck 1993, Levin 1993, Markoff 1993, Sproull and Kiesler 1991). There is notably less press coverage of what happens inside an organization once the Internet connection is made. What network applications are the most valuable for business? How does the Internet contribute to a company's information management strategy? What is the impact of global connectivity for companies of different sizes? These and other questions have just begun to figure in publications about the Internet.

CONNECTED TO THE FUTURE

Managers seeking the answers need to view the Internet in the context of other critical forces affecting the future of American business. We have entered a period where the old formulas for corporate success are no longer viable, and new solutions seem to have an ever-decreasing shelf life. Even the most advanced technology cannot offer a competitive advantage for very long these days without skillful and forward-looking management. An Internet connection is not an instant solution to the many challenges of the 1990s, but it can provide crucial benefits for any company interested in improving its communication capabilities (Maloff 1992). Even more important, it offers a head start in the race to integrate high-speed networks into all aspects of business.

The defining trend of the 1990s, from corporate board rooms to consumer playrooms, is connecting everyone and everything to everyone and everything else. Interactive television, cellular phones, modems, faxes, personal digital assistants—if it connects, it seems to be in demand. Convinced that this hunger for connectivity will continue, telecommunications and cable companies are investing billions to bring enhanced interactive communications to the American household. All types of businesses are installing local area and wide area networks to connect employees at different locations and to facilitate the exchange of electronic information with vendors and customers. Many of these enterprise networks, however, do not share the standards that allow the global Internet to transmit messages and data across international and organizational borders.

Companies already linked to the Internet receive the advantages of high-speed telecommunications and continuously evolving technology while learning invaluable lessons about the management of networked organizations. There are many lessons to be learned. We are just beginning to understand the impact of networked communication on our daily lives and our way of doing business. A networked society operates on different standards of speed and access to information. As more individuals and organizations connect to international networks, they are coming to expect an enhanced level of performance from service and information providers. A customer who is used to instant response time around the globe is no longer willing to wait days or even hours for a query to be acknowledged. Tomorrow becomes too late to find the answer or deliver the product: if one company cannot meet these expectations, a competitor with a network connection will be happy to oblige.

Paul Saffo, a Fellow at the Institute for the Future in Menlo Park, predicts the Internet and other networks will totally redefine today's corporation within a few decades. Internally, Saffo observes, the traditional corporate hierarchy will have to evolve into a more flexible organization that emphasizes teamwork, collaboration with business partners, and distributed decision-making. This in turn will require more active participation by technically sophisticated, highly motivated employees at all levels of the organization (Wylie 1993).

The organizational changes spurred by technology are converging with a transformation in the geographic boundaries of business. The emergence of a global economy means that developments in Asia and South America are just as important as those in Washington, D.C. Customers half way around the world may constitute the next big growth opportunity for any business. Whether the customer lives in Australia, Brazil, or China, the company needs to find a way to be there too. But the extensive marketing, sales, and customer support networks of multinational corporations are beyond the reach of most businesses eager to expand to a global marketplace. Connecting to the Internet creates an international presence for even the smallest company, allowing communication, data exchange, and support services to flow electronically at no incremental cost. Large corporations find that an Internet connection compares very favorably in cost and performance to dedicated leased lines for long-distance customer support or communicating with a small branch office on the other side of the world. In the continuing search for competitive advantage, the international capabilities offered by an Internet connection have become a vital tool.

Along with globalization, businesses face the challenge of keeping up with the rapid pace of technological change. With a premium on working smarter, innovating faster, and reaching farther than the competition, corporate investment in technology is being scrutinized more closely than ever to ensure benefits commensurate with costs. Every company relies on an array of technology to conduct its operations effectively. Software programs are needed for word processing, accounting, personnel management, inventory control, networking, computer management, communications, and graphics—and they will seldom integrate seamlessly. Whatever their business, companies must deal with an eclectic mix of hardware and software technologies that are upgraded or replaced frequently, and often need minor "tweaking" to perform at optimal levels. This combination of diverse systems and rapid-fire changes is difficult to manage. One systems manager at a medium-size high-tech firm acknowledged, "We just aren't big enough to have someone dedicated to keeping track of every piece of hardware and software. We have to get outside help to solve certain kinds of problems." The Internet, he concluded, "provides us with a real safety net."

It is impossible for most companies to have in-house experts for all the automated systems in place. Through the Internet, people with answers are easy to locate. Someone in another company using the same system may have the perfect solution to a vexing problem. Even better, the product support and engineering experts at the vendor are frequently Internet users who can send an answer directly through the network. Popular hardware and software platforms have generated their own Internet discussion groups where problems, bugs, and new releases are diagnosed and discussed in great detail. Often, lists of frequently asked questions and answers, covering the most common types of problems, are compiled and made available for everyone to consult. At the same time, attention to the needs of the customer and the quality of all aspects of customer interaction is recognized as an important contributor to corporate success. The Internet can also help in forging closer ties to customers. "Put the customer first," is the message at the heart of many fashionable management theories, but employees who are already coping with substantial demands in their daily work need motivation and resources to keep focused on customer satisfaction. One of the most effective motivators is direct contact with customers. When employees work more closely with the people who purchase their company's products and services, they work harder to provide excellent service in the first place. If something does go wrong, they take more responsibility for solving the problem. The Internet's many discussion and user groups provide an unparalleled opportunity to familiarize employees with the needs of customers on a regular basis, and to give them customer feedback about how products are received.

The atmosphere of information sharing and consultation fostered by Internet access also encourages employees to seek answers on their own. So many resources are available to solve problems, even relatively small ones, that there is less excuse for letting things go or passing them along to someone else. Most people find it gratifying to receive attention and positive reinforcement for sharing their expertise, so questions posted on Internet discussion groups typically attract multiple responses. The network establishes a new peer group that exists solely to share information and solve problems—a "virtual team" that can be a powerful demonstration of cooperative problem-solving. Seeing the world from the customer's point of view and learning to take individual responsibility for resolving problems with the company's product can become a conscious part of the company culture for improving customer service over the network.

The current popularity of "reengineering," or fundamentally restructuring, the work process within a company to dramatically increase speed, efficiency, and cost-effectiveness demonstrates that many managers recognize the imperative of change. But even the strongest proponents of reengineering admit that the majority of such efforts fail to achieve the desired results (Hammer and Champy 1993).

Reengineering requires not just new organizational charts, but a profound transformation of corporate culture. Many efforts to streamline work-flow or more drastically alter the nature of the work itself often encounter serious resistance from employees. This sort of reaction is one of the main obstacles to successful organizational change. In the end, if the people doing the daily work are not convinced, the reengineering process will be far less likely to meet its goals. Reorganization is a difficult concept to sell to staff, and radical work-flow changes are notoriously hard to implement, particularly when the basis of change is critical of existing work patterns and assumptions.

Internet use can give employees a broader context for thinking about organizational change, and can promote openness to new approaches to work. Regular Internet users spontaneously suggest new approaches to their work because of what they have learned through the network. A networked environment encourages employees to take the initiative, by gathering information, consulting with experts, and solving problems collaboratively. It transcends the traditional barriers of departments, management hierarchies, and even company boundaries.

Management analysts have suggested that businesses must evolve into "virtual corporations" or groupings of separate enterprises linked through high-speed networks (Davidow and Malone 1992). As more companies link up with business partners to collaborate on a particular project or to produce and market a product jointly, the virtual corporation will become the norm. Networks are the glue that can make such arrangements work. Virtual corporations, as a product of the age of connectivity, need direct, reliable communication links to develop and prosper. The Internet provides a standard for companies with diverse internal communication systems to exchange information quickly and efficiently. Even if the public Internet is not used by closely interconnected business partners, the Internet protocols are frequently the basis of interenterprise communication in the United States.

Strategic use of the Internet can help companies to meet the challenges of the nineties while preparing for the transition to the twenty-first century. Connecting to the global network is the first essential step. Companies planning to end the decade leaner and stronger, ready to set the pace into the next century, also need a strategy for mastering today's critical challenges. It may seem almost overwhelming to address globalization, technology, customer satisfaction, organizational structure, collaboration, and networking simultaneously. Faced with the inevitable turmoil of organizational change, managers could be tempted to wait for the future to take shape before plunging into uncharted territory.

Judging from the experience of companies trying to maintain the status quo, however, waiting is no longer the safest option. Those businesses that fall behind in the next few years may never recover momentum (Loomis 1993). Fortunately, there is no need to experiment blindly with new organizational structures. The pathway to the future does have a few signposts in today's corporate landscape—and the Internet is one of them. Managed strategically, the Internet offers more than just a global lifeline to the future. It can become a key ingredient to leadership in the age of interconnectivity.

MANAGING NETWORKED INFORMATION FROM THE BOTTOM UP

Executives have long recognized the importance of information for competitive advantage (Temin 1991). Extensive corporate investment in technology has been justified in part because computers generate copious amounts of internal information. Unfortunately, much of this standardized data is shaped into reports, sent to various levels of the company, and filed away without having any significant impact on decision-making

(McKinnon and Bruns 1991). Executive information systems for top-level managers attempt to address this problem by customizing the data to the management style and decision-making process of a particular organization and providing non-technical, simple commands to allow managers to display information in different configurations. Executive information systems, however, are time-consuming to create and expensive to maintain, putting them out of reach for most companies (Osborne 1992).

The problem with traditional models of corporate information management is that they are focused on the wrong end of the information spectrum. Too much emphasis is placed on generating internal information, and not nearly enough on integrating and utilizing external resources. Chief Information Officers and other information managers concentrate first on standardizing and controlling the information-processing requirements for various parts of the company, and next, if they are particularly forward-looking, on providing the information they think top managers need. They may spend time filtering, synthesizing, and selecting the most internal valuable information to transmit to decision-makers in the most useful form. Little attention is given to the flow of external information into the rest of the company.

According to management consultant and author Peter Drucker, the most important sources of information for competitive advantage and strategic decision-making come not from internal data but from the outside world (1993). In order to make better decisions, chief executives and top level managers require fresh information about trends in the economy and the marketplace, about the activities of competitors, new developments in technology, and new product opportunities. This information and its creative application provide the crucial new opportunities for companies to move ahead of their competition.

In a traditional, hierarchical corporate structure, external information does not readily permeate different levels of the organization. Top managers are responsible for remaining current with a broad range of developments outside the company, as well as for monitoring essential internal data. They are perched at the pinnacle of information access. The senior management group may have access to much of the same data, although the emphasis will be toward internal company information, including financial, production, and marketing trends.

Companies large enough to support dedicated research and development departments typically provide their researchers with a rich lode of external information, especially in the areas of science and technology. Many have established corporate libraries to acquire and organize the most relevant published materials and to access documents and special requests for information as needed. Even in this traditional model, researchers also maintain direct contacts with their colleagues in university or other corporate settings by attending conferences and keeping up with the literature in their field.

Marketing and sales staff, however, often concentrate their use of external information on areas that might assist with sales opportunities or development of new markets. Although marketing departments may utilize formal structures for information gathering, these are typically focused on a particular market analysis rather than on the broader business environment. Sales staff frequently rely on discussions with customers, attending conventions and keeping an eye on the competition, as well as personal networks. Engineers and technical and information systems staff require considerable external information about the systems and products relevant to the company, but this tends to be concentrated on the internal operation and on maintenance and development issues. In the traditional model, the least external information is available to support and production departments. The idea that employees at this level would benefit from direct contact with customers or an infusion of complex external information resources simply is not a part of hierarchical information management.

This model, which worked reasonably well when information itself was a somewhat scarce, competitive resource, is fatally flawed today.

In a networked environment, every level of every organization is awash in more information than it can possibly digest. No matter how energetic and forward-looking top executives may be, the pace of development and the amount of external information relevant to their company is exponentially larger than their ability to absorb and process it. This makes the traditional, hierarchal approach to external information highly dysfunctional. Those at the top are bombarded with more information than they can possibly handle, while people at other levels of the company have only limited access to external resources that could improve their decision-making and their overall contribution to company goals. These same employees are hard-pressed to find a context for new corporate strategies, or to understand the competitive pressures determining the future of their organization. Like other hierarchies, the stratified approach to information access no longer serves the needs of many companies.

Now consider access to external information resources in a company where most or all employees have Internet connections. Those staff who regularly use the network have access to far more external information than managers who are not on the Internet. For the first time ever, every department can retrieve information from sources as varied as federal economic bulletins, university technical reports, and electronic journals. Employees can seek expert advice from discussion groups on particular products and can often obtain free, public domain software to help them tackle routine tasks more efficiently. Technicians and engineers can communicate with peers and vendors to evaluate products and fine-tune implementation strategies. Customer support departments can monitor the discussions of their company's products on the network, and can provide answers or advice when problems are mentioned.

The Internet delivers what Peter Drucker calls the most important information resource, awareness of the world around them, directly to the desktops of all the employees connected to the network. Access to this much information all at once can be overwhelming, but it can also be tremendously empowering. With management support, information gives employees a vital tool for solving problems, taking initiative to make improvements in their work, and understanding how their job and their company fit into the larger picture. It transforms networked workstations into unlimited information generators. If information is power, and external information is the most powerful of all, then a dramatic power surge is possible for companies connected to the Internet.

The incoming information, of course, is only half of the equation. Managers have to integrate the model of distributed information access into a new corporate information strategy. According to Boynton, "Senior management can no longer afford to neglect the nature of their IT management architecture" (Boynton et al. 1992). How can the Internet contribute to this process? By encouraging managers to move away from traditional approaches to controlling information toward a coherent strategy for using expanded access opportunities for competitive advantage. Therein lies the real potential of the Internet.

Top management needs to understand that information changes have already taken place within organizations connected to the Internet. Failure to adapt to the networked environment can have unintended consequences for companies using the Internet. Managers who continue to depend on traditional external resources for decision-making may miss out on the valuable information available within their own organizations. At best, this can make them seem myopic. Recently, the CEO of a small manufacturing company already connected to the Internet decided to move the company to a research park location. He was sold on the idea partly because the research park developers touted the high-speed links to supercomputers and research centers offered in the new location. At the dedication ceremony of the new headquarters, he announced with great enthusiasm that his office now provided instant connections to Australia and Japan as well as research locations around the United States. Technical and systems staff looked at one another in disbelief. How had the CEO missed the fact that he already had that capability and more? After all, they had been sending him memos about the company's Internet connection for the past year.

Corporations do not have to relocate their headquarters to take advantage of the benefits offered by the Internet—but they do have to be prepared to make the most of fundamental changes in "who knows what" within the organization. Employees directly connected to the global network can provide their company with important competitive information. Each staff member using the Internet may be in contact with hundreds of outside people in the course of a day—including potential and existing customers, competitors, suppliers, and international partners. Well-informed employees can spot marketing opportunities, the emergence of new competition, unmet customer needs, and a host of other vital information—but only if the company has organized its internal information-sharing structure to incorporate their insights.

Businesses operating within the traditional model are slower to recognize these opportunities because of their preoccupation with information control. As Daniel Dern, editor of *Internet World*, observes, "Companies unfamiliar with the Internet have great reluctance, in fact, to joining the Internet as a community; aside from the perceived threat to security, they see unbridled e-mail and Usenet connectivity as a drain on productivity, and as another aspect of user computing they cannot control" (1993, 6). On the other hand, companies ready to move away from a hierarchical information access model and develop an information management strategy based on distributed information access can reap the benefits of a better motivated, more flexible, better-informed workforce. The information they derive from using the Internet in daily work can be integrated into plans for performance improvement in the key business functions of the company. The successful networked organization blends its internal and external information sources into a road map that everyone can read, all the way to the next century.

DOING BUSINESS ON THE INTERNET

This book captures a critical moment of transition in the commercial use of the Internet. Just a few years ago, doing business on a network designed to support research and development was a contradiction in terms. Today, commercial networks and corporate users are a major component of the global information highway. The combination of high-speed access to international resources, standards to enable data exchange among companies, global e-mail, and millions of apparently information-hungry users make the Internet an appealing investment for companies of all sizes and types. But precisely because it is in the process of rapid transformation and development, matching the potential of the Internet to particular business applications is a challenge for many organizations.

Thousands of businesses now recognize the strategic importance of networked information—yet relatively few are successfully using the Internet to gain competitive advantage. As the companies profiled in the following chapters demonstrate, it can be done. Forward-looking technical managers, CEOs willing to take a risk, entrepreneurs, and customer support specialists from Fortune 500 corporations and small start-up firms have all found ways to put the Internet to work for their companies. The insights they have gained in the process are integrated here into a discussion of the broader impact of the global network on key business functions, including communications, marketing, sales, product development, and customer support.

The companies selected for inclusion in this book are among the leaders in using the Internet for business transactions. More than sixty businesses already connected to the Internet were studied, ranging from America's largest corporations to one-person enterprises. The examples in each chapter are drawn from hundreds of interviews conducted either on site, on the telephone, or appropriately, over the Internet, giving equal space to large and small-to-medium size companies. Managers involved in navigating the Internet offered a wide range of models and networking solutions. The majority of respondents are directly responsible for the Internet connection in their organization, or have participated in the decision-making that led to network implementation. While some stressed that they were not "official spokespeople" for their organizations, their candor and willingness to discuss problems along with success stories make their observations more valuable than many formal statements and publications.

The insights of network practitioners, designers, and service providers comprise another important ingredient in the analysis that follows. One of the most striking characteristics of the Internet is the ethos of information-sharing that drives it. Any discussion of the network's value for business builds on the work of those who continue to add value to the Internet for all types of users. To learn from their experience, I followed the advice of O.B. Hardison Jr. in the introduction to his own book on technological transformation, *Disappearing Through the Skylight: Culture and Technology in the Twentieth Century.* "My method is simple. I have tried to listen carefully to what people involved in creating and interpreting cultural change say about what they are doing" (1989).

The chapters that follow present the results of careful listening to commercial users of the network, and provide concrete examples of how the network can enhance, and is enhancing, key business functions. Chapter 2, "A Manager's Guide to the Internet" launches the theme of using the Internet for competitive advantage and offers a management overview of the essential Internet basics, including the expanded options available from Internet service providers, the most important navigational tools, and strategies for locating useful business resources on the network.

Until very recently, high-speed global data exchange was the exclusive preserve of a select number of multinational corporations. By the end of the decade it will be a daily requirement for most American companies. Chapter 3, "The Desktop as Global Village" looks at how the Internet has transformed the communication strategies of both multinational and small regional businesses.

The network's contribution to all forms of communication, from basic e-mail to sophisticated marketing techniques to telecommuting, is considered in Chapter 4, "Reach Out and Touch—Everyone." The long-standing research support structure of the Internet has encouraged a rich vein of networked discovery and development. Chapter 5, "Transforming Research and Development" explores how many businesses have used the Internet to support high-powered corporate alliances and short-term product development efforts. Use of the Internet for sales and customer support is one of the most recent commercial applications of the network. The experiences of some pioneers in this field are considered in Chapter 6, "Customer Connections."

The Internet has also generated its own growth industry, as entrepreneurs move to provide software and services tailored to a networked environment. Chapter 7, on "The Entrepreneurial Edge," recounts some of the early success stories of new businesses based on the Internet. "Putting the Network to Work," Chapter 8, presents the challenges of Internet implementation, including security and training, from a management point of view, and profiles Internet postmasters at four major corporations. Finally, "Looking Forward" summarizes the incredible growth potential of the Internet and forecasts future developments in the world of networked information.

New technology frequently presents unfamiliar problems as well as immense opportunities. The Internet is no exception. Companies seeking an all-purpose, easy-to-use solution to all their communication and information needs are not likely to find it on the Internet—at least not yet. The global network was not designed for business use, and commercial applications are still in their infancy. Early business users had to cope with a technical command language and devote time to searching out elusive resources with few navigational resources. New directory and finding tools have been developed, but the sheer size and complexity of the Internet make it difficult to master. Network managers are still searching for improved ways to ensure the security of their internal data when connecting to the world. Definitive guidelines and standards for buying and selling on the Internet await development.

Business people using the Internet successfully are aware of these problems. Their solutions, and their conviction that Internet connectivity is one of the greatest strategic assets available to any company, are described in the chapters that follow. As the companies profiled here will demonstrate, doing business on the Internet is not just business as usual.

REFERENCES

Anderson, Christopher. 1993. The rocky road to a data highway. *Science.* 260:1064–1065. May 21.

Boynton, Andrew C., Gerry C. Jacobs, and Robert W. Zmud. 1992. Whose responsibility is IT management? *Sloan Management Review* 34(4):32–38.

Catlett, Charles E. 1993. Internet Evolution and Future Directions. In *Internet System Handbook*. Edited by Daniel C. Lynch and Marshall T. Rose. Boston: Addison-Wesley.

Cerf, Vinton. 1993. Testimony before the US House of Representatives, Committee on Science, Space and Technology. March 23.

Churbuck, David C. 1993. Good-bye Dewey decimals. *Forbes* 151(4):204–205. February 13.

Clinton, William J., and Albert Gore Jr. 1993. Technology for America's economic growth. White House: Washington D.C. February 22.

Cook, Gordon. 1992. The National Research and Education Network: Who shall it serve? Unpublished report available from cook@path.net.

Davenport, Thomas H., Robert G. Eccles, and Laurence Prusak. 1992. *Sloan Management Review*. 34(1):53–65.

Davidow, William H. and Michael S. Malone. 1992. *The Virtual Corporation*. New York: HarperCollins.

Dern, Daniel P. 1993. Meeting the challenges of business and public end-user communities on the Internet. *Internet World*. 4(5&6):4–9.

Drucker, Peter. 1993. According to Peter Drucker. Interview. *Forbes ASAP* 1993:90–95. March.

Elmer-Dewitt, Philip. 1993. Building the on-ramp to the electronic highway. *Time*. 141(22):52–53. May 31.

Gerber, Cheryl. 1993. Booming commercial use changes face of Internet. *InfoWorld* 15(15):1, 36.

Hammer, Michael, and James Champy. 1993. *Reengineering the Corporation*. New York: HarperBusiness.

Hardison, O. B. 1989. *Disappearing Through the Skylight*. New York: Viking.

Kupfer, Andrew. 1993. The race to rewire America. *Fortune* 127(8):42–61.

Levin, Jayne. 1993. Plugging Into Internet. *Washington Post* Business Section, May 17, p. 5.

Loomis, Carol J. 1992. Dinosaurs? *Fortune* 127(9):36–42. May 3.

Maloff, Joel H. 1992. Selling Internet service: An ancient art form on a new canvas. *Electronic Networking.* 2(3):17–23.

Markoff, John. 1993. Building the electronic superhighway. *New York Times* Section 3, January 24, pp. 1,6.

McKinnon, Sharon M., and William J. Burns. 1991. *The Information Mosaic.* Boston: Harvard Business School Press.

Osborne, Richard L. 1992. Information power in the private company. *Journal of General Management* 17(4):13–24.

Quarterman, John S. 1990. *The Matrix.* Burlington: Digital Press.

Rockart, John F. and James E. Short. 1991. The networked organization and the management of interdependence. In *The Corporation of the 1990s: Information Technology and Organizational Transformation.* Edited by Michael S. Scott Morton. New York: Oxford University Press.

Rogers, T.J. 1993. Testimony before the US House of Representatives, Committee on Science, Space and Technology. March 23.

Rutkowski, Tony. 1993. RE: Internet Past Present Future. Compriv discussion group. May 27.

Sproull, Lee S. and Sara Kiesler. 1991. Computers, networks and work. *Scientific American* 265(3): 116–123.

Styx, Gary. 1993. Domesticating Cyberspace. *Scientific American.* 269(2):100–110.

Temin, Peter. ed. 1991. *Inside the Business Enterprise: Historical Perspectives on the Use of Information.* Chicago: University of Chicago Press.

Weiss, William L. et al. 1993. Leading Telco CEOs jointly support Clinton-Gore technology initiative. Press release and policy statement released by Ameritech and other telecommunications corporations. March 23.

Wylie, Margie. 1993. Will networks kill the corporation? *Network World* 10(2) Supplement:9–12.

CHAPTER 2

A Manager's Guide to the Internet

> *This highly distributed, loosely controlled network is an absolutely perfect democratization of technology in service to organizations. And, in 1992, the Internet began to have a real, tangible effect on the operations of commercial enterprises, in addition to the educational and governmental organizations that had access to it all along.*
> —**Stewart Alsop**, Editor-in-Chief, *Info World*

Any lingering doubts about the Internet as a viable resource for business were swept away in 1993 by a veritable torrent of news about the commercial value of the network, including its selection as the Landmark Technology of the Year by *InfoWorld.* As the number of companies with Internet connections soared, products and services designed to make the network more useful to the business community were announced with great regularity. The first issue of *The Internet Business Journal* editorialized, "Companies that have no presence in this new arena will quickly fade from view" (Locke 1993).

Whether or not this particular prophecy comes to pass, a new era of business on the Internet is clearly underway. But strategic management of Internet connectivity within most organizations is still in its infancy.

The proliferation of Internet connections in business over the past few years can be compared to the spread of personal computers during the early 1980s. In both cases, the driving force was innovative departments latching on to a useful new resource to meet an immediate need, rather than centralized planning by top-level management. Researchers, network managers, and technical staff— especially those who had come into business from a university environment—had already experienced the power of global networking. They had come to rely on the Internet to supply vital information or links to colleagues in other organizations. Establishing an Internet connection for their own departments became a high priority, well before their companies developed any overall business policies about using the network.

Suzanne M. Johnson, an information technology manager at Intel, recalls that the first Internet connection at Intel was established by an engineering group. During its early years, the network was widely considered to be "the realm of wild-eyed engineers and computer scientists" rather than an integral part of Intel's networking strategy. The role of the Internet has changed significantly since then. Now the Internet serves as a model for improving the internal corporate, or enterprise, network at Intel. Johnson, like other corporate information managers, finds that many features of the Internet are valuable enough to transfer into the design of the corporate network infrastructure, because she believes Internet solves one of the greatest challenges in network design: providing interoperability between dissimilar hardware, software, and networks.

Interoperability, the ability to provide seamless connections among different communication systems, is frequently an elusive goal, even within a single corporation. The more networks a company operates, the more important an overall connectivity strategy becomes. Network analyst Tod Dagres notes, "As companies interconnect systems and networks, management becomes a challenge, if not a nightmare. The resulting enterprise internetwork is a collection of incompatible systems and networks with their own particular requirements" (1993, S9). The infrastructure and standard protocols that allow the global Internet to transmit data and messages among many systems around the globe can also be applied to the design of private corporate networks, facilitating internal data transmission and simplifying communication with the rest of the world. The widespread adoption of Internet protocols by enterprise networks is another indication that the network has a new status within the corporate technical management community. Instead of being viewed by many systems managers as a data security problem in the making, the Internet has been accepted as a core technology for future growth.

Acceptance by network managers and systems experts within the business world is just one stage in the metamorphosis of the Internet into an essential corporate resource. Still to come in most companies is appreciation by general managers and top executives of the network's true potential to improve organizational performance, including the all-important bottom line. Until the Internet becomes an integral part of corporate strategy, managers will continue to underestimate its capacity for providing valuable new opportunities in every area of business.

Even as the Internet is recognized as an essential resource by high-technology firms and major corporations with complex communication needs, managers in small and medium sized companies question its relevance for them. In fact, smaller companies stand to benefit substantially from a connection to the Internet. Davidow and Malone point out in *The Virtual Corporation*, that all types of businesses now depend on access to information to get the job done. In describing how companies can best position themselves to meet the challenges of the next century, the authors stress that information is the fundamental building block for any type of product or service.

In fact, they state, "Here at the end of the twentieth century, four decades into the computer age, it is increasingly obvious that the very nature of business itself is information. Many of the employees in any corporation are involved in the process of gathering, generating, or transforming information" (1992, 65).

If companies of all shapes and sizes have become equally dependent on information, then effective use of the Internet to obtain an information advantage should be a topic of vital interest to all managers. Across the board, those companies with the most successful Internet applications are distinguished not by size, but by well-informed managers who are willing to explore the ways in which Internet can add value to their business, and who are able to communicate their vision to employees throughout the company. Like most other evolving information resources, the Internet requires a well-considered strategy, and creative management to yield maximum benefits.

Short of sitting top executives down in front of networked workstations and demonstrating the power of the Internet directly, as many network managers would like to do, it is difficult to prove in advance that the Internet can make a measurable difference for any given company. The technical feats of super high-speed connectivity and multimedia transmissions are not convincing to management unless they are grounded in a realistic business plan. In addition to gathering basic cost and performance figures, Internet advocates within the corporation and managers interested in improving corporate performance need to understand how the network provides the opportunity to gain a significant advantage over competitors. The first crucial step is to become familiar with the Internet itself: How does this global superconnector really function? What are the organizations and the structures that support it? What are all those millions of Internet users accomplishing on the network?

INTERNET BASICS

Managers need a clear understanding of the Internet—not necessarily the technical details of its infrastructure, but a firm grasp of its primary functions and operation—in order to perceive how the network can best be used in a particular business setting. For a company planning an Internet connection, management involvement should begin at the early stage. Most of the technical details of connecting to the Internet will be addressed by systems or networking specialists or by the network service provider. These details, however, determine how widely available and how useful the Internet will be to the organization. Developing strategic goals for the Internet within a given company is a high level responsibility which requires a good sense of the mission and priorities of the whole organization, not just the networking and computer departments.

This section provides an executive overview of the Internet, rather than a comprehensive guide to its features. Managers not familiar with the network should read it for a brief introduction to terms and navigational tools that will be mentioned in later chapters in connection with specific business applications. Companies still not connected to the network will find the "Options for Access" section that follows helpful particularly in combination with Chapter 8.

Those who need more detailed information about the workings of the Internet have several choices. A number of recent publications offer an in-depth look at the history and growth of the network, explain its technical underpinnings, and guide new users through some of the intricacies of implementation and intensive network utilization. For practical advice on how to use the Internet, these books are highly recommended. Many offer extensive explanations of the resources that will be mentioned in this chapter. A selected bibliography of such titles is included in Appendix A.

Internet Then and Now

Getting to know the Internet presents a special challenge for corporate managers, even those with a technical background, because it was not originally designed with business use in mind. Many of the network's most fundamental and most idiosyncratic features reflect its origins in the government, technology, and research communities, which shared responsibility for its design and architecture in the 1960s and 1970s. The first phase of development, funded by the Department of Defense, centered on allowing researchers in different parts of the country to log on to remote computers for computational and data-sharing purposes. Early developers were already accustomed to an environment of arcane computer commands and complex operating systems. They were addressing the substantial technical problems of making diverse sizes and types of computers and terminals communicate and interoperate as smoothly as possible. Ease of use was simply not a priority.

Solving these problems required a new approach to linking computers: adding a standardized layer of information that could be sent from any type of terminal over network lines and be recognized by any host computer after passing through a piece of communications hardware called a file server. This layered approach allowed the conversion of data or text required for different computers to "talk" to one another to be handled automatically by the machines themselves-provided that each machine was able to recognize the same set of instructions, or protocols. The protocol developed for this purpose is known as TCP/IP, or Transmission Control Protocol/Internet Protocol. Communicating through TCP/IP was originally the basic requirement for, and is still a partial definition of, participation in the Internet.

Developers of the early TCP/IP implementations foresaw widespread applications for the protocols, but no one at the time quite anticipated the phenomenal demand for connectivity that was yet to come. A network document from 1982, recently circulated on Internet discussion groups as a "blast from the past," noted: "Currently the internet is fairly small. It contains no more than 25 active networks, and no more than a few hundred hosts....The guidelines currently recommended are an upper limit of about 1,000 networks. If we imagine an average number of 25 hosts per net, this would suggest a maximum number of 25,000 hosts" (Clark 1982). Contrast this with the current Internet estimates of more than 13,000 active networks and 1.5 million hosts, and some of the quirks of the Internet interface become more understandable.

The next wave of Internet growth came in the mid 1980s, when the National Science Foundation began to provide funding to encourage research and doctoral-granting universities to link their faculty and researchers to national supercomputer centers via the network. Between 1986 and 1991 the number of individual Internet networks had surged from around a hundred to over three thousand, an increase that brought qualitative changes to the Internet, not all of them welcome to its designers. In the *Internet System Handbook*, Charles Catlett notes that the newcomers had a different attitude toward using the Internet:

> A lot of people are crashing the Internet party. The immigration of noncomputer science researchers into the Internet community began with the NSFNET providing services to the university community at large. Corporations, community colleges, K–12 schools, and even private citizens are beginning to access the Internet, both in the US and abroad. These new groups of users include noncomputer scientists, as well as noncomputer literates, and they treat the Internet as a service, not necessarily as a shared community resource (1993, 719).

For most of its history, the Internet was almost exclusively the domain of government-sponsored or university-based research. As more and more users outside of the university began connecting to the network, the relationship of the federal government to the support of the network infrastructure became an issue. An "acceptable use policy" was developed by the National Science Foundation for all traffic that travelled on the portion of the Internet funded by the federal government and operated by the National Science Foundation (NSF). Companies wishing to utilize the NSFNET network "backbone," a high-speed connection linking supercomputer centers and universities around the United States, were asked to ensure that their activities on the Internet would further research and education, and not support for-profit interests. Specifically, the Acceptable Use Policy states:

> NSFNET Backbone services are provided to support open research and education in and among U.S. research and instructional institutions, plus research arms of for-profit firms when engaged in open scholarly communication and research. Use for other purposes is not acceptable. (National Science Foundation, 1992)

This policy attempted to establish some workable parameters for appropriate business use of the Internet. However, in practice it was often difficult to draw the line between educational and commercial use. Was it supporting the educational goals of the Internet to send announcements of new products over the network if that would help universities to keep their systems up to date and performing at peak capacity? Did researchers benefit from customer support services and delivery of software through the Internet, or was this a commercial service? Although a number of companies, especially those with research departments, did connect to the Internet and agree to the restrictions on traffic, the Acceptable Use Policy became a source of much confusion as well as a real barrier to business making the best use of the network.

From a business point of view, a major turning point occurred in 1991 when fully commercial Internet connections became available. First, the Commercial Internet Exchange Association (CIX) was established specifically to provide a nonrestrictive pathway for business participation in the Internet. The three founding members—General Atomics, which operates CERFnet; Performance Systems International (PSI), which operates PSInet; and UUNET Technologies which operates AlterNet—were soon joined by network providers around the country in an agreement not to restrict commercial traffic on those segments of the Internet operated and funded outside of the federal government. CIX membership now includes network providers from around the world. Later in 1991, Advanced Network and Service, Inc. (ANS) the company formed by IBM, MCI, and Merit, Inc. to provide the National Science Foundation high-speed backbone also announced a commercial Internet service called CO+RE.

These new commercial options made it possible for businesses to stop worrying about fitting into a restrictive definition of "acceptable use" and focus on what Internet applications make the most sense for an individual company—both strategically and financially. As Bill Washburn, Executive Director of the Commercial Internet Exchange, puts it:

> CIX has already had a profoundly important effect for business in promoting use of the Internet. When CIX came into being it put the business philosophy on the table as a real viable alternative to the Acceptable Use Policy/National Science Foundation concept of the Internet. The Internet has a significant role to play in the global business world; it's no longer just a means of scholarly communication and exchange. CIX brought business into the Internet ball game; legitimately and through the front door.

The next year brought another commercial option, as Sprint joined the list of Internet service providers. Bob Collet, Director of Internet Services and Systems at Sprint, recalls that the growth potential of Internet connections for business was becoming obvious at the beginning of the 1990s. He saw an opportunity for the Internet to do for business what the public switched telephone did in an earlier period. Now, he says, "companies can send mail and exchange multimedia instantly from one desktop to another, even continents away. That capability has an enormous impact on productivity and innovation."

Based on this conviction, Collet championed the idea of establishing SprintLink as a new business area, becoming something of an "intrapreneur" to convince management at Sprint that this would be a profitable venture. His efforts were successful, and SprintLink was up and running in 1992. Collet makes special note of the cooperation and advice he received from other members of the Internet community. In implementing the new service, he says, "The most amazing thing was the help we received from both partners and competitors in making sure that SprintLink was the best possible implementation." This help extended to very specific suggestions from around the world, he recalls, "We took the original design to groups like Merit and UUNet and network managers in the United Kingdom and Japan, then we changed it several times based on their comments and criticisms. It was a real demonstration of how interdependent we all are on the network."

The next significant breakthrough for business use of the Internet may be heralded by several announcements in 1993. Sprint's recent agreement with the Microelectronics and Computer Technology Corporation (MCC) to offer a platform for electronic commerce services on the Internet will provide companies with a new level of support for commercial activity via global networks. MCC has been working for several years to define and develop the tools for a fully functional commercial application on the Internet—one that would include directory services, security, advanced e-mail, and remittance capabilities based on open standards. Joe Sims, vice president of marketing and business development at MCC, expects that by 1994 close to five thousand corporations will have access to his company's Enterprise Integration Network, or EINet. Many of these companies will gain access to EINet through their participation in major consortia and trade associations. Electric utility companies, for example, have already indicated their intention to take part. Sims envisions EINet as adding the features necessary to make the Internet the preferred means for all companies to communicate, develop partnerships, carry out research projects, and conduct their buying and selling with each other. The need is so compelling, he feels, that EINet will eventually be joined by other, similar services, "This infrastructure is so important for the competitiveness of American business, that we have to provide advanced commercial functions over standardized networks. Someone had to get the next stage of development going. I do expect that at some point there will be others offering the same capabilities as EINet."

Meanwhile, a number of regional network service providers have expanded their scope of service to business by joining with MCI Communications Corporation in a new group, CoREN (the Corporation for Regional and Enterprise Networking). All these groups offer alternative pathways for commercial traffic on the Internet, allowing businesses to make full use of the global network without violating the National Science Foundation Acceptable Use Policy.

Options for Access

There are now so many ways for businesses to connect to the Internet that the main challenge is to find the best match between the type of service and company needs. Analysis of the potential competitive advantage that the Internet could provide in dealing with suppliers, revamping internal operations, and enhancing relationships with customers should help to determine the anticipated volume of Internet use throughout the organization. The connection options range from a very high-speed direct link to the Internet backbone to support data and information exchange between the company and a supercomputer site, or a high volume of multimedia applications, and continue at lower speeds down through a low-end option of sharing an Internet port with other users by using a dial-up connection running through regular phone lines.

Connection packages vary considerably from one network provider to another, and the range of services and price change frequently, so any published information about the cost of linking to the Internet should be verified with a representative group of service providers. Like everything else about the Internet, the number of network providers and the configurations they offer seem to grow at a rapid rate, making a comprehensive listing impossible. A list of the major commercial providers in North America is given in Appendix C. Membership of these providers in the CIX or CoREN as of July 1993 is also indicated. Any of the Internet service providers can quote up-to-date service options and prices for business connections.

As would be expected, the cost of Internet access is driven by the capacity and speed of the basic connection. The general rule is that the higher the bandwidth capacity and the faster the speed, the higher the cost to install and maintain the Internet link. Dedicated connections devoted to the use of one company are significantly more expensive that shared connections. Companies can choose from three basic options. The most expensive is a dedicated connection, which has the capacity to link an entire organization to the Internet and will require the installation of network hardware on-site as well as a special leased line. In the medium range is a dedicated dial-up connection, which can be run from a workstation with the appropriate software and at modem speeds over regular telephone lines. The least expensive connection is a dial-up to a shared line service, which may be billed on the basis of how many hours the connection is used each month.

A dedicated connection will provide significant advantages in performance. Companies that will frequently send large amounts of data through the Internet, or that need to connect a number of workstations and users, should consider their own dedicated line, which is leased through the network provider. There will be start-up costs for the line installation and purchase of networking equipment; these costs and the annual fee will vary with the size and complexity of the site and the speed of connection. At present, network providers estimate that an average corporation would pay around $1,00 per month for a dedicated connection (Rugo 1993).

If limiting up-front costs is a priority, then the connection itself can be scaled down to the speed and capacity needed in the short term, with an option to upgrade as Internet use increases. High-speed modem connections to the Internet, known as SLIP (Serial Line IP) and PPP (Point to Point Protocol) are possible through a standard telephone line at much lower cost than dedicated, leased lines—currently about $250 per month. This type of connection requires installation of the appropriate modem and software, and it has limitations in terms of the number of users supported and the speed of the connection, but many small companies have found it to be the most cost-effective way to participate in the Internet.

Dial-up connections to the network provider or another organization that offers shared Internet services are the least expensive of all; such services can run as low as $20 a month. Shared connections do not provide direct Internet access, but they do allow access to e-mail and may include many other network features, depending on the source of the service. This type of connection combines ease of installation with the lowest prices available—but without the advantages of a direct Internet connection. It has been the first step for many small businesses interested in becoming familiar with the Internet.

In addition to the physical connection, Internet providers offer a variety of service and consulting packages. The most expensive of these cover all the details of the Internet link, from complete installation and maintenance of all required lines and equipment to obtaining a network number and registering as a new Internet connection. For companies that do not want to dedicate internal staff and resources to these functions, but need to get up and running quickly on the Internet, this level of service will be attractive.

The preconnection phase is also the time to analyze the type of security that a company requires for its Internet connection. Most commercial users want at least the assurance that their own internal computer systems and networks will not be vulnerable to outside prying through the Internet. Businesses interested in using the Internet to transmit sensitive or confidential information will also want to investigate the encryption packages available through some networks to ensure privacy of data. Security and privacy options are discussed in more detail in Chapter 8.

Selecting a network service provider and determining the most appropriate Internet connection to support particular business objectives should involve a consideration of all the options available. The following questions can help to determine how well the various possibilities match a particular company's requirements. Discussing these issues will also help to determine the service attitude of the providers and their ability to understand company needs. At a minimum, businesses considering the Internet should obtain more detailed information about the following from each service provider:

1. What is the provider's total customer base and what percentage of that are business customers?

2. What is the size range of the provider's business customers. How many are comparable in size to your company?

3. Are all three types of Internet connections described above provided to business customers (dedicated, dial-up, shared access)?

4. How many commercial customers are using each type of connection?

5. What are the total annual costs in each category of connection and service for a company comparable to yours ?

6. Are both unrestricted commercial traffic and National Science Foundation traffic supported? Are there differences in cost for these options?

7. What are the responsibilities of the customer for equipment operation and maintenance under the various options?

8. What level of training is available and what does it cost?

9. What other networks will be accessible through this connection?

10. What security options are available, and what is the cost?

In order to remain competitive, many network providers have started to offer more substantial educational and training programs, customized security arrangement, and other services tailored for business customers. Training can be especially important for organizations with no in-house training program. It is in the interest of every business to talk to several potential providers before making a decision about an Internet connection.

Who's In Charge Here?

For a network that covers the globe and supports more than 1.5 million host computers, *the* Internet can be difficult to find. Thousands of separate networks comprise the Internet; each has its own identity, as do the dozens of network service providers. All this diversity can add up to confusion for Internet newcomers and prospective participants. Mary Riendeau, vice president at Software Tool and Die, which offers commercial and individual access to the Internet in the Boston area, tells the story of a manager who called to inquire about the Internet, listened to the basic introduction about connection requirements and service options, and declared, "Well, this all sounds very interesting, but I think I should have a talk with the **real** Internet before making a decision. Can you tell me how I get in touch with them?"

A logical question, and one that speaks volumes about the differences between the business world and the Internet culture. All the statistics on the mammoth size and the spectacular growth of the Internet would lead one to expect that somewhere, holding it all together, there is a tightly structured, centralized, supernetworked organization. The reality is quite different. Although the federal government, first through the Department of Defense and now through the National Science Foundation, has played a significant role in the network's funding and direction, the government is not the "owner" of the Internet. Nor are the research universities or the commercial network service providers. The world's largest network is an association of interconnected but separate network entities with government, educational, and commercial participation from around the world. It is governed not by a chief executive officer or corporate-style board of directors, but by a loose confederation of its component parts.

The most recent umbrella for coordinating and overseeing the workings of the network is the Internet Society, which was established only a few years ago. This professional, nonprofit organization was chartered to foster the continued evolution of the Internet through education, support for technical developments, and provide a forum for exploring new Internet applications. Membership in the Internet Society is open to both individuals and organizations, including corporations. Vinton Cerf, the president of the Internet Society notes, "The Internet Society does not operate any of the thousands of networks that make up the Internet, but it assists service providers by providing information to prospective users and involves product developers and research in the evolution of Internet standards. Corporate and individual, professional support for this organization is widespread and international" (1993).

Tightly controlled governance has never been as important to the Internet community as maintaining the infrastructure of the network and improving its operation. The nitty-gritty work this requires comes from a collection of task forces, research, and working groups, operating under the umbrella of the Internet Activities Board (IAB). The Internet Activities Board coordinates Internet design, engineering, and management with a special focus on the TCP/IP and other network protocols. It has two subsidiary task forces: the Internet Engineering Task Force (IETF) specializes in the operational and technical realm, and the Internet Research Task Force (IRTF) takes on the research questions required for future development of the network.

Membership in all these groups is open to the whole Internet community, with a cross section of researchers, software developers, engineers, faculty members, staff from the networks, and other interested parties working together with no distinction made about institutional or organizational affiliations. This cross-fertilization promotes lively dialogue regarding Internet policy and priorities. For the most part, differences of personal opinion are set aside in the interests of advancing the network as a whole. Expertise, information sharing, and vision are what count on the Internet working groups, not position or organizational background. The open structure is an asset to business, because it allows full participation in discussing and setting standards, many of which have an impact on internal corporate networks as well as the public Internet.

An Internet Toolkit

The influx of business and nontechnical users is already having an impact on the look and feel of the Internet. Innovations in navigational tools, directory assistance, and information services make the Internet easier to use and eliminate the need for remembering some of the specific commands and technical details associated with earlier access to the network. This section provides an overview of a few of the basic tools now available to Internet users and widely adopted by businesses already connected to the network.

A universe populated by millions of users searching for information in thousands of databases and accessing resources that may reside in any of over a million computers scattered around the world needs all the directory and information help it can get. The complexity of the global network combined with the frequently urgent information needs of business place a premium value on the tools available to users. Amazingly, for most of the history of the Internet, users had to resort to personal persistence and informal tricks of the trade to find what they needed on the network. Just as there is no official Internet "boss," there was no central place to turn for Internet directory and information assistance.

The advent of a centralized network information center called the InterNIC is beginning to remedy this situation. For the first time, the InterNIC offers Internet users a single-stop information service, which includes advice on getting connected to the network, suggestions on how to use the Internet more effectively, help in locating important resources, directory services modeled on the white pages for individual names and the yellow pages for business services, and registration services for organizations at the point of connecting to the Internet. Basic InterNIC services will be offered free to all Internet users for the next five years through the collaboration of General Atomics/CERFnet, AT&T, and Network Solutions, Inc. The Inter-

NIC opened for service in April 1993, and is funded by a five-year grant from the National Science Foundation.

The InterNIC is organized into three coordinated parts: directory and database assistance is provided by AT&T, information services are offered by General Atomics, and registration services are provided by Network Solutions, Inc. The three companies have pledged to work in collaboration to ensure a seamless and user-friendly approach to all the resources of the InterNIC. AT&T will produce an on-line "Directory of Directories" that will include pointers to such resources as computing centers, network providers, information servers, white and yellow pages directories, library catalogs, data and software archives, training services, and other Internet information. As part of its agreement with the National Science Foundation, AT&T will also provide fee-based consulting on database design, management, and maintenance to institutions and groups preparing information for inclusion in the Internet. All Internet users and hosts will be invited to list themselves in a directory at no charge. There will also be a yellow pages version of the directory where commercial users can include more information for a fee. AT&T promises to work toward accuracy and completeness of the entries by actively soliciting new listings and regularly checking and updating resources that are listed.

The information services component of InterNIC offers a referral desk service to answer requests for information about the Internet via telephone, e-mail, FAX, and hardcopy mailings. It also maintains an on-line information resource called InfoSource, which contains a variety of documents and resources about the Internet. Guides to using the network, lists of interest groups, Internet newsletters, tips on getting started, site security information, and much more can be searched by subject terms or by browsing the InfoSource table of contents. Items of interest can be retrieved over the Internet for local use. During its first two months in operation, the InfoSource logged more than three thousand contacts at its Reference/Help Desk; close to ninety thousand information files were retrieved.

The third type of assistance available from the InterNIC involves support for registering networks, domains, and other entities to the Internet community. New members of the Internet must register their host computers and networks. Many of the network service providers already assist new users with the registration process, and the InterNIC will work closely with domain administrators, network coordinators, and Internet service providers. The InterNIC will also be able to answer user questions about registration policy and the status of their registration request.

If the InterNIC fulfills its promise, businesses will start their first day of connectivity to the Internet with a well-organized and accessible world of information at their fingertips. While this happy state is still in the somewhat distant future, even in its start-up mode the InterNIC service is the best place for new Internet users to turn for on-line orientation, resource discovery, and directory information. A careful reading of the files posted on the InfoSource will go a long way toward answering most new users' questions. Contact information for reaching the InterNIC and searching the InfoSource is included in Appendix B.

Once connected to the Internet, most users want to locate its resources and information files as quickly and easily as possible. Even with the help of the InterNIC, mastery of the global network presents a formidable challenge. Internet veterans are familiar with functions such as "telnet," that allows a user to log on to and operate a computer attached to a remote system (for example, to search remote databases), and "ftp," or file transfer protocol, that facilitates moving files from one computer to another via the network.

A number of recently developed tools make these and other Internet procedures more straightforward for the novice user. Among the tools that have been widely adopted by business are Gopher, WAIS, and Archie. These have become standards for locating and transferring information, and are supported by the InterNIC as well as many other repositories of Internet resources. Many detailed explanations of how to use these tools are available, so just a general overview of their purpose will be provided here.

Gopher, developed at the University of Minnesota and named after the university mascot, was originally designed to give on-campus Internet users easier access to a growing number of internal and remote information resources. The Gopher software provides menus and pointers which can be customized in a few simple steps to suit individual or departmental information priorities, opening the doors to information files residing in computers around the world. This ease of use made Gopher an extremely adaptable tool for the distributed computing environment of the Internet. The software developers at the University of Minnesota offered Gopher at no charge through the Internet and many other organizations discovered its benefits. Enhancements and new versions of Gopher spread like wildfire, first to other campuses then to research laboratories, organizations, and companies.

With Gopher in place, Internet users have a ticket to a truly amazing variety of resources (Wiggins 1993). Figure 2.1 illustrates the first screen of a computer listing at the InterNIC's InfoSource under the heading "All the Gopher Servers in the World." Among the locations and types of organizations currently offering Gopher access to their electronic resources are universities, government agencies, research centers, and corporations around the world. Each of these hosts has created a hierarchical menu of resources of special interest to that location—all instantly accessible to the Internet user with a click or a keystroke. One way to begin exploring the incredible scope of Internet resources is to browse through "All the Gopher Servers in the World" for an hour.

As Gophers reproduced themselves around the world, it became quite difficult to figure out what Gopher among the hun-

```
                Internet Gopher Information Client v1.11

                   All the Gopher Servers in the World
 -->  1.  Search Gopherspace using Veronica/
      2.  Virginia Institute of Marine Science, College of William & Mary/
      3.   IST National Inst. for Cancer Research, Genova, (IT)/
      4.   Information Science Dep. - University of Milan, (IT)/
      5.   Tecnopolis CSATA Novus Ortus (Master Gopher)/
      6.  ACADEME THIS WEEK (Chronicle of Higher Education)/
      7.  ACM SIGGRAPH/
      8.  ACTLab (UT Austin, RTF Dept)/
      9.  Aalborg Universitetsdtatcenter/
     10.  Academic Position Network/
     11.  Academy of Sciences, Bratislava (Slovakia)/
     12.  Alamo Community College District/
     13.  Albert Einstein College of Medicine/
     14.  American Mathematical Society /
     15.  American Physiological Society/
     16.  Anesthesiology Gopher /
     17.  Appalachian State University (experimental gopher)/
     18.  Apple Computer Higher Education gopher server/

Press ? for Help, q to Quit, u to go up a menu            Page: 1/40
```

FIGURE 2.1   Gopher Servers in the World.

dreds available might provide access to particular information. Users needed an adjunct to Gopher that allowed subject searching of Gopher menus. A development team at the University of Nevada introduced Veronica in 1992 to address this need. Veronica overcomes the problem of finding one specific Gopher by providing a way to search through the menus in all Gopher servers according to key word or a combination of subject terms. Although Veronica doesn't search the contents of documents, it does serve to narrow down the field to the Gophers most likely to contain useful information about a particular topic.

WAIS, or Wide Area Information Servers, provides a different level of access to Internet resources, based on searching the actual text of files for which indexes exist. Users can query a WAIS server using natural language and they will receive a group of documents which match their query ranked according to how often the desired terms appear in the text. The combination of Gopher, Veronica and WAIS provides a method of locating and retrieving resources from the vast and quintessentially disorganized universe of networked information. World Wide Web (WWW) adds to this mix a useful hypertext capability, which allows the user to jump automatically from one document to another, and provides links between otherwise unrelated documents. Many other Internet tools, with expanded features, are now in development. The process of establishing road maps and navigational tools for the Internet is expected to accelerate rapidly in the next few years, as more companies invest in developing the network's potential for graphical and multimedia interfaces.

Access to free, public domain, software is close to the top of every Internet user's list of valuable resources. Many Internet sites, including universities and corporations, maintain extensive collections of free software and make these programs available at no cost to Internet users. With thousands of programs available for all types of computers, finding a particular piece of software can be like looking for a needle in an electronic haystack. Archie is the tool which helps users to pinpoint the computer locations of archives containing text, image, data files and software code available through anonymous file transfer. Some of the most popular software for business users are the programs used to manage communications with the Internet, including navigational tools, basic networking software for file servers and routers, and electronic mail managers. These and many other utility programs for all types of computing environments can be located by using Archie.

Can free software really be all that valuable, or are these Internet sources just pale imitations of the commercial versions which sell for hundreds or thousands of dollars? People who should know—programmers and systems managers—are enthusiastic about the quality of the publicly available software. One of its great assets is that so many organizations are already using the software available on the Internet, and improving on it. "Public domain software is actually better quality, in many cases," says one software engineer. "Because it is so widely distributed through the Internet, any bugs or glitches are reported and fixed right away by the user community. The improvement cycle is much faster than with most vendors, because there is a tendency to share enhancements freely."

The possibility of importing viruses through the network remains a major security concern, but system managers feel this need not be an issue with public domain software if the software's source code is examined for any problems before being installed. Virus detection programs are also available free of charge. Many companies, large and small, point to the availability of free software a major cost-saving and efficiency-promoting feature of the Internet.

A comprehensive list of Internet tools could encompass many more aids and resources that have been introduced to the network community over the past few years. New developments occur daily, and are best followed by participating in the network itself, which even beginning users can do with the help of the tools discussed here.

BETTER BUSINESS RESOURCES

When it comes to business information resources, the Internet is still waiting for its "killer application," the one compelling source that every company must have. The network offers a seemingly infinite array of texts, files, bulletins, reference sources, statistics, electronic journals, research reports, government information, and much, much more, but it is hard to pinpoint any one or two sources of universal value to business. Asked what Internet resource they find most helpful, most network regulars give high praise to the discussion groups related to their job or subject interest. This is often where they turn to keep up to date with new developments or to solicit help with a difficult question. With remarkable frequency, someone participating in the group will come through with an answer.

USENET, or NETNEWS, is the source of thousands of specialized discussion groups open to participation by the millions connected to the Internet, as well as by users of other networks. The discussion groups, or newsgroups, on USENET are divided into a number of distinct hierarchies, dealing with topics such as computers (groups labelled comp), science (sci), recreation (rec), and business (biz), together with hundreds of subjects grouped under miscellaneous (misc) and alternative (alt) categories. The notes posted to these groups range from the highly technical and informative to the silly and offensive. A number of the specialized computer, software, and technical groups are for serious discussion only and frivolous postings are not welcome. Groups in the recreational and alternative categories may vary wildly in their tone and content.

An Internet connection does not automatically include access to USENET, but most service providers offer it as an option. Many organizations arrange to obtain USENET files at no cost from a site already receiving them, and Internet standards are designed to facilitate this process. A "network news feed," which can include as many or as few of the USENET discussion categories as the company chooses, is combined with newsreading software to allow users to browse through the discussion groups, read those of interest, and post queries or answers back to the group. The software required for reading and distributing the newsgroups is available for many different types of computers and network configurations.

For companies interested delivering world and national news to the desktops of employees, ClariNet News is a popular Internet option. This service provides daily delivery over the Internet of all the information carried on wire services like UPI and news syndicates. The news is arranged in hierarchal categories similar to USENET, and tailored to a company's particular subject interests. Brad Templeton, the founder of ClariNet is profiled in Chapter 7.

Some Internet lists function explicitly to announce the existence of new resources—the InterNIC maintains both a Net-Happenings and a Net-Resources list for this purpose. Active participation in relevant newsgroups (accessible through a USENET news feed) and discussion groups (accessible by on-line subscription) is one of the best ways to find out about the resources of particular interest to business. A listing of all current discussion groups, complete with brief descriptions and instructions about how to subscribe is available on the InterNIC InfoSource.

A number of recent journals and newsletters are dedicated to providing information of special interest to business users of the Internet and there is every indication that periodicals focusing on business use of the network will continue to multiply. The *Internet Letter, Internet World, Internet Business Journal, Internet Report,* and the *Cook Report on Internet—NREN* all offer coverage of corporate applications of the Internet, regular listings of new resources, and analysis of business-related developments on the network. More information on these and other Internet publications is included in Appendix A.

What specific questions can be answered using the Internet? For experienced searchers, the network is now the obvious one-stop source for all types of information. Occasional "Internet Treasure Hunts" are designed to demonstrate that you can find anything and everything on the network—if you know where to look. A recent Internet Hunt focused on business resources, and challenged network users to find the following: the impact of the North American Free Trade Agreement on the domestic content of passenger automobiles; the phone numbers of all the meat packers in Tucson, Arizona with more than thirty employees; the states with the highest and lowest unemployment rates for June 1993; and the Republic of Korea's projections for economic growth over the next five years (Gates 1993). Participants in the Hunt reported a number of Internet sources for the requested information.

In fact, the network has information on most topics you can

imagine, and some that literally boggle the imagination. Nevertheless, many users find their first attempts at locating a precise piece of information to be rather frustrating. It is certainly true that the Internet's navigational tools don't yet offer the precision and reliability of many specialized information retrieval systems. For certain questions, there are many more efficient ways to find the answer. But the convenience and power of browsing sources located in many different locations at one time make the Internet an excellent starting point for all types of business information needs.

Federal Information

If any Internet business resource has universal information appeal, it is the publications and data available from the United States government. Some materials, such as the Securities and Exchange Commission (SEC) reports and the economic indicators, are so valuable upon release that businesses already pay to access them from third party vendors. Now the government has a mandate to make federal information available to the public in electronic format (Wilson 1993). Some of this distribution will take place over the Internet, making a network connection all the more valuable for many companies. The amount of federal information accessible on the Internet increases daily. Among the important resources already available are:

The Economic Bulletin Board, U.S. Department of Commerce
Contains press releases and statistical information from the Bureau of Economic Analysis, the Bureau of the Census, the Federal Reserve Board, the Bureau of Labor Statistics, the Department of the Treasury, and other government agencies. More than two thousand files are currently available, and new

material is always being added. This is where businesses turn for the daily release of Treasury rate quotations, State and Local government bond rates, regular producer and consumer price indexes, manufacturing and trade inventories, unemployment figures, and most other statistics related to the national economy. It is an invaluable source for the most current, most authoritative information. Now it is available, for an annual fee, through the Internet. For access information contact the Bureau of Commerce, Office of Business Analysis at (202) 482–1986.

Commerce Business Daily

A daily listing of all federal procurement invitations, research and grant opportunities, contract awards, subcontracting leads, sales of surplus property, and foreign business opportunities. The Internet version is available the day prior to print publication.

Federal Register

The source for new federal regulations, many with extensive background material from the responsible government agency, including a review of existing research in the area. The *Federal Register* also provides proposed rules, presidential documents, notices and reports on government meetings. It includes publications from the Office of Management and Budget and from the Securities and Exchange Commission, grant application instructions and deadlines, and notices of official agency actions. Both the *Commerce Business Daily* and the *Federal Register* are accessible on the Internet for a fee. Contact Counterpoint Publishing at (800) 998–4515 for information.

Government Accounting Office Reports

Background documents prepared for Congress and the White House on budget and transportation issues, food and agriculture, environmental protection and other questions related to national policy and budget initiatives. These documents are available by anonymous ftp from: cu.nih.gov

Library of Congress

Library catalogs from major research institutions and universities around world offer telnet access through the Internet. A list of U.S. and international libraries with access information is posted at the InfoSource; and to locate a particular book or journal title, the Internet-accessible catalog of the nearest university library is usually the best place to start a search. But for all-inclusive research information, there is no match for the Library of Congress. The Library's Internet available database contains the LC Catalog of book, journal, manuscript, microfilm, and other format titles. These can be searched by title, author, and subject. Also available are files on Federal Legislation that contain summaries, chronologies, and detailed status information for legislation introduced in the U.S. Congress since 1973. This is an invaluable source for tracking the progress of various bills and resolutions, and the information can be retrieved in a number of ways. Another file provides information on foreign laws and regulations, as well as journal articles on legal topics.

Marvel, the Library of Congress Gopher, serves as a gateway to extensive information from many other federal agencies. Using Marvel, one can search the Catalog of Federal Domestic Assistance, and the files of the Commerce Department, the Environmental Protection Agency, the Food and Drug Administration, the Justice Department (including Supreme Court decisions), the National Technical Information Service, the Patent and Trademark Office, and much more. The Library of Congress plans to continue updating and expanding this Gopher, which promises to become the essential tool for locating federal and statistical information of all types. To reach Library of Congress resources telnet to 140.147.254.3 or connect to the Gopher server at marvel.loc.gov.

Many more specialized resources in law, technology, medicine, the sciences, economics, and other subject areas can be located on the Internet. A comprehensive listing would range from agriculture to ZIP codes and cover hundreds of pages. Keeping track is a full-time occupation, since more information is posted on the Internet all the time. It takes some exploration and experimentation to determine which sources are the most valuable for a particular company (Cronin 1993). From a manager's viewpoint, no one source is as important as the ability to connect with specialists and peers, potential partners, and future customers anywhere in the world. Understanding these Internet basics provides a foundation for planning the network's strategic contribution to a particular business.

THE SEARCH FOR COMPETITIVE ADVANTAGE

Signing on to the Internet does not automatically endow a company with competitive advantage. Several important components are necessary to move from connecting to competing. The first is involvement by top management. The model for competitive advantage developed by Michael Porter at Harvard Business School highlights the necessity of managers becoming more knowledgeable about new developments in technology:

> Most general managers know that the [information] revolution is under way, and few dispute its importance. As more and more of their time and investment capital are absorbed in information technology and its effects, executives have a growing awareness that the technology can no longer be the exclusive territory of EDP [electronic data processing] or IS [information systems] departments. As they see their rivals use information for competitive advantage, these executives recognize the need to become directly involved in the management of the new technology. In the face of rapid change, however, they don't know how (1991, 59).

To gain competitive advantage through information, Porter advises that managers must understand not just the technology but also the "value chain" in which their company operates. In Porter's definition, the value chain for any business includes several basic components. The first is inputs—these are sources of information and technology, as well as suppliers of other goods and services to the company. The second component is the company's own internal activities that create a product or service. Finally, the value chain includes the distribution channel for the company's product, and the customers who ultimately purchase it. No matter what the company's area of business, information will have an impact on each activity along the value chain. In fact, Porter asserts that information technology is, "transforming the way value activities are performed and the nature of the linkages among them. It also is affecting competitive scope and reshaping the way products meet buyer needs. These basic effects explain why information technology has acquired strategic significance and is different from the many other technologies business use" (65). The search for competitive advantage through strategic use of technology first described by Porter and other management analysts in the 1980s has become imperative for business survival in the 1990s (Clemmons and McFarlan 1991).

The Internet can make a significant contribution to each component of a company's value chain. To uncover and evaluate new avenues for competitive advantage through use of the Internet, companies need to analyze their relationships with suppliers and vendors, the existing role of information in the organization of the company, internal production mechanisms, and the points of contact with customers.

Relationships with Vendors and Suppliers

Figure 2.2 illustrates the impact of the Internet on inputs from vendors and suppliers.

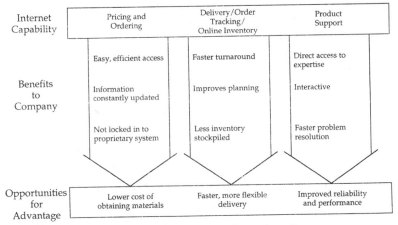

FIGURE 2.2   Internet Value Chain: Inputs from Suppliers.

The network provides fast, reliable connections to suppliers around the world. Companies can communicate with vendors in any location, without incurring additional communication costs. It is difficult to convey complex bids or cost estimates accurately over the telephone, and if the vendor is in a different time zone even scheduling telephone calls can be problematic. Large amounts of data are also cumbersome to transmit via telefacsimile. Even overnight delivery of information may be too slow when critical decisions are waiting to be made. Many vendors offer electronic pricing and ordering information to overcome these limitations. However, adopting one vendor's proprietary on-line system may limit a company's flexibility to change vendors.

The Internet connection offers all the advantages of a direct electronic link to vendors without requiring the company to commit to a proprietary vendor system, which might make it difficult to switch to lower-cost or more competitive suppliers in the future. With more vendors providing on-line pricing and ordering capabilities over the Internet, companies have a basis for comparing prices and delivery schedules of several potential suppliers. Up-to-date information is available whenever a company needs it, and ordering can be more efficient.

Electronic distribution of software, publications, and other items provides immediate access to these products. On-line tracking of orders and inventory ensures that companies are aware of delivery dates, and reduces delays in the distribution process. Many companies have found that product support over the Internet significantly reduces the time lost due to system performance problems. For some companies, the efficiencies and cost savings generated by dealing directly with suppliers over the Internet have more than justified their investment in the network.

Internal Operations

Some advantages of networked communication and information access for the company's internal processes are outlined in Figure 2.3.

The global connectivity of the Internet offers companies immediate savings in long-distance telecommunications. A dedicated Internet connection allows unlimited exchange of data and e-mail with locations around the world. Even a low-cost,

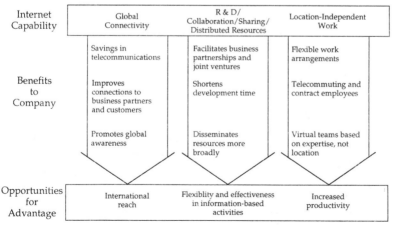

Internet Capability	Global Connectivity	R & D/ Collaboration/Sharing/ Distributed Resources	Location-Independent Work
Benefits to Company	Savings in telecommunications	Facilitates business partnerships and joint ventures	Flexible work arrangements
	Improves connections to business partners and customers	Shortens development time	Telecommuting and contract employees
	Promotes global awareness	Disseminates resources more broadly	Virtual teams based on expertise, not location
Opportunities for Advantage	International reach	Flexiblity and effectiveness in information-based activities	Increased productivity

FIGURE 2.3   Internet Value Chain: Internal Operations.

shared dial-up connection with an hourly use charge is more economical than long-distance telephone charges. In the longer term, the ability to exchange information quickly and easily facilitates the relationships with business partners and customers, encouraging more joint ventures. For employees, connecting to an international information source promotes global awareness. It allows companies to monitor economic and political developments in countries targeted for market or production expansion.

The information resources and discussion groups on the Internet also provide employees with direct access to virtually unlimited advice and information. By helping them to answer questions and retrieve relevant materials, the network connection can increase their productivity. Research teams are able to exchange data and discuss results with colleagues in other organizations. The Internet also facilitates more effective deployment of human resources. Network links support telecommuting and allow small, remote offices to participate more actively in companywide programs and contribute to joint projects. When project teams are being formed, managers can select members based on their expertise, without regard to geographic location.

Customer Relations

Contact with customers over the Internet is another area for potential advantage, as illustrated in Figure 2.4.

The Internet is a powerful tool for market research, for establishing new markets, and for testing customer interest in emerging products. Thousands of discussion groups and bulletin boards are available for keeping in touch with new developments through environmental scanning, as well as for direct contact with customers. Gophers and other tools allow compa-

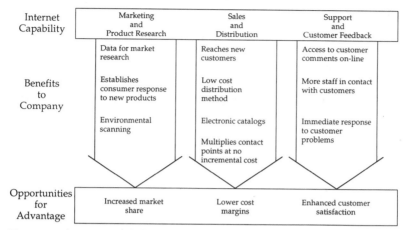

FIGURE 2.4 Internet Value Chain: Customer Relations.

nies to provide detailed product information, announcement of new offerings, and other public relations material for customers connected to the Internet. Manufacturers and producers of electronic information or software can deliver these items instantly to customers and collect payment on the Internet. Electronic catalogs offer products and services to millions of users browsing through the network. Vendors can offer on-line help services and product support without the additional expense of dedicated connections to customers. The Internet allows direct interactions with customers to be spread through many divisions of a company; technical and development staff, documentation providers, production workers, and researchers find out first hand how customers respond to company products. They can address problems and provide customer support as a team.

Strategic use of the Internet based on an analysis of the value chain encourages companies to focus on areas where they can measurably improve performance. If a company decides to distinguish itself through the quality of its customer service organization, the network can be a decisive asset in achieving this goal. If the emphasis is on developing and marketing innovative products, the Internet connection will contribute at a different point in the value chain. As the following chapters will illustrate, the benefits of the Internet will vary from business to business. One thing is certain, however. For companies seeking competitive advantage, the global network is an essential management resource.

REFERENCES

Alsop, Stewart. 1993. Editor-in-Chief's Landmark Technology: Internet. *Infoworld* (15)16:17. April 26.

Catlett, Charles E. 1993. Internet Evolution and Future Directions. In *Internet System Handbook.* Edited by Daniel C. Lynch and Marshall T. Rose. Boston: Addison-Wesley.

Clark, David D. 1982. RFC 814. Internet Request for Comments. July.

Clemmons, Eric K. and Warren F. McFarlan. 1991. Telecomm: Hook Up or Lose Out. In *Revolution in Real Time: Managing Information Technology in the 1990s.* Boston: Harvard Business Review Book.

Cronin, Mary J. 1993. Internet Business Resources. *Database* (16)6. December 1993.

Dagres, Tod. 1993. Pulling the right strings; Assessing the features and futures of net management tools. *Network World.* 10(7) Supplement: s9. February 15.

Davidow, William H. and Michael S. Malone. 1992. *The Virtual Corporation,* New York: HarperCollins.

Gates, Rick. 1993. The Internet Hunt for August 1993.

Krol, Ed. 1993. How to find resources on the Internet. *Network World.* (10)7:75–76.

Locke, Christopher. 1993. RFC/FYI—Editorial. *The Internet Business Journal.* 1(1):3.

National Science Foundation. 1992. NSFNET Backbone Services Acceptable Use Policy. Posted on the InterNIC InfoSource.

Porter, Michael E. and Victor E. Millar. 1991. How Information Gives You Competitive Advantage. In *Revolution in Real Time: Managing Information Technology in the 1990s.* Boston: Harvard Business Review Press.

Rugo, John. 1993. The emerging market for Internet services. Presented at Public Access to the Internet, John F. Kennedy School of Government. May 26–27.

Wiggins, Rich. 1993. The University of Minnesota's Internet Gopher system: A tool for accessing network-based electronic information. *The Public-Access Computer Systems Review* 4(2):4–60.

Wilson, David L. 1993. Clinton signs bill on electronic access to government data. *The Chronicle of Higher Education.* June 23, 1993: A15–16.

CHAPTER *3*

The Desktop as Global Village

> *For 20 years, we have been hearing and reading about the global village, a futuristic vision of how we will live in a wired world with instantaneous communication. Over the last two years, something remarkable has happened: The global village has become a reality.*
> —**Carl Malamud,** St. Petersburg Times

> *People talk about the "global village." Internet is already one... With the Internet you bring globalisation right up to your office or your home, literally at your fingertips.*
> —**Tommi Chen,** Business Times

It doesn't matter whether you are sitting at a work station in Washington, D.C., or typing at a terminal in Singapore. When you connect to the Internet, your window on the world offers the same dazzling prospect of endless information resources and instant global connectivity. As Tommi Chen, manager of the campus network at the National University of Singapore, recounts in the *Business Times*, the Internet facilitates electronic collaboration, delivers full text to the desktop, offers business resources, and much more. On the other side of the world Carl Malamud, founder of Internet Talk Radio and much-travelled network analyst (Malamud 1993), demonstrates the same enthusiasm in describing network capabilities to the readers of the *St. Petersburg Times*.

"Global village" has been applied to many different situations over the past few decades, some far afield from Marshall McLuhan's original concept of how computerized communication changes society. But it seems entirely appropriate that this phrase should become the description of choice for the Internet. The millions of people linked to the network not only have the common experience of using the same electronic tools and information resources regardless of location, they are also connected to each other in a new way, free to exchange ideas, solicit advice, consult, and argue, without regard to national boundaries.

As a window on the world, the Internet has been an important player in many of the most dramatic episodes of politics and conflict in recent years (Lynch 1993). When Chinese students demonstrated in Tiananmen Square in 1989, their aspirations and requests for support were detailed in Internet messages to colleagues in other countries. The events behind the fall of the Soviet Union were documented at terminals in Moscow and sent out over the Internet when other lines of communication were shut down. While missiles rained on Israel during the Gulf War, the Internet connections on desktops in Tel Aviv and Jerusalem brought news and reassurances to anxious friends and relatives around the world. Most recently, bulletins from Croatia have been channeled to the international community from Zagreb by a writer who says, "Electronic mail is the only link between me and the outside world" (Cooke and Lehrer 1993, 60).

Even without the drama of political upheavals, the daily interchange of technical assistance takes on the cosmopolitan flair of an international information bazaar as messages from all countries flow back and forth. A systems administrator in Brazil wants advice on getting TCP/IP up and working his company; suggestions are offered from Finland and Texas. A researcher in the Ukraine asks for help in establishing an independent network for his country while an economist in Australia announces a new source of information on worldwide employment. Countless e-mail messages circle the globe daily, creating bonds of common understanding and mutual assistance among citizens of the Internet who will probably never meet face to face.

The impact of high-speed global communication on research and education is already so profound that the Internet has been dubbed the second Gutenberg revolution. Engineers and researchers have exchanged data and shared discoveries over the network since its inception. Now the international scope of the Internet has started to transform education, even at the public school level. Internet connections in hundreds of classrooms demonstrate that students can use the video conferencing and e-mail capacity of the Internet to communicate with peers in distant countries, learning the importance of cooperating across national borders, as well as valuable computer skills.

Clearly, the Internet has become the highway of choice for a burgeoning flow of global communication about research, technology, politics, and education. These topics may seem remote from the daily concerns of managing a company, but in fact they are directly related. In *Turning Points* (1992), Charles J. Fombrun argues that "technological, economic, social, and political pressures" are the factors inexorably propelling every business into an increasingly competitive global environment. "Globalization," he contends, "forces economic competition, which, in turn, goads firms to be more efficient—to search for ways of reducing costs and improving revenues" (25). Global awareness, he concludes, is a precondition for any company interested in being around to do business in the year 2000.

There may be no better way for companies to ensure a clear window on the world than by participating in the global network. As Figure 3.1 illustrates, networks outside the United States have increased as a proportion of the total Internet community over the past two years. International connections

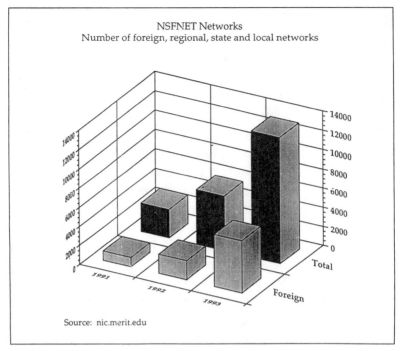

FIGURE 3.1   Total and Foreign Networks 1991–1993.

are expanding at such a rapid rate that the Internet has become the most popular and sometimes the only reliable source of data exchange and external communication for some countries (Quarterman et al. 1993).

Wherever a company makes its home, one of the fastest ways to transform employees into citizens of the world is to provide them with Internet addresses. That string of letters and dots, punctuated with the @ symbol, is a powerful passport to the global community, a membership card to a nonexclusive, international club that already encompasses more than a hundred countries and extends its reach daily. An Internet connection can open new avenues to international business partners, customers, and markets. For the first time, local and regional firms need not be constrained by the cost of long-distance data exchange. Multinationals, in turn, are discovering the value of the Internet to supplement their private internal networks. In the global village, all participants can and do benefit from sharing their network experiences and expertise.

GLOBAL VILLAGE, INC.

Global competition and multinational communication are already a way of life for America's largest companies. Comprehensive private electronic networks, or enterprise networks, link the far-flung subsidiaries and branch offices of corporate giants like IBM and Rockwell International. These internal networks safeguard proprietary business information while supporting the intensive flow of data inside the company. Increasingly, however, the focus is turning to communication with the outside world. For this purpose, many corporations have concluded that Internet gateways offer the most effective means of connecting with business partners, customers, and everyone else in the global village.

The need to keep in touch with the international marketplace is no longer confined to the largest corporations. Even companies with no plans for expanding outside the United States need to know what is happening in the rest of the world. Their competition, their next source of parts or supplies, and new ideas for their products will most likely be influenced by international events. Small companies, in fact, are more vulnerable than the big players to an unexpected turn of the tide on the international front.

The practical impact of a global economy is that events in the Middle East, China, or Japan will reverberate not just in the newspaper headlines, but also in America's shopping centers and manufacturing plants. Henry Wendt, Chairman of SmithKline Beecham, one of the world's largest multinational corporations, concludes that "the marketplace imposes a global imperative that cannot be evaded. Global economic integration requires a global response." As a result, he says, "even resolutely local businesses must now compete with global products and services in their own backyard. Stay-at-homes cannot secede from the global marketplace because the global marketplace is not elsewhere, it's everywhere" (1993, 52).

The transformation of the Internet from a network of researchers, government contractors, and universities to a heterogeneous mix of education, science, and commerce is not happening just in the United States. Commercial Internet links are thriving in many other countries, and the new customers signing up for service through providers like PIPEX in Great Britain and Internet Initiative Japan are primarily businesses. In every country, business planners have become aware of the importance of an Internet connection in establishing a presence in the global marketplace.

The more companies use electronic connections to communicate with customers and business partners, the less important their actual geographic location becomes. With an advanced communications network, a business can locate wherever conditions are most favorable to growth (Keen 1991). In this new environment, having the best connections to the rest of the world can provide strategic advantage to cities or entire countries in attracting new businesses. As locations compete on the basis of telecommunications and sophisticated information technology to attract new business, access to Internet connectivity has become an important selling point.

Singapore provides an interesting example of competing through connectivity—and the dynamic relationship between policy, commerce, and technology in the global village. Singapore promotes itself as "The Intelligent Island," and its National Computer Board has adopted a plan called IT2000 to transform Singapore into the information technology capital of Asia. Government agencies make every effort to smooth the pathway of multinational corporations wishing to use Singapore as a communication hub for the twenty-first century. The island's national networks connect companies directly to Singapore's import-export departments, the port authority, and other agencies to eliminate paperwork and speed the process of moving goods, services, and financial transactions through Singapore to the rest of the world. Despite this emphasis on technology, government officials were reluctant to allow Singapore residents direct connectivity to the Internet. The open, uncensored flow of information over the global network challenged Singapore's tightly controlled government planning and political environment (Rapaport 1993).

It is no coincidence that Tommi Chen, cited above, extols the benefits of the Internet for business. He, along with many others, made the case to government officials that Internet connectivity was an essential component of Singapore's competitive package of services. Planners like Chen believed that without unhampered access to the global network, business and research in Singapore would be at a disadvantage. Working through the National University of Singapore, he created Technet to provide connections to Internet for the research community (Ong 1992). Eventually the realities of global competition overcame, at least in part, the Singapore government's concerns about information control. Now the Internet is promoted as an essential resource for every business.

Closer to home, the Internet has become a factor in discussions of United States competitiveness. The Clinton administration's high-technology National Information Infrastructure initiative postulates that government and private investment in expanding the electronic highway will stimulate economic growth and give the United States a lead in developing the key networked industries and universities of the future. Working to get a jump start on this process, states like Hawaii, North Carolina and Virginia, as well as a number of North American cities, have included the Internet in programs designed to attract new business and improve the quality of life. Many locations have developed Free-Nets, community-based Internet nodes based on the model for community network access first implemented in Cleveland. Free-Nets provide access to local and international Internet resources for individuals, schools, libraries, nonprofit groups, and small businesses.

It is too early to determine whether there is any direct relationship between the Internet and regional economic growth. As noted in Chapter 1, there is still debate and disagreement about the best balance of government planning and commercial interests in expanding electronic access to the information highway. It is clear, however, that the Internet is having a significant impact on the companies already connected to it. The network has created new possibilities for the largest and the smallest companies to participate more actively in the global village.

MULTINATIONALS MAKE THE CONNECTION

A closer look at the experience of four multinational corporations provides valuable insights for any size business planning to participate actively in the global network. Even the most sophisticated internal corporate networks are no longer sufficient for the complex communication needs of multinational companies. Enterprise networks linking offices and employees around the world must be supplemented by gateways to the standard systems used by customers, business partners, governments, and universities. Multinational corporations may have similar motivations for linking to the Internet, but how they use it depends a great deal on distinctive corporate cultures and styles of work. Factors like management support, network policies, training, and ease of access make a tremendous difference in how much the Internet contributes to corporate success. When top executives promote Internet use and provide the resources for its implementation throughout the organization, the impact can be significant. Such is the case with Schlumberger.

Schlumberger

Schlumberger may not be a household word, but this $6 billion multinational company is most definitely a citizen of the global village. Schlumberger provides oil field services and a variety of high-technology measurement devices to customers around the world. From an early focus on bore-hole measurement, the company has expanded to become an essential player in the petroleum industry. Whether customers want vital data about existing oil wells, or technical support in exploring potential oil and gas deposits anywhere in the world, Schlumberger is in the business of finding answers.

The company's oil field service locations range from Oklahoma to Japan, South America to Northern Europe, and encompass a marine fleet of more than twenty vessels, drilling and pumping rigs, and research and manufacturing facilities. The corporation maintains extended communication links into remote parts of the world where other networks haven't penetrated—even mobile units like trucks and boats carry dish antennas that link them to satellites for communications. Wherever major oil deposits exist, or where exploration is underway, one of Schlumberger's many subsidiaries may be found.

The company also provides a full range of technology-based measurement systems, including design and manufacture of the meters used by gas, water, and electric utilities. Their products are essential to measurement systems as diverse as gas station pumps, automatic testers for computer chips, and the "smart cards" used in the French telephone system. The unifying theme for Schlumberger's complex of separate businesses and subsidiaries is a continued focus on petroleum services, systems, and measurement. Most of the company's products and services are information- and data-intensive. Their services in the oil field environment are evaluated on how quickly and accurately they can acquire and process data, and deliver results to the customer. Schlumberger maintains its advantage by keeping current with the latest technologies and inventing new ones.

Operating from more than two thousand offices, field sites, and research centers located in a hundred countries, Schlumberger is a truly transnational organization. It is part of corporate policy to hire employees from each country where Schlumberger does business in proportion to the revenue generated by that region. Once they have mastered a particular aspect of the company, employees are encouraged to transfer to different locations and divisions to broaden their understanding of the overall business. The result is an extremely diverse work force with an international outlook.

Schlumberger's distributed structure makes it a challenge to find ways for geographically scattered staff to work together in close collaboration and keep informed about evolving projects and priorities. Management often attacks critical problems through task forces made up of employees from different locations. This brings people into contact with one another and promotes a strong flow of information throughout the company. But it also creates another problem—how to get the work of the task forces accomplished without having staff spending all their time traveling to distant meetings.

Bill MacGregor, a scientist at the Schlumberger Laboratory for Computer Science in Austin, Texas, seeks network-based tools that multinational task forces and projects can use to get the job done. MacGregor tests and evaluates a variety of "shared workspace tools" designed to enhance information-sharing and collaborative work in offices around the world. His task is made more manageable by Schlumberger's active participation in the Internet.

MacGregor observes that his company's interest in the Internet is not just a geographic convenience. Global networking is a natural outgrowth of Schlumberger's pursuit of the best technology solutions for international research and communication. In part this stems from continuing the tradition of promoting technical staff into management positions; most senior managers at Schlumberger come from the engineering component of the company and make every effort to keep current with new developments. Company culture stresses creative applications of technology to improve existing operations and make breakthrough discoveries.

Senior managers at Schlumberger are fully aware of the potential of the Internet, and are regular users of the network. For a growing number of employees, a laptop computer with modem is the first item packed for business trips and the last one put away in the hotel at night. On the road, the network keeps Schlumberger employees connected to discussions and decisions that must move forward, even while participants themselves may be constantly on the move.

This combination of long-distance travel and electronic teamwork puts a premium on information-sharing at all levels of the company. The Internet is a valuable tool for bridging the differences among locations and promoting a common culture. Even the small details of making frequent travel a little less stressful and a lot more effective are part of the company's networking plan. Some Schlumberger locations are establishing their own local Internet Gophers, featuring pictures and profiles of the people who work at that office and news about current projects, as well as the kinds of information appreciated by visitors: recommended hotels and restaurants, maps, tips on finding one's way from the airport. MacGregor would like to see every Schlumberger location offer this kind of on-line orientation, so travelling staff can arrive for a visit already somewhat familiar with essential features of the community.

The Internet has been a component of Schlumberger's strategy of technical innovation for more than a decade. Since the early 1980s, the company's research laboratories in the United States, working on collaborative projects with academic scientists, used the Internet to exchange e-mail and research findings. Even at that time, the company saw the advantages of client server technology, and began to plan for broader applications of TCP/IP networks for internal as well as external communication.

In 1986 Schlumberger established a corporate network group charged with improving connectivity for all company locations. The first step was to build an X.25 packet switched network because that technology fit best into the realities of the commercial and international network world of the time. The internal X.25 network quickly expanded to include more than five hundred hosts connecting Schlumberger sites around the world. Now, however, its growth is limited mainly to remote sites and some countries in Africa, South America, and Southeast Asia that have not developed the infrastructure to support TCP/IP networks. The network strategy of choice for Schlumberger as a whole is to move all its internal communications to a TCP/IP architecture similar to the structure of the Internet. Locations in the United States and Europe are moving quickly to convert to Schlumberger's TCP/IP backbone. This is where the company plans to invest in future bandwidth capacity and enhanced networking capabilities, including voice and video.

Like other companies, Schlumberger has made the commitment to building its internal connectivity on a TCP/IP base to link its many locations most effectively to one another and to the rest of the world. Connectivity to the Internet is there for every Schlumberger location that wants it, but Bill MacGregor has observed that it usually requires some external motivator for individuals to appreciate the value of the global network and take the time to learn how to use it effectively. "In many cases," he says, "sites will get Internet access and not really know how to use it fully; people don't automatically understand how to get to the resources or deal with network discussion groups. Some other sites are still using the X.25 connection and don't see any reason to change to TCP/IP. Even among people who do understand what the Internet can do in theory, there has to be a jump start to get them to be active users in practice."

What distinguishes Schlumberger's approach to the Internet is a well thought-out strategy for providing that "jump start" on the global network. Scott Guthery, a scientific advisor with Schlumberger's Laboratory for Computer Science in Austin, Texas, has primary responsibility for working with company locations around the world to encourage more use of the Internet. Guthery has opted for the technical career path offered by Schlumberger to a small group of highly skilled people within the company who devote their time to keeping up with the latest developments in technology, figuring out how new technologies can contribute to the company and spreading the word to Schlumberger locations that might benefit from adopting these advances.

Scientific advisors take the initiative for moving new ideas around and generating discussion, encouraging coordinated change and innovation within the company. As Guthery puts it, his job is to "run threads of technical coherence through the company." Sometimes this involves connecting projects in different countries when it becomes clear they would benefit from closer collaboration or a new technology.

Guthery decided the Internet would be his personal technical specialty, because the network offered so many potential benefits to Schlumberger. As the official Internet expert within the company, he takes responsibility for providing training and information about the network. He encourages Schlumberger sites to get on to the Internet if they aren't connected, and shows them what can be accomplished when they are. Guthery devel-

oped a special Internet tutorial for the company's annual software conference a few years ago, and this provides the core of a
traveling workshop that he now takes to other Schlumberger
sites.

At an Internet workshop, Guthery introduces Internet basics,
reviews the specific instructions needed to get going on the
network, and illustrates how using Internet can change the
approach to work. Among the reasons he presents for using the
network are:

- exchange e-mail with customers and colleagues

- get commodity code

- track standards

- technology watch

- ask questions and get answers

- send and receive documents

- conduct business; for example buy software, order parts

- learn about unfamiliar technologies quickly

Guthery receives invitations to each site from local managers,
rather than dropping in as an "outside expert." Once on location, he talks to technical staff in advance to get a sense of the
questions that might arise. After making his presentation and
answering questions, he takes the time to go around and sit
down with people at their machines to introduce the Internet
in a more personal way. This provides an opportunity for
hands-on use of the commands and functions and demonstration of specialized resources. Guthery's experience has been that
the Internet is not that easy to learn just by reading about it or
hearing a presentation; people have to get their hands on the
keyboard and learn by doing.

A traveling workshop is just one strategy for spreading the word about the Internet. Because network resources keep changing and evolving, Schlumberger dedicates one of its internal bulletin boards to Internet news; Guthery posts information about the latest developments there.

In addition to the benefits of communication and collaboration for Schlumberger's widely scattered locations, the company has identified the Internet's rich archives of publicly available software as a valuable tool for speeding development projects. Using software code already available on the Internet is part of an overall company strategy to accelerate development and encourage more standardization of the process of writing software. Guthery emphasizes the benefits of integrating existing software from the Internet into Schlumberger development projects as part of his presentation on network resources:

> One reason I was asked to take the Internet program on the road was so that people in all the sites can get used to the idea of importing [software] code rather than writing it all themselves. In designing new applications, we have to be system integrators not just system builders. That means getting used to relying on standard components for writing code. All the code now available on the Internet makes it possible to find most of the utility programs ready made.

To keep up with new software resources, Guthery participates in Internet and USENET groups that discuss and evaluate public domain software. He perfects his skills at locating appropriate software, both for his own use and to derive tips that can be passed on during his training sessions.

As Guthery spreads this strategy around the company, he has begun to hear some gratifying success stories. Because people now know about the availability of public domain software and how to find it, when a software program is required for a new project, they make an effort to find usable code on the network instead of starting from scratch. He has collected examples of projects where the existence of usable public software made it possible to move more quickly through the development process.

The Internet also supports Schlumberger's dissemination of information to customers. The data gathered from oil wells, seismic surveys, and other on-site measurements are extremely time-sensitive. It is essential to send results to customers as quickly as possible; typically, major decisions are waiting to be made. At the same time, much of the data is extensive and complex to interpret. Once security concerns are carefully addressed, the Internet provides an excellent vehicle for transmitting very large data files quickly and reliably. Most of the customers using Schlumberger services already have Internet connectivity. For security reasons, their private Internet systems, like Schlumberger's, are isolated from the public Internet so they can see out but other users can not see in.

To handle security issues, Schlumberger set up a special SNIC (Schlumberger Network Interconnect Center), a secure rendezvous point where data can be placed at the customer's request as soon as it is transmitted from the field. Like many other Internet applications, this concept is proving to be even more useful than expected. Now that the exploration and measurement data can be made available on the network, customers and Schlumberger engineers can look at it interactively. When a customer needs clarification or more data, Schlumberger can respond immediately. The same mechanism can support collaborative research work—in the future, data available at the SNIC will be used to support research groups with scientists inside and outside of Schlumberger working together on joint projects.

As the interest in collaborating over the Internet continues to grow, Bill MacGregor looks for future enhancements of the network resources for overcoming the limits of time and space, including applications of audio and video:

We are experimenting with video over the Internet as one element in a suite of collaboration techniques. Because Schlumberger is such a distributed company we are always in the midst of projects involving people in different locations. I have looked at a variety of tools that could help with this collaborative process, things that will allow people in different locations to work together over the network in the most effective way possible. When they are working on a project, the company has found that people want tools that are easy to use and fade into the background—the focus should be on the collaboration and the information being shared, not on the tools that support their work.

A reliable and high-quality audio connection is extremely important for distributed projects. The quality of audio over the Internet is not always acceptable and MacGregor feels they haven't found a good solution yet; project groups rely on phone lines for audio conferences. He does not expect a rapid growth for international videoconferencing until the tradeoff between image quality and price of bandwidth improves. But he has already seen some instances when even the existing tools have proved their value, "Talking heads aren't a priority, at least not when people already know each other and have worked together closely," he says. "It makes sense to use a video connection when it's important to 'meet' the other party; customers seem to have a very positive reaction to the video link, so one good application is setting up customer meetings."

MacGregor anticipates using the video capability of the Internet more when the cost of bandwidth comes down. He sees it facilitating communication among Schlumberger staff working on similar jobs in different locations around the world. Video connections could be especially useful for the types of responsibilities that don't normally involve extensive travel. Facilities managers, for example, rarely travel to other sites of the company, but do have many issues in common with their peers. Sharing information and becoming familiar with the layout of other sites using a video link would be very useful and could provide ideas for more efficient facilities management. Librarians at the different Schlumberger locations meet only once a year, but their services increasingly depend on coordination of physical and electronic resources. Video meetings would help them to plan more effectively for future delivery of information.

Schlumberger's strategy for global competitiveness includes using the Internet to speed development projects, to serve customer information needs more effectively and to foster a sense of community and collaboration among the company's far-flung locations. However, Schlumberger recognizes that employees won't spontaneously find value in the Internet, so it has dedicated resources to ensuring that people understand the network's functionality and are able to use it effectively in their daily work. As connections expand and applications like video become more sophisticated, Schlumberger expects to increase its use of the Internet to maintain a leadership position in a field where technological innovation and global communications are fundamental to success.

IBM

When the name on the door says International Business Machines, you know that a multinational outlook is ingrained in the corporate culture. But sometimes, the bigger the corporation, the more self-sufficient it can attempt to become. At its peak size in 1986, IBM employed more than four hundred thousand people around the globe in its own microcosm of the global village. It not only had an extensive internal network connecting this far-flung empire, it created its own standards for that network and encouraged other companies to adopt them in order to do business. From inside IBM in those days, it was entirely possible to feel that the center of international connectivity was somewhere near corporate headquarters in Armonk, New York.

Howard Funk, a technical assistant in the office of IBM's Vice President for Science and Technology, had the insight to propose in the early 1980s that IBM needed a bigger window on the rest of the world. While the research division, with its scientific and university ties, had already established Internet connections (see Chapters 5 and 8), the corporate division relied on the internal IBM networks and e-mail systems for its communication needs.

Convinced of the importance of the Internet for all of IBM, Funk set out to change corporate policy. In 1985 he proposed establishing an Internet gateway that would give corporate and marketing staff access to the external network for communication and educational purposes. At that point the prospect of moving beyond the internal IBM network to an uncontrolled universe of unfamiliar protocols had little appeal, and the proposal was not approved. Among the many concerns raised about the Internet, according to Funk, were security problems, the cost of establishing and maintaining a gateway, and whether or not it would really add any significant functionality to the existing IBM networks.

Over the next five years, a lot happened to change the scope of the Internet and the attitude of IBM. Networking and distributed computing overtook the mainframe computing industry, while customers began looking to open systems and international standards to replace their proprietary installations. At the same time, the international and research participation of the Internet community surged forward, revealing the power of a networked environment. When Howard Funk reworked his proposal for an IBM Internet gateway at the end of 1989, it took only a few months of discussions about policy and procedure for the concept to be approved. There was, however, no special funding or staffing allocated to the task of introducing hundreds of thousands of IBM employees to the capabilities of the Internet.

Taking responsibility for the gateway, Funk set up an automated registration process based on the internal IBM mail system. Initial interest in the Internet connection was limited to people who were already motivated to use the network for communicating with customers or business partners. Connectivity for individuals initially required a specific justification and management approval, which slowed down the process and added an extra layer of administrative review. After more than seven thousand users had registered under this policy, with only one instance of approval being denied by management, Funk requested a simplified process. Once the administrative review was removed, the number of employees requesting a connection increased significantly.

With increasing Internet popularity, especially among the employees in marketing and customer support, questions about the type of traffic being carried over the network were raised. IBM had started out with a research connection, which was subject to the provisions of the National Science Foundation's Acceptable Use Policy. With over a thousand new Internet connections each month being registered throughout IBM, it was clear that use could not be effectively monitored. Management made the decision to shift the corporate gateway to commercial status to allow broader business use of the network in 1992. According to Funk, switching from research to commercial status was a clear winner. "There was every reason to go commercial; the difference in cost for the commercial option amounted to almost zero," he recalls. "There was no way to effectively enforce noncommercial use with the spread of connections throughout the company, and high stakes were involved if IBM was seen as transgressing."

The commercial connection led to another spike in the number of network participants. When Funk described the new Internet connection on internal e-mail, he immediately received

2,500 requests for information on the implications of less restrictive use policies, an indication that at least some employees were poised to take advantage of the global network to expand their communication and support for customers over the Internet.

Security concerns also limited the utility of the network for many employees during the first two years of Internet connections. The initial gateway was limited to e-mail use only, with no capability for file transfer or direct telnet to remote computers. Because funding for the Internet was limited, it was not possible to set up the network configuration that was needed for a secure implementation of file transfer for several years. A 1992 survey of Internet users within IBM provided the impetus for creating a more secure gateway.

IBM employees using the Internet were overwhelmingly positive about the network's impact on their ability to communicate with peers and with customers. Figure 3.2 illustrates the major categories of use recorded by survey respondents. The great majority indicated that their technical vitality was enhanced by the Internet's global interconnectivity. The size of the Internet community within IBM was growing more quickly too, with new users requesting connections at a rate of about 1400 a month, even though the survey indicated that almost 65 percent of users had learned of the Internet's availability only through word of mouth.

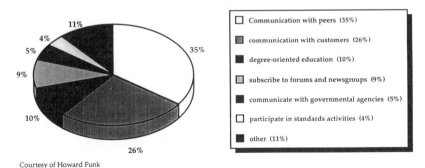

Courtesy of Howard Funk

FIGURE 3.2   IBM Internet User Survey (1992).

The survey results supported Howard Funk's impression that IBM's connection to the Internet was having a positive impact on productivity, even though the absolute numbers of Internet connections remained small in relation to the size of the company. The survey also made it clear that employees wanted to be more active users of the Internet. More than two-thirds said they wanted the ability to transfer files from the Internet and to use its telnet function as soon as possible. Many respondents made comments urging expanded Internet access and describing the importance of the Internet for their work. This provided enough evidence to move forward with the next phase of implementation: a secure gateway to allow file transfer and telnet capabilities for at least some users.

By May 1993, thirty thousand IBM corporate staff had been connected to the Internet, and the registration rate continued to climb. Howard Funk feels that his mission to create a dynamic link between IBM and the rest of the networking world has been accomplished. He is especially pleased at the positive feedback he gets over the network from active Internet users at IBM:

> I get at least one or two messages every day, from people who see the benefit of being connected and want to let me know they appreciate it. Just today, I got a note from a user saying he had used ftp for first time. It saved him nine months on his project because he was able to find and download data through the Internet that would not have been available in any published form until next year. If you take examples like that and multiply them by thirty thousand and more regular users, it really begins to make a difference.

Funk sees recent changes in IBM policy that make him optimistic that the Internet culture is taking hold. IBM's internal Internet directory of employees connected to the network is now accessible to outsiders who want to locate the e-mail address of an IBMer—a level of access to internal information that Funk is certain would never have been considered a few years ago. He hopes the next step will be to provide even more information about IBM to Internet users. This would be a profound change from the closed doors that previously met outsiders seeking company information on-line. Until recently, employees were not allowed to include their e-mail addresses on business cards, but now cards sporting an Internet address have become a statement about having the right connections.

For the first three years, basic information about the Internet gateway was distributed on internal IBM networks, but most employees who requested connections were encouraged to do so by word of mouth, or by a customer already on the network. Now there is a more formal program to publicize the availability of the Internet to all staff, and to talk about what can be accomplished by using it. There is a growing trend for executives in the company to use the Internet and to understand its value.

With IBMs work force pared down to fewer than three hundred thousand employees and its operations being challenged from competitors on all fronts, linking up with the rest of the world had started to look different by the early 1990s. But culture is a hard thing to change. And Howard Funk, Internet advocate, has joined the ranks of IBM retirees. Before leaving, he acknowledged that it would probably be impossible to get any one person to fill all the roles he has taken on as Internet administrator, policy setter, trainer, negotiator, and change agent. But he is confident that having opened the window to the global community, IBM will not want to close it again. How quickly this window becomes a doorway to the future will depend on the work of other Internet activists within the company—and there are signs that these are increasing in number.

David Singer, a researcher at IBM's Almaden Research Center in California, describes himself as a typical Internet user. "I read news groups, send and receive e-mail, import files, look at weather maps—the same things millions of other people are doing on the Internet." Singer is also instrumental in spreading the resources of the Internet to the rest of the company. He serves as the news importer for IBM, providing a gateway from USENET to the internal IBM mail system. He is personally committed to the Internet as a gateway to the world, and is encouraged to see more and more people in the company becoming active users.

Singer also thinks the Internet has potential for making IBM information available to the rest of the world. In 1993 he decided to try to get an OS/2 Gopher server up and running on an experimental basis. After some "playing around with Gopher at home," he developed a prototype, then found a colleague in IBM England who was interested in creating an enhanced version that could be put up at Almaden in a public, though still pilot, project.

The first information loaded on this prototype Gopher was rather eclectic. For test purposes, some background on the Almaden Research Center, including directions on getting there, a collection of OS/2 information and various items of interest to ham radio operators (like Singer himself) were included. After just a few months of unadvertised operation, the server was attracting hundreds of users daily, and several other groups in IBM contacted Almaden to ask that their materials be added. Now the server offers information from IBM Latin America's IBMLINK system and the IBM Client/Server White Papers, as well as fixes for OS/2 software. The number of connects is up to six hundred a day, with OS/2 and ham radio files currently attracting the most attention, although Singer continues to be somewhat mystified at the large number of people who access the file of directions for getting to Almaden.

Now that it is up and running, the Gopher server doesn't require that much of Singer's attention. It runs on a modest PS/2 Model 80 machine that sits in the corner of his office and quietly fields requests and offers information to anyone in the world who chooses to access it. When he looks at the Gopher statistics, Singer can determine the Internet address of those connecting to the server. So far, educational users predominate but that may be partly because many access it indirectly through the original Gopher at the University of Minnesota.

The experimental Gopher has provided IBM with a viable model for distributing information through the Internet. Singer personally sees lots of advantages and no significant drawbacks to this mode of communication with the world at large. What happens next may be a good indication of IBM's changing relationship with the global village.

Oracle

The landmark green glass towers of the Oracle Corporation in Redwood Shores, California, are a continent away from IBM headquarters in Armonk and probably even more distant if measured in terms of cyberspace. With revenues of $1.2 billion in 1992, Oracle's focus on integrated, portable software is based on a culture of networking and distributed computing. The 1992 Annual Report features distributed computing applications from some of the sixteen thousand Oracle customers in ninety-two countries, reinforcing the company's message that "the network is the computer."

An internal, private Oracle network links thousands of staff members and subsidiary companies in forty-five cities around the United States and more than fifty countries around the world. This private network is the company's nerve center, channeling e-mail messages, news releases, product announcements, and data, as well as vital project, planning, and development information throughout the company.

According to Tod Grantham, manager of International Network Services for Oracle, the boundary between the private internal network and the public Internet is often transparent to the employees at remote locations; the main issue is participating in the electronic community. "Electronic mail is so indigenous to the Oracle culture, that access to the network is the single most important qualifier for offices in considering themselves either first class citizens or, almost literally, non-entities." From the network planning point of view, however, there are significant cost and local access barriers to providing a private link to the Oracle communications system for subsidiaries in the Far East and South America. The local telecommunications systems may not be able to provide dedicated data lines, or the amount of data to be exchanged may not justify the costs.

Grantham, with responsibility for making and maintaining network connections to Oracle subsidiaries in ninety-six countries, finds that an Internet connection is often the best choice. "It's fast and cost effective," he says. "It gives offices which were out of the loop of electronic information within Oracle the communication links they are requesting."

Oracle has linked subsidiaries in countries like Costa Rica, Argentina, and Taiwan to the Internet through the local network service providers. Once connected to the Internet, these Oracle offices can communicate electronically with the internal Oracle network and also reach out to the rest of the global community. Because the Internet has become so pervasive, it is often the first step considered by Grantham when evaluating connectivity requests from Oracle sites around the world.

The Internet is also an important communication and support mechanism for Oracle in the United States. The International Network division staff scan the Internet for databases and resources that have special relevance for Oracle. When they find something of general interest, they download it to their local computer, then make it available to anyone within the company who needs the information. One example is the Request for Comments (RFC) files which are regularly posted on the Internet to update participants about new networking developments, standards, and other information. These comments allow software developers and engineers in Oracle to keep up with new developments in the business. Since this and other files are freely available, Grantham's staff simply import and manage them as local resources.

Current awareness is an important factor in maintaining the competitive position of high technology companies, and so is keeping existing systems functioning at the highest level possible. Many of the Internet newsgroups and discussion groups have direct relevance to Oracle's products, so monitoring those groups and responding to queries is a priority. An Oracle users' discussion group on the Internet numbers more than seven hundred participants from many different countries and organizational settings. Participants use the group to exchange information about what works best for them, to ask for specific help, to trade operating tips and to evaluate new Oracle products. It is a high-volume, high-energy group and participants are not reticent in expressing their opinions. A compilation of Frequently Asked Questions, known on the Internet as a FAQ, includes positive comments about the advantages of Oracle products, but also candid observations about problems past and present.

The International Network Division has also found that more of the companies that sell products to Oracle are using the Internet for customer support and services. Oracle's own worldwide support organization is actively preparing to provide a mechanism for Oracle customers to use the Internet for obtaining software patches, bug corrections and electronic updates.

Like other companies, Oracle has considered the security requirements for protecting their internal computer system from outside penetration through the Internet. Technical solutions to address such security concerns have been tested and have demonstrated their effectiveness. It does, however, take some additional investment in configuring a secure network and adding the layer of protection or "firewall" that prevents outside users from entering the company's private systems. A firewall, in Internet terms, is the physical or logical mechanism used to isolate traffic on the Internet from internal company networks. The International Network Division at Oracle has recommended a more robust firewall for the company's gateway, to open up Internet access for worldwide support services and for all Oracle employees.

Grantham, however, echoes Howard Funk in noting that it is sometimes an uphill battle to obtain resources for expanded Internet access. He sees the need to educate top management about network benefits, so that the Internet will be recognized as a stragetic resource for the whole corporation. Unitl that happens, his efforts are focused on improving Oracle's global connectivity as effectively as possible.

Rockwell International

Every regular Internet user has a favorite anecdote about how the network brings the world to their desktop. Ted Sickles, manager of data networking at Rockwell International, recalls an incident in May 1993 when he was visiting a Rockwell site in London:

> I checked my e-mail, and along with the more routine messages, I found a request from a person somewhere in China asking for information about a particular chip that Rockwell manufactures. I didn't know anything about that topic, but I used e-mail to forward the message to the appropriate person back in Newport Beach, California. He contacted the Rockwell support people in Japan, and they were able to reach the person who made the original query with an answer via the Internet. There's no way to provide that kind of responsiveness without global connectivity.

Sickles defines his responsibility at Rockwell as providing Wide Area Networks to facilitate communication throughout the company and between Rockwell and the rest of the world. He maintains the Internet gateway that gives all Rockwell business units their Internet connectivity. The internal Rockwell network is also based on TCP/IP architecture so that the company sites, or research campuses, connected to the internal network can have easy access to the Internet. At present, about sixty-five locations around the world are connected; as Sickles' own experience illustrated, if you are using a computer at a Rockwell site in London, you can easily communicate through the network to a location in Tokyo, California, or anywhere else Rockwell has a research and development facility.

The Internet gateway at Rockwell has been functioning since the late 1980s. In his role as manager, Sickles foresaw that the connectivity to the external world offered by the Internet would be an important trend for the future at Rockwell and other companies. Even though there wasn't a huge demand for expanded Internet access at the time, he decided to put the gateway in place and provide a central point of access to the global network. Now the Internet is an absolute necessity for Rockwell, as many aspects of the business emphasize collaborative development and partnerships. "We rely on working with research institutions," Sickles says, "and the Internet is a convenient, quick, practical, and capable way to connect scientists at Rockwell with research scientists at universities for joint projects. It is also very useful for communicating with other companies."

For ad hoc communications and short-term collaboration, Rockwell uses the Internet very heavily. More recently, other divisions of the company have started to make use of the network to distribute product information to customers. For extensive contract work or long-term projects, Rockwell will typically implement a dedicated TCP/IP network that is compatible with the communications systems of its development partners.

Sickles has observed that while employees may be slow to take advantage of the capabilities of the Internet, over time, people begin to make more effective use of the resources available to them:

> When we put in a LAN-to-LAN connection to a campus, people approach it as just a mechanism to communicate via e-mail; that's primarily what they have in mind. So at first there is a fairly low utilization of the global network capabilities. But as soon as users get accustomed to e-mail, they appreciate the importance of exchanging relevant data and you can see file transfer activity picking up. Pretty soon, people start working more closely on projects as a long-distance team. That's when online interaction starts to go way up.

Another responsibility of Data Networking is to balance productivity and effectiveness in using the Internet with the need for network security. Sickles observes that the ultimate measure of security would be to have no connection at all to the outside world, but that is not possible for a company today. He works to provide Internet security without making the internal safeguards a barrier to realizing the benefits of global connectivity. The major component of an effective security system is the attitude of administrators toward the importance of maintaining security. If users don't understand the need for security, and won't take some responsibility, all the system tools in the world cannot make up for it.

All of Rockwell's major business areas—electronics, aerospace, automotive, and graphics—benefit from the opportunities for collaboration offered on the global network. Sickles sees even greater use of the Internet as business processes within the corporation continue to evolve:

> In looking at the value of the Internet for the rest of the 1990s, I see an important shift taking place right now. We

are really pushing inter-enterprise connectivity as a priority. Rockwell wants to be able to communicate with other companies electronically even if those companies are not yet customers or suppliers. We want to have the capability of connecting to potential business partners, and making new alliances whenever the opportunity arises. To accomplish that, we have to maintain a gateway to the rest of the world. The Internet is a global point of presence for Rockwell.

Despite their different approaches to the Internet, these multinational corporations illustrate many of the key factors and potential problems in implementing and using the global network. Management support and the resources to provide full Internet access while addressing security concerns are important first steps. Once these are in place, the network still needs an advocate to make a companywide impact. Even many technical employees benefit from a program of publicity, information, and training about how the Internet can enhance their productivity. Articulating specific goals for using the network, such as streamlining development schedules through use of public software or improving communication among different locations provides a focus for initial training. On the other hand, lack of management support often translates into limited Internet access and missed opportunities. The largest companies need to make special efforts to ensure that all divisions are aware of the Internet.

NEW WINDOWS ON THE WORLD

It is perhaps not surprising that multinational corporations with branch offices and customers around the globe find many advantages in linking to the Internet. But these companies, which typically are more attuned to the importance of international connections, are not the only citizens of the global village. The Internet can bring the world to the doorstep of much smaller companies and help them do a better job in the process.

Greenville Tool and Die

Greenville Tool and Die builds automotive sheet metal stamping dies in a small town in western Michigan. When completed, the dies are shipped to a stamping plant, where they are placed in presses to stamp car parts for Ford, General Motors, Honda, Chrysler, and Toyota. It is a small business—136 people work in two shifts at the Greenville plant.

The manufacturing process here, as elsewhere, has become heavily computerized. Computer communications are a big part of the everyday work, from the beginning to the end of the design and casting process. Orders for parts are downloaded from customers over a modem connection. A die designer using computer assisted design (CAD) programs designs the dies for the requested parts. All the material data for the die is then transferred to a database and ordered by generating faxes to each supplier. After the die is assembled and test parts run, statistical process control comes into effect. Parts are created from the dies and are placed onto check fixtures where a computer measures many points and records the data. This data is sent to the customer where it must meet certain specifications. It can take more than a year to build the dies for a single part, so customers request progress data on a regular basis. Since all the time worked on a job is entered in the computer, the percent of work that has been completed can be calculated using estimated total hours. This estimated progress data is often sent to the customer electronically.

Greenville Tool and Die has actively pursued computerization of all phases of the business. Linking to the Internet was a logical extension of the company's use of computer-assisted design, fax, and modem communications. Sometimes, managers at Greenville find themselves waiting for other, larger companies to catch on to the advantages of Internet. Steven Meinhardt, Greenville's system manager, feels that all the data now transferred to customers and other sites over phone lines or by fax could be done more quickly and effectively using the Internet. As more of their customers connect to the Internet, Meinhardt expects the amount of data transmitted over the network will steadily increase.

John Latva, Greenville's CAD programmer, has found that the Internet saves significant time during the design process. "It is essential to our whole business that the CAD programs and software are running at peak performance. If these programs don't work, the die doesn't get designed, and everything is delayed all down the line." Good response time is critical to the company's success, he says. "We don't have long lead times in this kind of work, and often we are trying to get something into production the next day. Problems with the software interfere with production and manufacturing—so they have to be fixed in a hurry."

Greenville Tool and Die works with CAD software from ComputerVision, a computer-design firm, and John has found that the Internet makes their relationship work much more productively:

> Because we are both on the Internet, we can act as a beta test site for their most advanced software. ComputerVision transmits the software over the network, we load it and put it through the process. If there is any problem, we can send back a problem report on the Internet and an engineer there will be looking at the same information I have on the screen in front of me. That speeds up the whole time-frame to

production. It used to be we would have to phone in a problem report, only to find out that the detailed specifications were needed before it could be solved by ComputerVision; then we would rush to send them by overnight air and wait two or three days to resolve the problem. If you call a programmer on the phone these days, it's hard to get a real person and a return call in less than a day or two."

The Internet cuts that response time down to two hours—a major improvement in productivity for Greenville.

The company has benefitted from other features of the network as well. Steve Meinhardt downloaded a gateway program from the Internet to route the company's e-mail to and from their internal network. He regularly uses Archie to locate and download public domain software programs, including an e-mail program that enables any one of the forty-three work stations in the company to have Internet access. According to Meinhardt, the Internet has made a great difference in almost every aspect of the work at Greenville. "Internet has actually become a global extension of our in-house e-mail system. It takes no extra training for people to use it, which is a big plus," he says. "A lot of people are very active Internet users now; even ftp isn't that difficult. I had heard of the Internet, but never realized the vast amount of data out there. Resources are virtually limitless and free for the taking."

The Internet has put this small plant in rural Michigan in touch with a community of resources and technical support that never would be available without a network connection. Employees have integrated the network into their daily work, finding new ways to use its resources and waiting, sometimes impatiently, for some of their larger customers to begin taking advantage of its potential to speed up their part of the design and manufacturing cycle for new automobiles.

In the meantime, there are notable indications that Greenville has joined the global community. Steve Meinhardt recounts a recent example with obvious enthusiasm:

When I first downloaded the Pegasus program, I wasn't sure if there would be adequate support for this type of free software. But I found out there was no reason to worry. When I did have a few questions, I e-mailed them to David Harris, who programmed this excellent program. The next day, I got to work at 7 a.m. and he had already sent the answers back by e-mail. When I looked at the header of his message, I saw that his mail was sent out at 11 a.m. the same day I was reading it. He happens to live in New Zealand, which is twelve hours ahead of us. So my software questions were not only answered, they crossed a time zone halfway around the world. That's what makes the Internet so amazing.

SSESCO

Neil Lincoln couldn't agree more. When he started SSESCO (Supercomputer Systems Engineering and Services Company) in 1989, one of his first priorities was to get an Internet connection. His small business includes hardware and engineering consulting and equipment testing for large corporations around the world, as well as developing software used for the modeling done on supercomputers, so he knew that an Internet link was essential.

His expectation was that SSESCO would use the Internet to access the supercomputer center at the University of Minnesota, and other supercomputer centers around the United States that are linked by the National Science Foundation. SSESCO develops software for studying atmospheric conditions, pollution, and underground water resources, applications that require intensive data analysis. Software developers at SSESCO use the Internet to transmit data to supercomputer centers, to test the models created by their programs, and to make any software changes necessary, before delivering the program to customers. Staff can run a complex model through the Internet to a supercomputer center, look at it "on the fly" over the network, and make adjustments on-line. This, however, is just one aspect of the Internet at SSESCO.

All fifteen staff members have direct Internet access at their work stations, so they can stay in touch with customers and keep up with technical developments on a daily, sometimes hourly, basis. SSESCO opted to pay for a commercial connection to the Internet so the company can transmit software over the network to customers around the world. When problems are reported, employees can upload the affected code, analyze it, and fix it with a minimum of delay.

Lincoln feels that providing all staff with Internet access and encouraging them to discover and share the network's resources contributes to his company's productivity as well as to the individual motivation and problem-solving abilities of each employee. In his experience, "once a company provides broad access to the Internet, there is an almost exponential increase in use of the system. Some executives think the Internet only offers the marginal newsgroups, or peripheral discussions and they can't see that it is worth their own time and effort to learn about the network." Lincoln disagrees. "That's much too narrow a view. The Internet is definitely changing our world. Once we have a real data highway in place in this country, people will have options for all kinds of activities in their homes and schools, as well as at work. Companies have got to be part of it all."

SSESCO has done its part to share Internet resources with the global community. When Chinese students made their historic stand at Tiananmen Square in 1989, the company provided a link to transmit information from China to friends and supporters in the United States and other countries over the Internet. The company still hosts a China Watch newsgroup to update scholars and others on events in China. In true global village fashion, the system maintenance for the newsgroup is conducted over the Internet by a user in Hong Kong. Lincoln says that China Watch continues to generate a lot of traffic on SSESCO's Internet link, as people from around the world use it to keep in touch with one another and with current political developments in China.

AT HOME AND AT WORK

Just as the Internet makes the location of electronic resources transparent to the user, it also makes it possible for employees to work independent of the company location. Individuals working at home or in a one-person office far from company headquarters are a small but growing percentage of the American work force. The number of people working in home offices has been estimated to be as high as 39 million (Lomuscio 1993). While many of these are self-employed, more and more are "telecommuting," or using the power of telecommunications to perform work usually done in a traditional corporate setting. With connections through a work station to both the main office and customers, employees can often be even more productive by telecommuting than by going to the office every day.

Internet provides the flexibility for small companies as well as large corporations to deploy staff anywhere. John Cotter, director of engineering services at Wingra Technology, a twenty-person software firm in Madison, Wisconsin, has discovered the value of the Internet in bringing people together on the desktop, rather than at the airport or conference table:

> The Internet has eliminated lots of plane rides for software developers. It actually speeds up the development of new applications because there is less dead time devoted to travel and meetings. Now the staff use e-mail to focus on issues that need to be resolved in a new software program, and they

exchange source code over the Internet with other development partners around the country. The Internet also allows for people in any location to become part of the staff at Wingra on a contract basis. We have been able to keep talented people who moved to other states working on important projects by using Internet connections. It is just like having them on the staff in terms of their contributions to the software—they just never have to show up at the office.

Cotter feels that having staff work over the Internet is a great benefit for technology-based companies that need to retain highly skilled staff for specific projects and applications. It would not be cost-effective to provide a dedicated company connection to distant staff, and the exchange of copious amounts of program code make other forms of communication prohibitively expensive, but the Internet offers many low-cost options for individual access.

Bolt Beranek and Newman (BBN), a high-technology firm in Cambridge, Massachusetts, is one of the many larger companies experimenting with telecommuting and long-distance project management over the Internet. Staff may temporarily relocate to be close to a client site during a major project or set up field offices in new locations, or may simply be interested in the opportunity to change locations without changing jobs. Steve Groff, director of telecommunications at BBN, sees the Internet as the perfect way to facilitate what he expects will be a growing interest in telecommuting on the part of both employees and companies. "It makes perfect sense for us to use the capacity of the network to locate employees wherever we need them. The Internet allows us to set up single-person offices on a temporary or permanent basis, and to have a presence in key locations where we couldn't justify a full scale branch office." Groff confirms that telecommuting has a positive impact on productivity. "The employees who are working from a distance tend to be very productive."

How does telecommuting work from the employee's point of view? Craig Partridge had already worked at BBN for ten years when he decided to move to Palo Alto for personal reasons. BBN offered him the chance to experiment with telecommuting so that he could continue working on a major research project for the company, and he decided to give it a try. So far the experience has been positive. Partridge is fully connected to the main office in Cambridge. He has access to a secretary at BBN who forwards through the U.S. mail materials that are not available electronically. He participates in a project team that holds a weekly telephone conference to supplement the e-mail messages and file sharing over the Internet.

The hardest part, Partridge feels, was learning to maintain a one-person office; finding supplies, setting up files for the inevitable paper documents, establishing a routine for handling the tasks someone else usually takes care of in a large company. A trip back to Cambridge once every three months keeps Partridge in touch with the rest of the company and lets him talk face-to-face with key people. He feels that knowing the company and his managers very well makes him comfortable with working long distance; he is already part of the culture at BBN and doesn't worry about being integrated the way a new employee might. The Internet allows him to be even more productive technically—and to keep a job he otherwise would have left.

The availability of multimedia applications on the Internet makes it possible to develop even closer communication between remote locations, for telecommuting and other applications. The network has always had the capacity to carry audio and graphic information. More companies are beginning to take advantage of this capacity as the lower price of equipment and software makes it affordable to put videoconferencing on the desktop rather than in specially equipped conference rooms.

BBN, for example, developed the PictureWindow Desktop Video Conferencing System and started to market it in early

1993. According to the developers, this package is designed to "operate with equal ease between offices and between continents over networks using Internet Protocol (IP)." With the software installed in a workstation linked to a video camera, users can simply connect to other system users and initiate a video/audio conferencing session. One of the early tests of the system was to broadcast the Internet Engineering Task Force meeting in July 1992 to a hundred sites in North America, Europe, and Australia.

Carl Howe, the project manager for PictureWindow development, believes this is the first product of its kind priced realistically for the desktop market. He envisions companies with multiple locations using it for communications between offices, to keep staff in touch with what is happening at distant sites, to encourage informal conferences to solve problems on the spot, or to demonstrate new products to potential customers.

Telecommuting over the Internet means that workers can stay in touch with new developments in technology, international news, announcements from other companies, and all the other resources on the network, in addition to communicating regularly with the home office. Without ever leaving home, telecommuters can be well-connected to the rest of the world. With the advent of inexpensive and widespread video over the Internet, even "face-to-face" meetings with distant offices will be possible.

GLOBAL CHALLENGES

Surviving the test of international competition and thriving in a global economy are tough challenges for any company. The world is getting smaller and changing faster at the same time that customers are becoming more discriminating and looking for the added value in every purchase. As companies increasingly convert their work force and priorities from basic production of goods to provision of services, the role of communication increases in importance. New business strategies like partnerships, collaborative research and development, and virtual teams, all place a premium on information being transmitted, received, and clearly understood by all participants. Managing communication across time zones, language and cultural differences, and uneven technical development make the process even more complex. In this environment, new management tools are essential.

Use of the Internet encourages employees to be active citizens of the global community and to think of themselves and their company in the context of international developments. For an individual, or for a corporation with a work force in the hundreds of thousands, a global perspective can be as close as the nearest work station. As we approach the uncertainties of the twenty-first century, the international scope of the Internet may be among the most important of all business assets.

REFERENCES

Chen, Tommi. 1993. The Global Village. *Business Times.* May 10.

Cooke, Kevin and Dan Lehrer. 1993. The Whole World is Talking. *The Nation.* 257(2):60–64.

Fombrun, Charles J. 1992. *Turning Points: Strategic Change in Corporations* New York: McGraw-Hill.

Keen, Peter G. W. 1991. *Shaping the Future: Business Design through Information Technology.* Boston: Harvard University Press.

Lomuscio, James. 1993. When a Commute's from Bed to Desk. *The New York Times* Section 13CN: 1. April 4.

Lynch, Daniel C. 1993. Historical Evolution. In *Internet System*

Handbook. Edited by Daniel C. Lynch and Marshall T. Rose. Boston: Addison-Wesley.

Malamud, Carl. 1993. *St. Petersburg Times.* Sunday, City Edition: 1D, March 7. 1993. *Exploring the Internet: A Technical Travelogue.* Englewood Cliffs, N.J.: Prentice-Hall.

Ong, Lynette. 1992. Line to the World. *The Straits Times.* 3. July 14.

Oracle Corporation. 1992. *Annual Report.* Redwood Shores, California.

Quarterman, John S., Gretchen Phillips and Carl-Mitchell Smoot. 1993. Internet Services and Access Worldwide. Paper presented at "Public Access to the Internet" John F. Kennedy School of Government. May 26–27.

Rapaport, Richard. 1993. Technology Islands. Singapore: Still Onward and Upward. *Forbes ASAP.* 78–88.

Wendt, Henry. 1993. *Global Embrace: Corporate Challenges in A Transnational World.* New York: HarperBusiness.

CHAPTER 4

Reach Out and
Touch—Everyone

> *There were a lot of good reasons for my company to get on the Internet, but in the end what did it was that I got tired of feeling like a back-water hick every time I went to a conference and someone said "I can send you that on the Internet. What's your e-mail address?"*
> —connected@last.com
>
> *In the high-tech world, if you're not on the net, you're not in the know.*
> —The Economist

Ever have the feeling that you are out of touch with what is happening in the world around you? Well, if you are not on the Internet yet, you may be right. Those millions of Internet users don't necessarily know more than you, but they certainly have some impressive connections. Ask any one of them how many e-mail messages were waiting for them this morning, how many newsgroups they follow, or how often they exchange information with people in different time zones.

What does all this have to do with business? Whatever other advantages a company gains by linking to the Internet, every organization will benefit from the massive boost in external connectivity provided through the network. Just as "location,

location, location" defines value in real estate, in business today it's connectivity that equals competitiveness. As this chapter illustrates, the right connections can help companies to reduce costs, obtain better service, speed up crucial development projects, and increase their overall efficiency. The Internet also connects businesses to the rapidly expanding interactive marketplace—and provides some important lessons about how to navigate this new terrain successfully.

For some companies, gaining e-mail access to the rest of world is justification enough to invest in an Internet connection. Rich Gircys, is vice president of InfoServ Connections, which provides Internet access for more than three hundred clients in Northern California. "For many small businesses," he says, "E-mail is the first and often only reason to connect up. One important advantage of the Internet is that businesses can have a company-selected Internet address instead of the impersonal number that other on-line mail services provide. It's important to identify themselves and their company by name, and Internet allows them that personal touch." Gircys sees the interest in Internet addresses every day in his business. "There's not a single company connected to InfoServ that doesn't also have a unique Internet domain name registered; this is clearly something that matters to people."

Even if you aren't moved by the prospect of sending messages bearing your unique signature to destinations around the globe, there are strong economic arguments in favor of electronic mail. Barry Shein, president and guiding spirit at Software Tool and Die, a Boston-based company offering commercial and individual access to the Internet, puts e-mail at the top of his list of "Ways to Convince Your Boss to Connect to the Internet." Shein points out that companies spending significant amounts of money on postage, phone bills, and faxes are likely to enjoy measurable cost savings by substituting electronic mail for even a percentage of that communication. Once an Internet connection is in place, there is no incremental cost per message—no matter what the destination or the length.

Mentor Graphics, an Oregon high-technology company, saw the opportunity for lowering its communications costs as soon as it connected to the Internet. Support for its electronic design software requires a worldwide customer service organization, since more than half its annual sales are outside of North America. Development teams and customer support departments in Europe need to be in constant contact with the company's Oregon headquarters, as well as with development partners and customers. Before the Internet, frequent international faxes and phone calls generated a substantial telecommunications bill. Half of that cost reflected communications between various Mentor Graphics locations. With the network in place, most internal communication takes place over the Internet. As a result, the company's European offices reduced their telecommunications costs by more than 50 percent in the first year of Internet connectivity.

Internet communication provides other significant advantages for all types of business. No more missed phone calls, or second guessing the best time to call another country. E-mail gives the sender control over the content and the timing of each message. Large groups can be reached as easily as a single recipient. Information can be expressed in any number of ways including through graphics, data files, audio and video. A move to e-mail over the Internet allows businesses to expand their connectivity as well as save money. This may be the reason that Internet users tend to develop a superior attitude toward the traditional means of business communication. The signatures appended to many network messages include the sender's postal addresses labeled as "snailmail," while the phone number is tagged as "gabmail"—a pronouncement that these are inferior alternatives to the *real* way to exchange information; instantly and electronically

Electronic mail's value as a communications time-saver has made it one of the fastest growing applications in business. The

Yankee Group estimates that fifteen million people are already using internal electronic mail in United States companies, and projects that the number will climb to thirty-eight million users by 1995 (Reinhart 1993). But the differences between proprietary e-mail systems mean that companies cannot use their internal system to communicate with the outside world—or sometimes even with other parts of the company. Connecting to the Internet offers small companies a low-cost alternative to maintaining a private internal network, and gives large companies a new avenue to communicate with partners and customers. Hewlett Packard, like most major technology vendors, now offers customer support over the Internet even though it also maintains one of the world's largest internal networks—an acknowledgement that many customers prefer to communicate with them via the Internet (Farrow 1993, 62).

The high level of customer support now available on the Internet provides another incentive for companies to establish their own connection. That was the rationale David Spector, a vice president for technology services at J.P. Morgan in New York, used to convince his boss that joining the Internet made financial and organizational sense. Like Hewlett Packard, J.P. Morgan has its own extensive dedicated network, linking fifty-seven locations in more than forty countries. Even with all this in-house communications power, Spector made a convincing case for the Internet:

> It wasn't an easy sell, because a lot of people in the firm were concerned about connecting J.P. Morgan to an external network that they didn't control. I had to demonstrate the value of the Internet and show the advantages it would bring. I finally wrote a long white paper describing how the Internet could improve the quality of support we receive from our vendors in the technology area. J.P. Morgan has a very wide range of hardware and software, and keeping it up and running is essential to the whole operation. We are

always dealing with new releases or bugs or configurations that don't quite work the way they are supposed to. Without the Internet, it was difficult to get consistent support and fast problem resolution from manufacturers.

Based on discussions with J.P. Morgan's major vendors, Spector projected that an Internet connection would significantly increase the productivity of the firm's systems and technical support staff since they could use the network to interact directly with vendors' engineering departments. The delays involved with sending problem reports via overnight delivery would be eliminated because information and files could be exchanged over the Internet.

J.P. Morgan has been connected to the Internet for over a year, and the service improvements that Spector predicted have taken place. Now he can get in touch directly with the engineers and customer support people at the appropriate vendor as soon as he spots a technical problem. Because support is available on-line, the turnaround required for resolution is usually measured in hours rather than days. But this is not the only benefit Internet has brought to the firm. As Spector knew would happen, once Internet connectivity was in place it became invaluable for many other applications. "Now that everyone on the MORGANnet can use the Internet," he says, "I see hundreds of uses of the mail system every day. It has become second nature for a cross section of people in every section of the firm; traders, economic researchers, and planners as well as technology people."

There are limits to using the network for financial transactions and trading, and Spector doesn't expect to see this kind of application until better standards are set for security and privacy on the Internet. He believes that many companies are also waiting for some of the sticky issues of acceptable use to be clarified before committing themselves to essential business operations on the network. J.P. Morgan is interested in the future of the Internet for financial exchange; it has joined a financial information and securities consortium working with the federal government to develop and apply standards for networking all financial industries.

In the meantime, Spector is convinced that the firm's Internet connection is one of the best investments around:

> J.P. Morgan is in the information business. We remain competitive only to the extent that we have the best information available. The Internet provides us with a major interface to information about the rest of the world. It represents the cutting edge of connectivity, and J. P. Morgan realizes it must be a leader in cutting edge technologies to compete and serve clients effectively.

Another financial giant, the Charles Schwab Corporation, also expects its investment in the Internet to yield significant dividends over time. Information and communication systems are at the core of Schwab's success as a brokerage and investment firm. The process of buying and selling securities is highly automated. While Charles Schwab, Inc. operates a network of nearly two hundred branch offices for the convenience of its customers, most financial transactions are not handled face-to-face. Instead, the company uses a combination of phone and on-line communications to handle the enormous volume of daily transactions generated by its 2.2 million customers. Schwab account representatives can transfer customer orders directly onto a terminal, and can typically complete the transaction while the customer is still on the phone. Twenty-four hour access to accounts is provided from telephone service centers in Indianapolis, Denver, and Phoenix. Customers are also encouraged to use the company's on-line information services to check on prices, account balances, and to initiate orders (SEC 1992).

Keeping all these high-volume transactions moving smoothly is a top priority—without connectivity, the whole business would grind to a halt. Several years ago, Schwab embarked on an ambitious program to improve information management. The company established a schedule for moving its internal information and financial systems off the huge mainframe computer installation that required constant upgrades and into a distributed computing environment. Even though the mainframe-based system still functioned well, it had a voracious appetite for the largest, fastest, and most expensive hardware on the market. With customers coming on-line daily and branch offices opening on a regular basis, Schwab needed a more flexible platform to grow and expand its computing resources.

Rob Rizk is an expert on systems integration in the information systems division at Schwab headquarters in San Francisco. He has already worked three years on this massive project to "re-architecture" the entire computing environment, including its network capabilities. In the course of negotiating with various vendors, testing software, and selecting the best distributed platform, Rizk quickly realized that connecting to the Internet was essential:

> It seemed that there were significant delays when vendors had to address a problem that took them away from their keyboards. Working with new software, you always need patches and fixes, and testing new equipment means there are a lot of specific questions. Before the Internet connection, we were dependent on faxes or overnight delivery of tapes. The Internet was essential to keep the momentum of the project going. Without it, every development problem would have meant shutting down for a whole day, instead of getting a quick answer over the network.

The Internet proved its value during the project development stage, but Schwab's long-term plans for the network involve far more than improving vendor support. In fact, says Rizk, the project team has worked to facilitate Internet access for everyone in the company, by designing the new internal communication network on a TCP/IP base, so different Schwab locations can easily connect to the Internet. The information systems division is the earliest group to link up, but eventually anybody with an IP-addressable work station will be able to connect directly to the Internet. Rizk believes that connecting will have a major impact on the company. "As we learn more about how we can use the Internet, it will open up a whole new avenue for communicating with the rest of the world."

Schwab is already encouraging departments to make the most of their Internet connections. Training sessions and technical brown bag lunches have been designed to make the company's 4,500 employees comfortable with the network, and to emphasize the potential uses for connectivity. A customized graphical interface will serve the same function, substituting easy to use point-and-click commands for the most popular Internet functions.

Because it comes as part of a major restructuring of computing and communications within Schwab, Rizk expects that the new Internet connection will quickly have an impact on the way in which the company does business. "People will find reasons to use it that we haven't even thought of yet," he says. "We want them to experiment with the potential of the network, so we are trying to build in the flexibility to accommodate as many different applications as possible."

Flexibility and experimentation could well serve as the mottos for every company connecting to the Internet. Whether the original motivation was to save money with electronic mail or to get better service from technology vendors, or any of a dozen other reasons, many companies already using the network are convinced it has more than paid back their initial investment. However, businesses that use the Internet only to do familiar tasks faster or cheaper are missing the most important advantage the network has to offer. Those ready to experiment have discovered that the Internet's value is proportional to their willingness to use it to transform their own organization's communication and marketing strategies—the essence of how they reach out to the world around them.

FROM CONNECTIVITY TO COMMUNICATION

Mastering the Internet culture and implementing a viable program for reaching new customers and disseminating company information requires more planning than using the network's e-mail capabilities and vendor support connections. Managers who have heard about the limitations and quirks of the network may wonder whether the effort required to move beyond basic Internet connectivity is really worthwhile. It is difficult to justify rethinking existing marketing practices in order to experiment with the electronic marketplace. If the stakes were limited to just a few Internet discussion groups, any company's status quo might look more appealing.

However, there is growing evidence that businesses will have to make a number of organizational changes to meet the challenges of the information age. As customers become more selective, and more difficult to satisfy, many experts have concluded that the old marketing strategies don't work any more. In *Mass Customization: The New Frontier in Business Competition*, B. Joseph Pine writes:

> For an expanding number of industries, the world is an increasingly turbulent place. Customer wants and needs are changing and fragmenting. Product life cycles are getting shorter; keeping up with technological change is becoming more difficult. Basic requirements for quality and service levels go up as the competition gets tougher every year (1993, 131).

Like the decision to rearchitecture computing and communications at Charles Schwab, Inc., changes in marketing orientation are based on a vision of the future. Schwab recognized that the information systems that had performed well in the 1980s didn't have the capabilities necessary to sustain dynamic growth. Even though the transition to distributed computing requires a major effort, it will strengthen the company's competitiveness. Firms that do not have the foresight to upgrade their information systems will soon find themselves at a disadvantage.

Marketing strategies that were successful in the 1980s cannot be expected to achieve the same results today. Companies that hesitate to adopt new approaches to the market run the risk of losing touch with customers altogether. *Fortune* magazine describes communication with customers as the crucial difference between companies that successfully use technology to improve business performance and those that encounter problems:

> The common ailment of the corporations that got hit on the head by two-by-fours—particularly IBM, Digital, and Compaq—was distance from customers. They ended up making products customers didn't want. The lesson here, that applies to every industry, is that successful companies depend utterly on customer feedback. At winning outfits from GE to Wal-Mart, a primary goal is to create structures—from flattened management to E-mail systems linking employees with customers and suppliers—that increase that closeness (Stratford 1993, 70).

Viewed from this perspective, the challenges presented by the Internet are not part of the problem but the beginning of a new solution. Companies faced with demanding customers, aggressive competitors, rapid product cycles, and ever more focused target groups will find that mastering the culture of the Internet is a valuable asset in designing an innovative marketing strategy for the information age. Developing a successful program for communicating with customers on the network can become the foundation for transforming traditional marketing into a new interactive style of "intermarketing."

THE ART OF INTERMARKETING

Any place where millions of people a day turn for information, entertainment, and advice offers enticing prospects for commerce. Add the fact that this particular locale is doubling in size every year, and the attraction becomes almost irresistible. For some networkers, the phrase "commercialization of the Internet" conjures up a specter of bandwidth cluttered with home shopping groups and slick advertisements popping up willynilly on computer screens. These users dread the day when the tremendous communication power of the network is overshadowed by commercials.

But the Internet is not about to become the world's biggest electronic shopping mall, even if the legal barriers to commercial traffic, such as acceptable use policies, are removed. For one thing, the network has a strong culture of free discourse, and a bias against anything resembling a sales pitch. Some of the most vocal advocates for relying on private companies instead of the federal government to expand the Internet are also avid opponents of flooding the bandwidth with the electronic equivalent of junk mail.

A second and even more compelling reason is that traditional forms of marketing and selling simply don't translate all that successfully into a networked environment. Figure 4.1 illustrates some of the key differences between advertising and networked information. Advertising, the mainstay of most companies' marketing strategy, was designed to be broadcast to a large number of potential customers at once, through billboards,

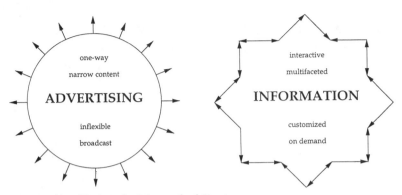

FIGURE 4.1   Fitting the Networked Environment.

printed ads, television, or radio spots. Good ads place a premium on delivering a short, memorable message. Their focus is narrow, because only a small amount of information will fit into the available time or space. Often the content is not information at all, but an image of some intangible quality the company wants to project about itself or its product.

Attempts to disseminate this type of advertising on the Internet are likely to be met with such a negative reaction that thoughts of making a profit are engulfed in the "flames" of criticism that come from all quarters. The safest response is a hasty retreat and perhaps a posted apology. Companies familiar with the network culture have already adopted information-based approaches for reaching customers on the Internet, and go out of their way to avoid any appearance of unwanted advertising. Newcomers jumping in with a commercial message are more likely to raise a firestorm. Since the norms and tolerance level differ from one Internet group to the next, ads can seem successful in the short run. The "biz" discussion groups, for example, frequently contain company-specific pro-motional material. But the Internet is heavily populated by individuals and groups with an aversion to using the network for unsolicited advertising, especially on topics unrelated to the focus of their discussion. For most of the discussion groups operating on the network, a commercial message will not be welcome.

Joe Andrieu found this out the hard way. After a positive experience with buying and selling various items on USENET's "misc.entrepreneur" newsgroup, he decided to experiment with marketing beauty products through the Internet. He selected a number of target discussion lists, then posted a message describing an amazing new beauty cream, and asking to be contacted for ordering information. One of the groups he sent the posting to was BUSLIB-L. Now, business librarians may be as interested in beauty products as the next potential consumer, but they don't want to hear about them on a discussion group dedicated to exchanging information about electronic reference sources. Instead of orders, Andrieu got peppered with critical messages pointing out that he had no business intruding on this discussion group. A few days later, he made a final appearance—apologizing for his inappropriate posting and requesting that negative responses cease and desist.

Asked to summarize his experiences with trying to reach customers on the Internet, Andrieu, who has decided to get out of the network marketing business for a while, was willing to share his hard-won lessons:

> This is what I have learned from my time on the net. Blatant self-promotion is highly discouraged, as is improper placement of ad-like material. However, most groups will accept minimal commercial activity if it may be beneficial to some parties of the newsgroup. There are also some groups dedicated to business transactions, like all of the biz groups. With the commercialization of the net by [commercial service providers] PSI and ANS in 1990, restrictions and antipathy to commercial use has eased considerably. In misc.entrepreneur, I have received many positive replies, and not one negative. No longer is commercial activity a crime, but wasting net resources is. And

in most groups ads are considered annoying noise, and not information.

Andrieu represents an extreme mismatch between the message and the intended audience. Few companies are likely to make such an egregious error. But his experience does reflect the cultural differences among the thousands of discussion groups connected to the Internet. Since many groups do encourage information exchange that includes suggestions for specific products, the line between advertising and information can be a source of confusion. One good rule of thumb is that unsolicited, blatant advertising is seldom, if ever, appropriate outside of the explicit biz and entrepreneurial groups where Andrieu started. Recognizing that a deluge of electronic advertisements could have a negative impact on the utilization of network resources, as well as on the tempers of the recipients, some network service providers that do not otherwise restrict commercial traffic have specific rules against unsolicited advertising. Even without such rules, it is only common sense to avoid a form of communication that will often backfire. As Barry Shein reflects, "It's usually a mistake to start out on the Internet by annoying all your potential customers."

Broadcast-style advertising doesn't fit on the Internet because it dumps a one-way message on an audience with interactive capabilities. People operating in a networked environment are committed to active communication, to exchanging ideas and information with others in the electronic universe. Such exchange is fundamental to the popularity of USENET and the other Internet discussion groups; the opportunity to play an active role has attracted millions of participants, and strained the capacity of the network at regular intervals. From the early days of the Internet, when electronic mail capability was added more or less as an afterthought, planners have tended to underestimate the number of people who want to use their connectivity primarily to interact with others.

Companies interested in turning connectivity into effective communication need to adopt a model appropriate to this interactive environment. The critical components of a successful model are a high percentage of relevant information and a high level of interaction with the customer. Figure 4.2 compares different approaches on the basis of these two components. Traditional advertising spots, as expected, are lowest for both information and customer interaction. Printed materials such as brochures and detailed product specifications can provide a lot of information to the customer, but with little opportunity for interaction and feedback. "Infomercials," the long, documentary-style commercials, have made a place for themselves on television, but also lack significant interactive features.

Marketing approaches such as phone contacts with customers can be highly interactive, but are typically focused on an immediate sales message rather than information delivery. A new hybrid of multimedia commercials are appearing on the early

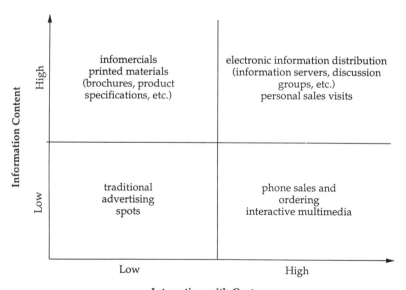

Interaction with Customers

FIGURE 4.2   Information/Interaction Matrix.

prototypes of interactive television channels. Ford, for example, has started offering viewers the choice of customizing their advertising to feature more information on one of four car models (Tierney 1993). Interactive commercials offer customers more control over the content of the message, but they are still quite limited in the amount of information that can be conveyed.

Electronic information distribution excels in conveying a high information content. Because it is designed for a network environment, electronic information has the flexibility to be posted in answer to a specific question, shared with a relevant group, or stored in large quantities at an Internet-accessible location for retrieval as needed. The amount of information that can be made available to customers is practically unlimited. Entire catalogs, detailed product specifications, extensive reviews of performance, examples of successful applications, and anything else a company wishes to share with customers can be digitized and maintained at a relatively low cost.

The interactive component of network marketing is a second important feature. Internet navigational tools like Gopher allow customers to locate and select exactly the information they need, in as much detail as they wish. From the customer's point of view, the information is tailored to their interests and available whenever they want to consult it. The same tools can provide a mechanism to interact directly with the information provider by making comments or asking specific questions on-line.

The advantages for business are considerable. Information that would be prohibitively expensive to produce and distribute in print can be posted to a network file server at very little cost. Frequently material that has been stored on a company's internal information system can simply be moved over to the public server. Changes in product specifications and new developments are available on-line as soon as they happen. Large numbers of customers can access the information at the same time. Reaction to new products and services, otherwise difficult to track, are registered directly on the network. Questions can be answered and complaints averted or resolved by the people in the company best able to deal with them. In addition to explicit customer feedback in the form of questions and suggestions, the server generates valuable data on which pieces of information are being consulted, and how often. For the networked environment, this model emerges as a clear winner.

Once companies commit to a strategy of using the Internet to communicate with customers, they face both technical and organizational questions. On the whole, the technical issues of electronic information distribution are the more straightforward. Any company with the expertise to maintain an internal information system will be prepared to deal with the technical requirements for providing information on the Internet. There are a number of well-tested techniques for distributing networked information, each with their own features and advantages. Among those most frequently used are:

- **Anonymous ftp servers.** These can store everything from typeset documents to graphics to source code for software programs; they are a cost-effective way to make large quantities of information available on demand. They require that the customers find their way to the server, and execute some commands to locate and transfer the files they want.

- **Gopher servers.** Gophers have the advantages of ftp, with the accessibility of one of the Internet's favorite tools; they can easily be linked to other Gopher servers in thousands of locations, and can be searched by subject interest.

- **Newsgroups.**

These include more than 2,000 discussion groups that make up USENET. Topics and discussion norms vary considerably from group to group; so does the number of people participating—typically many people are reading these groups without actively posting to them. There is a complex approval process to start a new group, but often customers will initiate the process because of the perceived value in having a support group for a particular product.

- **Mailing lists.**

Interactive discussion or announcement only groups cover a wide variety of topics. There are three basic types of mailing lists: unmoderated (subscribers messages are posted directly to everyone on the list), moderated (a designated person receives and screens all messages before posting), and digested (messages are gathered and posted in batches). For the customer, a brief e-mail request is usually all it takes to be added to a mailing list. It is easy to start one on any topic by simply announcing it and providing subscription directions.

- **Electronic newsletters.**

These are distributed on-line by publishers to a list of subscribers. The number of titles is growing

dramatically, with the range of
information typically mirror-
ing print publications, although
more hypertext and electronic
navigation features are starting to
emerge.

Adapting these tools to a company's network and hardware capabilities is not difficult for anyone already administering an Internet gateway. Within a few weeks of deciding to distribute information over the network, a business can establish a presence on the Internet. In fact, it is almost too easy to set up a network information server first, and worry about where the information will come from later. A number of companies have discovered that having the distribution vehicle ready to ride the electronic highway in no way ensures a smooth flow of high-quality information. Once the obvious sources are tapped— product announcements, press releases, print newsletters, company profiles, employee contact lists, frequently asked questions—it takes creativity and commitment to keep the existing information current and provide additions on a regular basis.

MARKETING FOR EVERYONE AND FOR ONLY ONE

This is the time to remember that interactive communication on the Internet should serve as the foundation for expanding the standard organizational approach to marketing. One stage in the process is to broaden the responsibility for keeping customers well informed. In *The 6 Imperatives of Marketing*, Allan Magrath observes, "Marketing is everyone's job, not just those with marketing titles on their doors. Marketing is an orientation, not an organization" (1992, 1). A great strength of intermarketing is that it puts more people than ever in direct contact with customers. Using the Internet as a springboard, departments not normally involved in marketing can become familiar with customer needs and concerns. This familiarity doesn't just help to generate better quality informational postings—it also moves the whole organization closer to the customer point of view.

Groups in research and development, technical support, manufacturing, and other areas can develop a stake in a company's reputation for top-quality interaction with customers. The organizational challenge is not so much to convince these groups to share responsibility for information distribution as to coordinate their input with an overall information strategy and avoid duplication of effort. Companies that have long-standing Internet connections may discover that many employees are already using the Internet to answer customer questions and participate in discussion groups. Frequently they are doing this on their own initiative; the marketing and sales departments are not aware of it. It is not unusual for employees to forge ahead of company policy once they have become accustomed to the interactive capabilities of the network.

Ensuring a steady flow of quality information is only one part of the intermarketing process. Equally important is establishing the identity of the intended audience. Thinking about communication with the millions of Internet users as one homogeneous group is both overwhelming and pointless. There is in fact very little that most of the thousands of networks that make up the Internet share, except the communication protocols that link them together. While that makes it counterproductive to "broadcast" a message to all fifteen million networkers at one time, it does provide some vital marketing information. In the interest of getting closer to customer groups, it is worth taking the time to become familiar with the many subcultures of the network.

Businesses frequently invest significant resources in market research to obtain the kind of feedback that is readily available on the Internet. In *The New Marketing Research Systems* (1993), David J. Curry points out that the most important trend of the 1990s is "micro marketing." Because consumers demand products targeted to their individual tastes, companies must customize their offerings to fit the profiles of increasingly smaller segments of the market—all the way down to the individual consumer. Companies lacking the information and flexibility to reach the micro market level will find that products designed for everyone may actually appeal to no one.

Despite its enormous size, the Internet is already segmented very neatly into micro markets, and its subgroups come conveniently labeled according to their particular interests, ranging from amateur radio to gardening to travel, and including about every imaginable technology product. Companies wanting to appeal to a particular market or group of customers can monitor and participate in these interchanges at will. Unlike high-powered market researchers, participants in Internet groups obligingly hold their discussions in a public forum. This means that opinions, likes and dislikes, response to product offerings, and emerging trends can be monitored. Many groups have even created archives of earlier discussions, that are readily available for searching over the Internet, in case it is important to find out how attitudes have changed over time.

The complex infrastructure of the Internet makes it a market researcher's dream, once the divisions of interest and subject groupings are mastered. But market data is not the only benefit of using the Internet to reach out to customers. Moving your organization from the most detailed level of Internet market analysis to an overall strategy for improving communication with customers is the goal of "intermarketing." Interactive marketing opportunities are not limited to the Internet; they are expanding as fast as new technology brings interactive, high-speed connections to homes, schools, and offices. The steps outlined below are geared to distributing electronic information over the Internet, but can be applied to any networked environment. The key is to use the network to inform people, answer their questions, and respond to their suggestions. Essentially, the customers are offered a full spectrum of information choices, then allowed to make up their own minds. Each step of an intermarketing program should help to increase the level of useful information available to the customer, and to the company.

1. **Identify the audience.** The Internet offers a number of opportunities for finding out more about the audience you want to reach. The top-level divisions of USENET provide a starting point, especially for companies with a science and technology focus, or with products revolving around hobbies and recreation. But whatever the product, there is likely to be a relevant group somewhere on the Internet. There is no need to guess; using the network's search tools and then following the discussions in likely groups will quickly reveal which groups are a good match for a particular company. Even without posting a message, companies will learn a lot about the norms and culture of the network by monitoring a number of groups.

2. **Negotiate company-wide participation.** The more people in the company who are connected to the Internet, and who take part in providing information or responding to customers, the better. Participating departments have a chance to showcase their expertise, and to find out first-hand how the consumer views their efforts. Potential contributors range from top management to employees on the front lines. In addition to posting information, many company experts can contribute by answering specific customer questions. Some companies are concerned that the amount of time employees spend following and participating in Internet discussion groups may detract from productivity. This is

more likely to be a problem when there are no overall guidelines for using the network "officially" to locate and communicate with customers. Developing a coordinated approach and a clear set of expectations for productive participation in discussion groups will help keep Internet use focused on company goals.

3. **Feature essential information.** More than anything else, the quality of the information determines the long-term success of intermarketing. Whatever is posted to the Internet must be accurate, current, and clear. It should express what distinguishes a firm's products and services from those of other companies. People want to know more about development breakthroughs and future plans. They are interested in what other customers have been able to accomplish with new products, as well as suggestions about how to deal with problems. The type of information included should be adjusted as the company observes how the customer responds.

4. **Open communication channels.** It should be easy for customers to respond through the network with reactions to new products, company services, and future directions. In addition to tracking how frequently the information is accessed, Internet file servers can provide features that encourage direct comments and discussion. It is important to build in interfaces that encourage feedback. These can include suggestion boxes; prompts for comments and questions, with responses posted on-line; and other formats for dialogue.

5. **Respond to customers.** Soliciting feedback implies a commitment to respond appropriately. To encourage a flow of two-way communication it is important to provide some response to all suggestions and comments; if the volume is large, this responsibility can be distributed throughout the

company. Questions of general interest can be re-posted to a discussion list or server together with the response, or included in a Frequently Asked Questions section. Sometimes the best response is a new procedure or a change in policy. Discussion within the company of negative feedback can stimulate departments to work together on innovative solutions to problems.

6. **Monitor the results.** The way customers use the information available through the Internet will provide guidance on designing the next generation of electronic communication. File servers can track how many people look at each file, how long the average session lasts, and what combinations of information are popular, as well as recording the origin of the query. This and other data can be used to keep improving the quality of the information and the interactions with the customer.

Rob Raisch, president of the Internet Company, has created a business by making other companies' databases available over the network. Understandably, Raisch sees limitless growth opportunities on the Internet—provided companies are committed to using appropriate marketing techniques. He feels that any product that has worthwhile information associated with it is a good candidate for network exposure. "Here you have millions of people already on the Internet, searching around for interesting things to do," he says. "They are going to be happy to find useful information about products, and more detail about the companies that sell them."

For instance, Raisch has discussed with automobile manufacturers the feasibility of a Gopher server to bring together all the detailed manufacturing information, performance standards, and surveys that might appeal to potential buyers. The server could include pictures, parts information, and the numerous details that are too expensive to reproduce in a typical print advertisement. Raisch is convinced that many consumers would take the initiative to access such information if it were conveniently available on the network. He predicts that the network distribution approach will be the solution of choice for many manufacturers in the future. "Preparing a print catalog for this specialized type of information and mailing it to large groups is extremely expensive," he notes. "And every time the product changes, the descriptions are out of date. The same level of detail could sit quite comfortably on a Gopher, and be updated in real time, as soon as changes are made. Plus, on the Internet the customers come to you."

The next group of businesses turning to the Internet and other interactive media, he feels, will be "companies that stand for something," because they can use the network to share information about their cause or philosophy, without even mentioning a specific product. Raisch looks for rapid growth of Internet awareness among companies that have leveraged this form of "identity public relations" to develop an image of social responsibility. Prime examples are the Nature Company, the Body Shop, and Ben and Jerry's—companies known for taking a corporate stance. It would be in character for such companies to put their information out on the Internet, because they espouse many of the same values that have come to be identified with the network. At the same time, concludes Raisch, it would sell their products: "If a company represents itself properly, and shows itself to be a good citizen of the global Internet community, customers will be attracted and will find that company's products appealing."

Intermarketing may sound good in theory, but does it work in the real world of deadlines, downsizing and demanding customers? Companies that have already started a program of interactive information distribution on the Internet are fully aware that it is not a perfect solution or a substitute for other marketing efforts. But ask if they and their customers are happy with the results, and the answer is a resounding yes.

MAKING IT HAPPEN

Apple

Jim Chou, a consulting engineer for Apple's Higher Education division, figured that someone had to get the ball rolling. He realized that almost all of Apple's higher education customers were already connected to the Internet. They used the network every day to communicate with colleagues, conduct research, and keep current with new trends. It was time for Apple to develop a strategy for reaching colleges and universities over the Internet. Noting that the University of Minnesota Gopher software had been adapted by many other campuses, Chou decided that Gopher should be Apple's vehicle of choice for communicating with the higher education market.

Once that decision was made, it took Chou about a week to define the scope of an Apple Higher Education Gopher, and work out the technical requirements. Then he proposed the idea to his vice president and general manager, requesting approval to move forward with a development effort. Two weeks later, a pilot of the Apple Gopher Server was up and running at the University of Minnesota.

Chou and his colleagues worked closely with staff at Minnesota, the development site of the original Gopher, to add new features to the Apple server. The most important enhancement made it a vehicle for two-way communication with the higher education community. For example, most Gophers offer read-only information, but Apple's version has been programmed to encourage users to post comments and information to a discussion section via a special e-mail address. The contents of the server have also been planned with faculty and academic administrators in mind. In addition to product information and specifications, the Gopher offers electronic versions of Apple's higher education publications and a cluster of "discipline groups," chaired by faculty members from various colleges.

These groups focus on technology issues of special interest to business, language, health science, and the other disciplines. Macintosh users are invited to share their stories about innovative applications of technology in the classroom and tips for teaching with computers.

The typical response from users has been "This is great. Give us a lot more information." Which leads Jim Chou to conclude that the real work starts after the Gopher server is up and running:

> We need to be more active in coordinating and updating the information that is made available on Gopher. Each department in Apple should maintain its own section and add new material directly. That requires a new level of commitment; we have to get departments that are not used to thinking about the Internet to buy into this project. It will take exciting material and regular updates to keep people coming back again and again.

Moving the Higher Education Gopher from pilot to permanent status requires a corporate commitment of resources and a recognition of the Internet Gopher as a viable avenue for marketing. Chou has promoted the pilot project within the company by pointing out its advantages over other types of marketing:

> I tell them how many people will be looking at this Gopher on a monthly basis. It will be much better than any printed magazine, because of size of the readership, and because we are able to track what users are accessing most often. That's a great advantage—you can never tell what people are actually interested in when you send them a newsletter. This is a chance for every department at Apple to get their message out to higher education, to keep information completely up to date, and to get instant feedback.

The message seems to be getting through. Apple has started publicizing the Higher Education Gopher, and is considering how to adapt it to other markets. With a proven product in hand, it is time to consider enhancing its effectiveness. The use of graphics and multimedia to demonstrate new products is already a technical possibility, but Chou is concerned about the impact of large-scale distribution of video. "Apple could run video across the network today," he says, "but it might bog down the server and create a logjam for people trying to download a file. We have to keep in mind the current status of the Internet, and work with that."

As options expand for using the Internet, Chou is confident that Apple will be ready to turn them into reality. He envisions a natural transition from posting product information and encouraging feedback on the Gopher server to demonstrating software capabilities and delivering products on-line. The message attached to Apple's Gopher server reflects his optimism:

> *Please keep in mind this is an evolving project, it will grow and become more sophisticated. Content will be added on a continuous basis with improvements using graphics and illustrations to accompany text in the future, along with software that is represented in the publications.*

Meanwhile, Apple is increasing its activity on other Internet fronts. In addition to the marketing efforts in higher education, the company maintains an anonymous ftp server available to all customers. This dedicated machine is used to distribute any technical information or software that Apple wants to make publicly available; it provides access to key technologies like HyperCard that make Apple products more attractive and samples of other software. The server typically handles two to three thousand connections every day.

The company also encourages its employees to be active contributors to the Internet. Erik E. Fair, the Internet postmaster at Apple, is well known for his work in developing network standards. Steve Cisler, another active Internet participant, shares information on the Internet through detailed meeting reports and informative postings to discussion lists. Dale Mead makes it a point to respond directly to every customer comment or question about Apple that he spots on the Internet, or to forward the message to someone he knows will take responsibility for finding the answer. When these examples are multiplied by the thousand of Apple employees who regularly use the Internet, the impact is significant.

Digital

> Customers are telling us that it's easier now to reach them on the Internet—and that's where they are looking for more information and services. If customers are going to be on Internet, it behooves Digital to do business the way the customer wants to do it (Russ Jones).

Russ Jones, the Digital Equipment Corporation's public forum marketing manager for Unix marketing, has a long and somewhat ponderous title. Fortunately, his definition of the job gets right to the point: "I make sure Digital is on the leading edge of using the Internet as a communication vehicle." Actually, the Internet is not the only electronic marketing channel of interest to Digital; Jones is also responsible for working with opportunities on CompuServ, America Online, and other networks. In his opinion, however, the Internet, with its dramatic increase in the number of customers, and types of organizations now connected, has become the one marketing channel that no company today can afford to ignore.

Jones sees the Internet as a vital tool for Digital to get information quickly and directly to customers to help them understand more about specific products. The company uses the Internet to post concrete examples of how existing products can be used more effectively, and encourages customers to share information and questions about new product configurations. It also provides a forum for them to contact Digital developers to discuss questions about product functionality. The premise is that the more information customers have about products, the more satisfied they will be with them.

Like many other technology companies, Digital has been forced by rapid changes in the computer marketplace to rethink its overall strategy. Jones sees participating in newsgroups and maintaining freely available resources on the Internet as the building blocks of a new marketing and customer support system. The traditional customer information seminars and invitational meetings have to some extent been replaced by the electronic forums that target specific groups of customers with information relevant to their current needs. Says Jones:

> With the advent of new Internet services, we have a flexible environment for getting information to where people are, rather than trying to get customers to come to us. The big advantage of using the network has been to move our world out to meet the customer. Now that barriers to commercial activity on the Internet have been removed, the network has diversified to include a commercial community, and that is reflected in Digital's planning for future services.

Digital Equipment has always worked closely with the education market, cultivating a strong base of customer support in colleges and universities. The company's association with research and education made the Internet a natural communication channel even before commercial activities were contemplated. Many of the Internet's developers of the Internet were Digital customers; and Digital employees also participated in development efforts, contributing to the Internet Engineering Task Force, and helping to develop protocols such as ftp mail. Jones feels this history of involvement created a lot of good will from people who know and remember that their favorite piece of public domain software came from the DEC software server. Now it is essential to turn this good will into new business opportunities.

Digital's on-line software archive was one of the earliest Internet addresses. The company has now added product information to the same file, and is working on making it available in as many Internet formats as possible. Gopher, WAIS, and World Wide Web access will allow more users to locate what they want, at the same time that Digital dramatically increases the amount of product information supplied on the network. The goal is to make a much greater percentage of the material that has been provided to customers in printed form available electronically.

Growth in customer interest has paralleled this growth of the product information available on the Internet. Readership of the biz.dec newsgroup climbed to more than eight thousand in the Spring of 1993, reflecting an increase of 20 percent over the first quarter of the year. During that same period, Russ Jones estimates that forty thousand pieces of product information were accessed by customers using Digital's information server.

Digital's strategy is based on the conviction that distributing interactive information on the network will bring the company closer to the customer. According to Jones:

> The Internet creates a direct relationship with the customer, allowing many departments at Digital to hear and respond to user questions as soon as they are raised, rather than having them filtered through several layers. The sales force at Digital has found that the Internet makes them much more effective in answering specific customer questions. Instead of making standard customer calls, and distributing general printed information, the representatives can focus

their face-to-face meetings on the most important issues and solutions for that particular customer.

Digital has used the Internet to distribute its press releases and product announcements to editors, consultants, and analysts since the early 1980s. These announcements are also posted to the biz.dec group of USENET, along with new services, information on seminars and sales promotions, activities of DEC partners, and other information. A Frequently Asked Questions posting tells customers everything from how to find Digital phone numbers to how to locate public domain software. The same information is available via ftp at Digital's file server (gatekeeper.dec.com), or via electronic mail, for those customers not set up for file transfer.

Digital is sensitive to the Internet's aversion to junk mail and blatant ads, so the promotional announcements are posted only through the biz groups or mailing lists for people who have asked to receive the information directly. The company's newsletters are now focused on the electronic customer, and are also distributed through mailing lists, ftp, and newsgroups. Everyone who works at Digital can have access to the Internet, and it was a vital part of the development environment before it began to contribute to the company's marketing efforts. Thus, there are many Digital employees who contribute to newsgroups and answer customer questions on their own.

More business units inside Digital are developing plans to tailor their network information and services to the needs of particular industries (such as health care), or to more specialized technical groups. Jones recognizes the need to be innovative and forward-looking in providing expanded Internet services, and he knows it will take creative planning to maintain Digital's head start in this area. "Now that more and more companies are recognizing the potential of the Internet, just maintaining our current services doesn't give us a competitive advantage," he says. "Digital has to work at being the first in the industry to offer a unique service, and then be prepared to see other companies copy us."

What Digital hopes to gain from its intensive use of the Internet is more permanent than a short-term technical advantage—the company is aiming at new and better products based on improved communication and responsiveness to customers.

Any size company can develop an effective strategy for Intermarketing. In fact, Internet access gives even the smallest companies a chance to use the information resources that were once the exclusive domain of the high-technology world. Communicating and interacting with customers on the network relies more on creativity, flexibility, and responsiveness than on corporate muscle power. Establishing a presence on the Internet can be a breakthrough opportunity for a small company, putting it in touch with a market otherwise out of its reach.

Getting closer to the customer is probably one of the most important benefits of using the network, according to Victor Rosenberg, president of Personal Bibliographic Software, Inc., in Ann Arbor, Michigan. "The Internet has profoundly changed the way we work," he maintains. "Intensive use of electronic mail and customer-oriented discussion groups creates an electronic community of users. This is where we get our ideas for new programs and products—by communicating with customers over the Internet."

The world of publishing and bookstores, where once the printed word reigned supreme, is also starting to recognize the potential for reaching customers through the Internet. Quantum Books, a technical and professional bookstore in Cambridge, Massachusetts, started by using the Internet as a supplement to its regular mail-order service two years ago. The response has been tremendous; with the store's focus on computer books, the Internet connection provided a great match with existing and potential customers. The network makes it easier for customers to send in orders or queries, and provides a vehicle for the store to send out information of interest about new books or special events such author appearances.

Quantum has also established a Gopher server to encourage readers to browse through their latest offerings. The retailer is able to highlight specific titles, and to feature the most important books on certain topics. The bookstore is aiming to get its whole inventory of about twenty thousand titles on-line so that customers will be able to search for titles of interest and order them in one easy step.

Readers are encouraged to send e-mail to the store asking for recommendations of titles on specific topics. The staff member who handles the Internet mail, receives between seventy-five to a hundred messages a week. The messages vary from requests for specific titles to general questions. The service representative feels this kind of service is ideal for Quantum. "It's what a lot of customers have been asking for, and that makes it important for our business. The books we sell deal with cutting edge technology, so we have to be on top of technical developments." The Internet connection is a particular boon for foreign customers, who can send e-mail messages, clarify requests, and finalize orders without the expense of phone calls or the delays of postal service.

Like all companies that put customer service first, Quantum is careful to be respectful of the Internet culture and to focus its postings on providing useful information rather than direct advertising. The key is knowing who reads which discussion groups, and matching the distribution of announcements to the interests of a particular Internet list. Sometimes there is a mismatch, and the list participants will make it clear that future announcements are not especially welcome. But this is a rare occurrence. Quantum has found that the Internet expands its ability to reach customers, with orders up and use of the Internet informational postings growing weekly.

Thanks to the initiative of one staff member, who is a home user of the Internet, KKSF Radio in San Francisco now has a new Internet Gopher featuring playlists, general station information, locations of record stores that carry KKSF music, and more. Network users are encouraged to send comments and questions about programming, information about upcoming events, and even technical questions via e-mail. Many newspapers, including *The Boston Globe,* have a regular column on electronic communication and now feature Internet addresses in polling readers for opinions.

CONCLUSION

These few examples attempt to capture the positive impact of using the Internet to reach out to the electronic marketplace. By the time you read this book, there will certainly be many new examples, but the essence of intermarketing will remain the valuable information and innovative ideas it bring can to both a company and its customers.

By connecting to the Internet, companies gain full access to the universe of interactive networking and information exchange. If a primary corporate motivation is saving money on communication costs, the experience of other businesses indicates that significant savings are possible, especially in international communication and data exchange. Companies interested in qualitative improvements in communication with customers face a challenge of a different magnitude. Success will hinge on management willingness to experiment with a new approach to marketing that focuses on providing information and interacting frequently with customers over the Internet. Intermarketing is a long-term strategy requiring company-wide commitment to putting customer interactions and information at the center of the marketing process.

Using the Internet to interact with customers is just one stage in the transition to intermarketing. Fortunately, it is a process that generates its own rewards—better-informed customers and companies better able to serve them.

REFERENCES

Curry, David J. 1993. *The New Marketing Research Systems: How to Use Strategic Database Information for Better Marketing Decisions.* New York: John Wiley & Sons, Inc. 1992.

—. The Good Network Guide: Being One of Us. *The Economist* 325(7791):20–24. December 26.

Farrow, Rik. March 1993. Hooking Up to the World. *Unix-World* 10(3):61–64.

Magrath, Allan J. 1992. *The 6 Imperatives of Marketing: Lessons From the World's Best Companies.* New York: Amacom.

Pine, B. Joseph, II. 1993. *Mass Customization: The New Frontier in Business Competition.* Boston: Harvard Business School Press.

Reinhardt, Andy. 1993. Smarter E-Mail Is Coming. *BYTE* 18(3):90–108. March.

Securities and Exchange Commission. 1992. Form 10–K, Annual Report. The Charles Schwab Corporation.

Stratford, Sherman. 1993. The New Computer Revolution. *Fortune* 127(12):56–80. June 14.

Tierney, John. 1993. Will They Sit by the Set, or Ride a Data Highway? *The New York Times.* 1, 20. June 20.

CHAPTER 5

Transforming Research and Development

> *What it all boils down to is one critical activity: collaboration. We didn't invent it—but we made it instantaneous.*
> —**Jim Fitchett**, CIO, Harvard Medical School

What do researchers at Bellcore, GE Medical Systems, Motorola, Intel, and hundred of other corporations have in common with the doctors at Harvard Medical School? Three elements that have become fundamental to cutting-edge research in the 1990s: a commitment to scientific inquiry, a growing interest in collaborative projects, and a connection to the Internet.

Products that change our lives, from chemical compounds to miracle medicines, from computer chips to cellular phones, often require a slow, painstaking process of discovery. Each breakthrough entails solving myriad separate problems, sometimes over a period of years. But the image of the scientist seeking solitary solutions in an isolated laboratory is as outdated as the vacuum tube. Science today is more often a collaborative venture based on team work and pooling of vast amounts of data. For the millions of researchers connected to the Internet, the communication power of the network has transformed the nature of their work (Broad 1993).

American corporations are embracing collaborative research for financial and strategic reasons. Multimillion dollar investments in separate research and development facilities in the tradition of IBM Research, Bellcore, and Xerox Parc are being scrutinized and often scaled back as part of overall corporate downsizing (Corcoran 1992). More than ever, company executives and shareholders expect basic research to make a measurable contribution to the organization's bottom line. Research projects that do not lead to viable, competitive products are increasingly seen as an unaffordable luxury by companies in the midst of reducing their work force and cutting other expenses.

At the same time, the breakthrough discoveries that may ultimately create a whole generation of new products must start with basic scientific inquiry. One way to lessen the expense and risk of research and development is to work in collaboration with other organizations. Private industry has often looked to partnerships with university-based scientists and with government to accelerate the pace of development. Now, this view of collaboration is expanding to include former competitors who are willing to join forces on particular projects at the basic research stage or in joint product development (Rotemberg and Saloner 1991).

The increased interest in research partnerships also reflects lessons corporate America learned from the tough international competition of the past decade. Japanese companies demonstrated a particular talent for transforming research innovations into product improvements during the 1980s. Analysts observed that Japan placed less emphasis on pure research and more on getting products quickly to market. Japanese companies often transformed the results of basic research carried out in American laboratories into competitive products much faster than was possible in the United States. Speed of innovation and steady quality improvements allowed Japanese companies to capture the lion's share of the market in many areas of electronics and manufacturing. Using a collaborative model in which a group of companies worked together on various aspects of a major development effort, Japan was able to speed the pace of innovation with a significant total investment but less burden on any one company (Levy and Samuels 1992).

Even the U.S. corporations most committed to innovation and development can no longer afford to support their multi-million dollar research operations in isolation from the realities of the marketplace. A faster pathway from laboratory discoveries to profitable product applications has become the number-one goal of corporate research. Successful research and development today depends on bringing the resources of many organizations together to work on a seminal problem, in the hope that a solution will create new opportunities for all participants (Badaracco 1991). After a history of competitive, independent work by corporate laboratories and research centers, companies are beginning to invest more of their research dollars in collaboration.

Developments at IBM exemplify the changing landscape of American corporate research. AT IBM research centers in Yorktown Heights and Almaden, the laboratories where scientists once pursued specialized projects far removed from the daily concerns of marketing, manufacturing, and product design, are now teamed with other divisions to encourage a focus on the end products that may result from their discoveries. Increased use of the Internet is one of many indications that a new strategy is taking hold. Through its participation in the Open Software Foundation, for example, IBM works closely with Hewlett Packard, Digital Equipment, and Siemens in Munich on a Distributed Computing Environment (DCE) project. Dave Bachmann, an IBM scientist in Texas, sees the Internet as essential to this and other collaborative work. "Networking is critical to the very existence of shared development," he says. "Almost all our interaction for DCE is done over the Internet. There is a weekly conference call, but all the important work is done by e-mail."

IBM's new partnerships have also extended to Japanese companies. A joint effort with Toshiba to develop the flat panel displays essential to smaller notebook computers was described in glowing terms by James McGroddy, Director of IBM Research, in an article on the new IBM: "This is enormously successful financially and technically. So what if it's half Toshiba. We have to get used to IBM being involved with a wide variety of companies" (Wrubel 1992, 44).

Taligent, a joint venture between IBM and Apple, was formed in 1990 to create an object-oriented operating system capable of running on a variety of platforms. A technology alliance with Motorola and Apple to develop powerful RISC (reduced instruction set computing) microprocessors has resulted in a new line of PowerPC products being designed and fabricated jointly in just twelve months—a shorter production cycle than IBM could have achieved independently. These and other partnerships indicate that IBM has made collaboration an important part of its comeback strategy (Brandt, Rebello and Burrows 1993).

A growing number of corporations participate in research consortia, joining in new alignments between government, universities, and industry. A recently announced consortium of Armstrong World Industries, Raychem Corporation, Rohm and Haas, and the 3M Corporation will work with Sandia National Laboratories to improve the processing of polymer blends and alloys with the goal of producing new and more economical resins. Another alliance of seven manufacturers, seven universities, and three federal agencies has been created to improve the precision casting of metal alloys commonly used in the aerospace industry (NIST 1993). Such consortia rely heavily on networked communication.

These and similar projects use the collaborative power of the Internet to help ensure American competitiveness in bringing technology to bear on applications in manufacturing. With more than eighty corporate participants, including Bellcore, GE, 3M, Motorola, Apple, and IBM, the Microelectronics and

Computer Technology Corporation (MCC) is one of the country's most broad-based industry consortia.

Joe D. Sims, vice president for marketing and business development at MCC, believes that in order for American companies to remain competitive, they must put more emphasis on collaboration and networking. Sims acknowledges, "It may sound like just buzz words, but virtual organizations will actually be the infrastructure that allows American business to flourish in the next decade. The Japanese model of *keiretsu* doesn't transfer all that well into our dynamic culture, but electronic connections do." The payoff from these connections, he says, is that "different companies can pull together an organization in a short time, address a market need, and produce a quality, price-sensitive product by using high speed networks." The strategic use of global networking for collaboration is an important priority for MCC:

> Perhaps the most important information systems challenge and competitive business opportunity for the coming decade will be universal, broadband interactive networking. Coming on the heels of very low cost/high value computing, which emerged in the last decade, the impact will be enormous. MCC's research will enable members to realize the business potential of this development.

The increased emphasis on collaborative research and development, even if the short-term motivation is strongly financial, does foster a qualitative shift in the organization of corporate research in America. The benefits of enhanced communication links among research laboratories, cross-fertilization among disciplines, and exposure to outside ideas will have the greatest immediate impact on corporations making significant investments in research and development. The climate of shared discovery resulting from such collaboration, however, is now open to many companies through their participation in the Internet. As Jim Fitchett, chief information officer at Harvard

Medical School, notes, the Internet did not create collaboration—that was a factor in many earlier discoveries. But by
making communication of research findings literally "instantaneous" and available to all, the network has profoundly altered
the future conduct of research, whether it takes place in a
corporate or a university environment.

As Figure 5.1 illustrates, even research scientists use the
Internet for a variety of reasons. In 1993 Thomas J. Cozzolino
and Thomas H. Pierce of Rohm and Haas Company conducted
a survey of network users in the chemical field. More that 50
percent of the respondents listed communication using e-mail
as their primary activity on the Internet. Accessing bulletin
boards and mailing lists was the next most frequently mentioned
activity, while one third of the respondents explicitly mentioned
collaborative research as a primary reason for using the network.
One chemical company respondent noted:

> I personally feel I do the work of 2–3 people due to access
> to the Internet. Almost all my research is begun by querying
> other researchers that read USENET for references, sugges-

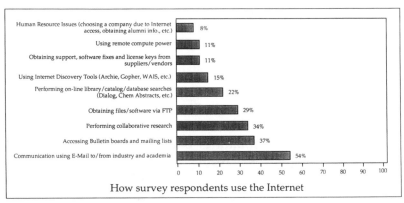

How survey respondents use the Internet

From: Internet Survey Results
      Posted to CHMINF-L, April 1993
      Chemical Information Sources Discussion List

FIGURE 5.1   Use of the Internet: Chemical Industry Survey (1992).
Thomas J. Cozzolino and Thomas H. Pierce

tions, or software that are applicable to my research. To date I have never been disappointed. Some responses are not useful but I have found that there is usually one or two responses that is exactly what I need to make progress on my research (Cozzolino and Pierce 1993, 23).

With connections to the Internet, researchers keep up with new discoveries as they happen in laboratories around the world. They communicate in real time with colleagues working on similar projects, or hear about a relevant discovery in a different discipline. Real-time updates on new approaches to a research problem can save substantial periods of trial and error. As the lines between scientific disciplines like biology, chemistry, engineering, computer science, and physics begin to overlap, specialists working together on interdisciplinary teams can benefit from the insights of each discipline—whether the team members work for the same organization or in different countries.

From its inception, the Internet was designed to facilitate "big science" by giving researchers access to the most powerful computing facilities available, first for defense-related research and then for other university-based projects. The National Science Foundation network connects supercomputer centers around the country to one another and to regional networks that now provide connectivity for most U.S. colleges and universities. Research problems that involve modeling, visualization, and other data-hungry applications can often be solved using supercomputing resources via the Internet. Such problems are not all focused on abstract mathematical hypotheses. They can be as real-world as determining the best aerodynamic shape for a new car design or testing alloys and chemical reactions to produce a better aluminum can, and frequently involve cooperation between industry, government, and university research.

The Internet also links many corporate research divisions directly to supercomputer centers for dedicated research projects. U.S. Steel, for example, connected to the Internet in 1990 to allow scientists and engineers at their Technical Center to do cutting edge computational work on important engineering issues related to the efficient production of high-quality steel products. Most of the work requiring supercomputer power is in the field of computational fluid dynamics—analyzing the flow of liquid steel in continuous casting equipment. Other work simulates the hot rolling process and explores ways to improve the design of food cans manufactured from U.S. Steel tin plate.

PURSUING SCIENTIFIC DISCOVERY

At the frontiers of discovery, many research problems are too big for any one company to tackle single-handedly, and too important to leave unsolved. The Internet provides a mechanism for very different types of organizations to pool their knowledge in the attempt to overcome current scientific limitations and achieve significant breakthroughs. Instead of racing against competitors to assimilate proprietary information, organizations share their resources over the network in the interests of a collective solution. This is not to say that corporations are giving up on competition or product development when they join a collaborative project. They are just recognizing that advantage will come at a different stage of the process—after the basic problem has been solved.

Two research projects among the thousands that have been tackled with the help of the Internet—improving medical diagnosis and treatment through computer imaging, and locating untapped oil reserves—serve to illustrate how the global network can help push forward the frontiers of science.

Medical Imaging

The delicate vessels and neural complexities of the human brain still conceal some of their most important secrets. Yet when surgery is needed for trauma or disease, successfully navigating the brain's uncharted territory may be a matter of life and death. At Brigham and Women's Hospital in Boston, Ron Kikinas, M.D., the director of the Surgical Planning Laboratory and associate professor of radiology at Harvard Medical School, is leading a project to transform the output of magnetic resonance scanners into three-dimensional maps of the human brain.

To carry out his data-intensive research on the digital processing of diagnostic medical data, Kikinas has an impressive array of technology at work in his twenty-person laboratory. Imaging data is input, processed, and analyzed on twenty-five high-powered, networked workstations and two supercomputers linked to six MR (magnetic resonance) scanners and four CT (computer tomography) scanners. "It sounds like a lot of horsepower," he acknowledges, "But for some of the applications here, it's barely enough."

That makes the laboratory's Internet connection a vital resource. A research partner at the Cancer Research Institute in Heidelberg, Germany, carries out an important piece of the project by using the Internet to log onto the computers in Boston. Colleagues in Switzerland collaborate on the segmentation of various structures in the brain and exchange data with Kikinas over the network. His Internet mail directory includes more than a hundred people with whom he regularly exchanges e-mail and data related to his work. Many use the Internet to communicate with the laboratory daily. Among his close collaborators are the scientists at the GE Research and Development Center in Schenectady, New York.

With orders totaling $3.6 billion in 1992, GE Medical Systems is one of the world's largest suppliers of diagnostic imaging equipment. Medical Systems products include the magnetic resonance scanners and computer tomography scanners used in the laboratory by Dr. Kikinas as well as in hospitals, clinics, and research laboratories around the world. Together with x-ray, nuclear imaging, and ultrasound equipment, these tools provide essential medical information to support diagnoses ranging from the existence of tumors to the stages of fetal development. Transmitting the voluminous data such equipment produces from one location to another is well-suited to the high speed and bandwidth of the Internet.

Now, GE is working with researchers like Kikinas to make this high-technology equipment even more valuable to surgeons and diagnosticians. By mapping the output of the scanners onto very precise, three-dimensional models of internal organs, medical imaging software can help doctors to pinpoint the exact location of a tumor or injury and plan the most effective pathway for surgical intervention. Ideally, the images would be produced not just in advance of the treatment, but also in real time during an operation to guide the surgeon as quickly and precisely as possible. The result would be minimally invasive surgery:

> Computerized axial tomography (CAT) scan, magnetic resonance imaging (MRI) and other inputs would be combined to create a 3-D computer image of a patient's body. Then, during the surgery, the 3-D computer image could be viewed by a doctor or medical technician while an ultrasonic device could be used to guide the surgical instrument and update the 3-D surgery. By allowing the doctor to precisely identify a cancerous area, for example, such a system would limit the extent of a surgical procedure (Hughes 1993, 55).

GE Medical Systems is in business to create the equipment and the software that will make such applications a reality. Just producing the platform for high-powered medical imaging is not enough, however. Long-term success in this area requires intensive collaboration to design and test advanced applications in the real world of patients and treatments. In planning and improving their imaging products, GE Medical takes into account the experiences and needs of practitioners and research scientists at hospitals and clinics around the world.

The Internet provides essential connections between researchers at GE Medical Systems and scientists in hospitals and universities engaged in developing new applications for imaging. Those who are working on collaborative projects, for example co-developed software, can send the source code back and forth through the Internet for changes and additions. Scientists at GE find that the network has significantly reduced the time lapse between research teams in different locations starting a project with a new idea and turning it into a finished application.

The Internet also allows clinical sites to send images back to GE for additional analysis. Most research projects include efforts to derive more useful data from the computer-based images already being used for diagnosis. Over the network, GE scientists can try different approaches to data analysis, generating software to create three-dimensional images, or rotating the images to see if this new look will help with diagnosis.

Harvey Klein, a scientist at the GE Research and Development Center, has been working for almost seven years on medical imaging projects—improving the ability to "look" inside the human body to make a diagnosis or carry out a surgical procedure. Klein uses the Internet to communicate with over a hundred research sites that are working on some aspect of image processing and surgical planning, and sees it as a requirement for his work. Without the network, this level of collaboration would be impossible. There are, for example, fifteen installations in Japan and twelve in Europe that carry out all their communication with Klein over the Internet, as well as numerous research partners at hospitals and universities in the United States.

Creating accurate 3-D images for even one part of the body requires a huge amount of data and computation. But with the ability to exchange and compare data over the network, scientists can focus on a particular problem and contribute their findings to the whole, literally changing the face of medical diagnosis. The Internet will also make the benefits of such discovery more widely available, eventually allowing smaller hospitals and clinics to transmit images of difficult cases to research hospitals for real-time consultation and diagnosis.

In addition to direct communication and collaboration with medical imaging research around the world, GE Medical Systems sees the potential for other Internet applications. They expect to expand their use of distributed information through bulletin boards and other features as they become more comfortable with the security and administrative issues outside the research center environment.

A logical next step would be to use the network for customer support. Currently, GE has modems attached to its equipment in various clinics in order to dial in and correct software problems on-line. The Internet would provide a faster and more powerful option. Scientists at GE have been giving top management demonstrations about the benefits of participation in Internet, showing what can be accomplished through collaborative work with research partners in hospitals and laboratories. As with other large companies, the next breakthrough depends on increased management understanding of the network's potential benefits for the whole organization.

Global Basins Research Network

The diagnostic equipment guiding a surgeon's incision would seem to have little in common with the rigging needed to explore the ocean floor for oil deposits. In fact, both areas depend heavily on generating and analyzing large amounts of data that can be transformed into useful computer images. Like medical imaging, geological research requires intense collaboration among scientific disciplines.

The Global Basins Research Network (GBRN) provides another example of the Internet helping to solve large-scale research problems. According to Roger N. Anderson, senior research scientist at Columbia University's Lamont-Doherty Earth Observatory and co-director of the Global Basins Research Network, the United States is rapidly coming to the end of its traditional petroleum resources. "If something new isn't discovered soon, all the major fields in the U.S. will be played out very soon, including the Alaska North Slope onshore and offshore and the Gulf Cost" (1993). Anderson points out that unless the United States can develop innovative methods of discovering and tapping significant new oil deposits within its national boundaries, our country will be left without adequate petroleum reserves by the year 2010.

Working through the collaborative framework of the GBRN, Anderson and his fellow scientists can develop and test new methods for locating huge underwater oil fields, based on computer visualization of all available seismic, geophysical, and geochemical data gathered over time from a likely deposit site. Massive amounts of such data are collected into integrated databases at different locations, and then computer models track the movements and interactions of key elements used to predict the location of oil. Finally, the computerized results are put to the test with on-site drilling to confirm whether oil will indeed be found where the computer models predicted it.

From its inception, the Global Basins Project has involved close collaboration among universities, corporate participants, and the U.S. Department of Energy. The list of distinguished participants reads like a who's who in the disciplines of geology, geophysics, geochemistry, and related earth sciences. University researchers from Columbia, Louisiana State University, Pennsylvania State, and the University of Colorado have joined forces with organic geochemists from the Woods Hole Oceanographic Institute and Texas A&M's Geochemical and Environmental Research Group—all linked to one another through the Internet. Corporate participation is equally impressive, with twelve major oil companies providing support: Agip, Amoco, ARCO, Chevron, Conoco, Elf Aquitaine, Exxon, Mobil, Pennzoil, Shell, Texaco, and Unocal. In addition, a number of high-technology companies are providing support and technical advice, including Advanced Visual System, Inc., Landmark Graphics Corporation, and Sun Microsystems.

Each participant in the project has essential contributions to make. Much of the information needed to locate and "visualize" new oil deposits through computer imaging has been created in separate research projects. Jeff Nunn of Louisiana State University is co-director of the Global Basins Research Network. Nunn describes the role of the Internet from his perspective as an active researcher:

> I have been involved in two Internet collaborations involving GBRN. The first is a collaboration between Cornell University, Computational Mechanics Corporation of Knoxville, and LSU. We are developing a 3-D Finite Element Code to describe fluid flow and chemical reactions in sedimentary basins. . . . Each group has developed their own pieces of software, remotely installed them on machines at the other sites and debugged them in conjunction with researchers at the other sites. . . . I have just started a similar collaboration with Hypermedia Corporation of Houston, which develops object-oriented databases. They have remotely installed software on a machine at LSU, and once it has been refined here, we will remotely install the software at all the GBRN sites. Once the software is installed at all the sites, we will have a database that is accessible to all sites over the network.

Without the use of the network, the distances between sites would be a formidable obstacle to cooperation. Through the Internet, all the partners can look at the same data interactively, and work together to solve the many issues related to such complex modeling and processing. For Roger Anderson, the Internet is fundamental to the success of the Global Basins project:

> As an Internet organization, GBRN is one of the first of a new generation to disregard 'red brick walls' and connect needed expertise regardless of geographic location. . . . The benefits of such collaboration can be enormous to the industry as a whole, because these new dynamic technologies are also applicable to international basins where migration is currently active (Anderson 1993, 87).

LEADING EDGE TECHNOLOGY

Almost every discipline and every major corporate research laboratory can provide numerous examples of the Internet's impact in facilitating cooperation and advancing the pace of research. In even the most competitive of businesses, the walls between companies have been penetrated by the power of high-speed networks.

Motorola

Leadership in the competitive world of electronic equipment, systems, components, and services requires a major commitment to research and development. Motorola's corporate mission is "to grow rapidly, in each of its chosen arenas of the electronic industry, by providing its worldwide customers what they want, when they want it" (Motorola 1992). When it comes to products like semiconductors, cellular phones, and microprocessor units, customers typically want the advantages of tomorrow's technology now.

In addition to its internal research initiatives, Motorola looks to partnerships with other companies to speed the process of turning basic research into new products. The technology alliance with Apple and IBM that produced the PowerPC is just one example of many joint research projects now underway. Collaboration to advance technology and develop new products extends around the world. Motorola's strategy includes both competition and cooperation in some of its key product areas. According to its 1992 annual report:

> The Semiconductor Products Sector experiences intense competition from numerous competitors, including Japanese companies and several other companies around the world, ranging from large companies offering a full range of products to small companies specializing in certain segments of the market. The competitive environment is also changing as a result of increased alliances between competitors. . . . Management believes that Motorola's commitment to research and development of new products combined with utilization of state-of-the-art technology will allow the Sector to remain competitive (1992, 3).

A partnership with Philips Electronics has resulted in a joint chip design center in the Netherlands to accelerate the development of integrated circuits for multimedia products like interactive compact discs. In another project, Motorola cooperated with Thompson Consumer Electronics to introduce a closed-captioned television microcontroller, a chip that can be included in new television sets to provide access to closed-captioned services for millions of hearing impaired television viewers. In keeping with the rapid growth of markets in the Far East, Motorola also works closely with companies in Hong Kong, China, and Japan. By the end of the decade, the company projects significantly increasing its international sales and services, especially in China.

In order to maintain its leading edge in rapidly evolving markets, the company invests almost 10 percent of every sales dollar in product development and technological advances. In 1992, that amounted to $1.31 billion allocated to research and development on sales of $13.3 billion (1992, *Annual Report*, 22). More than thirteen thousand professionals are engaged in research activities throughout the company. Like researchers everywhere, they need access to the Internet.

The Motorola Computer and Semiconductor Groups obtained the earliest connections to the Internet to participate in specific research projects. When a broader Motorola Internet connection was being considered in 1989, management expressed concern for security. Ensuring that internal company data was not at risk through the link to the Internet became a top priority in the implementation process. The whole company has about 110,000 employees worldwide in fifty-seven countries; some use modems and dial up access to network, so the total number reached by Motorola's enterprise network is close to 85,000 around the world. Motorola engineers worked to develop a first-rate security system that improved on the standard Internet security. A double firewall, the recommended standard for security, puts two separate and unconnected mechanisms between the Internet and the internal network. The security of the Motorola firewall is further enhanced by two mechanisms that operate independently: an access control list, plus a special software application for connecting to the Internet.

Dr. Hermann Tai, who helped to implement Internet connectivity for Motorola in 1989, recalls that research support was the primary rationale for joining the network. He explains, "So many Motorola scientists were conducting research on chip design and other projects that required extensive visualization and simulation resources that they needed access to the super-computer at the University of Illinois at Urbana. The research departments also wanted the capacity to get into other systems and download data files and other large information resources from external computers." From the beginning, he says, "There was also great interest in e-mail connections, to enable the researchers to keep in touch with developments around the world."

Tai rewrote Motorola's internal e-mail system to make it Internet-compatible so that the internal mail network could connect more easily to the Internet. Even with the special priority given to security and the complexity and size of Motorola's internal networking, the implementation process went smoothly. By the fall of 1989 Motorola had a corporate gateway to the Internet up and running. Tai is pleased to note that there has been a measurable increase in Internet use throughout the corporation, and that researchers often com-ment to him on how important the connection is to their work.

In addition to the specific research applications, Motorola has realized a number of value-added benefits from its corporate Internet connection: companywide participation in the many newsgroups and bulletin board services, and use of the network timing protocol to keep all the internal company networks synchronized. Users can also take advantage of the Internet's other capabilities, such as Archie and directory services. The Motorola gateway is set up to allow one-way telnet to the world without compromising security; any host internal to Motorola that is registered to the Internet host/server can use the Internet as a full gateway to the external world.

Les Shroyer, vice president and chief information officer at Motorola, believes that the Internet is one of the most powerful means available today for all parts of the technical community to keep in touch with colleagues and new scientific developments. He observes that at Motorola and most of its development partners, the majority of scientists and engineers have become accustomed to using the Internet. Using the network in their projects has become second nature:

> There is a whole new generation of people who are as comfortable communicating through a keyboard as face to face. Networks have become the preferred method of communication for exchanging scientific data and carrying out joint projects. The Internet definitely promotes knowledge sharing and professional interaction here. Motorola's use of the Internet is primarily for our development and research work, rather than on commercial applications. With a focus in high technology, including communications, computing platforms, and other electronic communication devices, the company has an interest in the network both as a platform for testing products and a vehicle for research and collaboration. Between us, our suppliers, vendors, and customers, there is a high premium on a rapid, robust flow of communication. That's what the Internet delivers.

Shroyer, who is taking on the responsibility of network systems for the wireless data group of Motorola feels that a link to the Internet will be important for wireless communication in the future, especially in an age of global communication, when the standard business card must include an Internet address and probably a few additional languages on the back.

In his experience, communication vehicles like discussion groups and bulletin boards on the Internet indicate that despite the competitive environment of high-technology research, collaboration is a fact of life. Requests for help in solving a particular problem will generate overnight responses and advice from people at many companies. In Shroyer's opinion, "The Internet fosters the problem-solving and collegial nature of the industry—people are cooperating as well as competing all the time."

This combination of cooperation and competition raises some important questions for network managers. Randy Buchholz, Motorola's global operations manager, is responsible for global issues regarding corporate-wide networking policy at the company. He wants to "take down the walls" between internal groups in the company and improve internal communication by standardizing and optimizing the enterprise network design. At the same time, however, it is important to ensure that the external wall remains as tight as possible. Maintaining secure Internet access is part of an overall networking strategy. As an engineering-focused company, Buchholz recognizes that Motorola needs to participate in research and development collaboration, and access information through the Internet to keep up with new developments. Even with many new joint development projects underway, Buchholz feels it is important to remember that one business group's technology partner may be another group's competition. This means that network managers have to consider how to address the interface with the outside world in a coordinated manner, so that the information that should be internal to the company stays that way. Buchholz concludes that connectivity must be based on a secure internal system for companies to succeed. "It is going to be an information-based world," he says. "Today's companies will survive into the year 2000 only if they can optimize their information exchange and be able to secure their most important asset; the information inside their computers."

Intel

In the semiconductor industry, competition is a way of life. Staying at the top requires constant product improvement, as successive generations of computing await the powerful new chip designs that will take complex applications in stride. Like Motorola, Intel recognizes that its leadership and profit margins depend upon the quality of its research, noting in its 1992 Annual Report that "Intel's competitive position has developed to a large extent because of its emphasis upon research and development" (Intel 1992).

With an expenditure of $779 million for research and development in 1992, and more than five thousand employees devoted to research and development around the world, Intel engages in a large number of joint development projects to ensure its competitive position in the years to come. Support for this research collaboration comes in part from the company's Internet connections.

Intel is a member of the ten-year old SRC (Semiconductor Research Corporation), which plays a key role in supporting silicon-based technology research at universities and encouraging interindustry cooperation. "The only place research into silicon-based technology is increasing is in our universities, and that's because of SRC," says SRC president George Sumney, "Plus, we now have the strongest link between industry and the universities that exists anywhere in the world" (Burrows, 1992, 47). As a member of SRC, Intel works closely with a number of other companies on basic research in the industry (Robertson 1992). The company's computer assisted design (CAD) groups collaborate with universities on the development of algorithms and software; most of this work takes place on the Internet.

Jeff Sedayao, Intel's Internet postmaster, knows that the number of active Internet users has increased significantly in the past few years. He estimates that eighty thousand messages go in and out of the Internet gateway at Intel each week. Any employee at the company can send and receive mail, but file transfer is limited to certain systems, so network staff can track down any problems that arise. Sedayao has been keeping track of Internet use since 1987; in addition to the annual doubling of mail traffic, bytes for file transfer are growing exponentially.

When he talks with groups at Intel that are setting up servers and access points to the Internet, they are highly interested in research and development with other companies. According to Sedayao, joint development projects generate intensive use because they usually require extensive use of file transfer as well as e-mail.

Even though Intel's use of the Internet is still heavily oriented toward research, Sedayao has observed that the introduction of new tools like WAIS and Gopher have made the network more accessible throughout the company, "It's not just for engineers any more." The Internet has started to play a role in customer support, for example, in distributing software patches over the network, a capability many customers had specifically re-quested. Archie is one of the tools that Sedayao includes in his list of personal Internet favorites. "It's just a wonderful tool; Intel has an anonymous ftp server in Archie now. When you use public domain software, you can have the source code to change things or fix them. I actually think that much public domain software is better than what vendors provide."

The availability of quality public domain software has also had an impact on Intel's approach to software development. Some people will check on the Internet now to determine if software has already been written. That way, developers don't reinvent the wheel, and it saves a lot of time that can be devoted to other aspects of the project. Sedayao believes that the trend at Intel and elsewhere is more interaction between companies. He has seen first hand that the Internet makes information sharing among consortia and other cooperative research groups easier to manage and more productive, and he expects to see a continued increase in the use of the Internet at Intel, as more departments become involved in collaboration.

According to the *Internet Letter*, IBM, General Electric, Motorola, and Intel are among the network's "power users," defined as the "top 150 companies sending the most traffic through the NSFNET backbone in June 1993" (Levin 1993).

As research collaboration continues to expand, this select group can be expected to rely even more on the interconnection power of the global network to support its work. For the thousands of other companies that may never reach the level of "power user," the Internet still offers important benefits in terms of speeding the pace of product development and encouraging partnerships. The experience of these companies is an important part of the transformation of research and development on the Internet.

PRODUCTIVE DEVELOPMENT TEAMS

Breakthroughs in basic research are essential to shaping the products of the future, and corporations using the Internet for collaborative research have an advantage in the search for scientific discoveries. Turning innovation into new and improved products is the lifeblood of every company, and here the Internet has also proved to be a critical component for success. Developing new products can be faster and more cost-effective when partners share information over the network. Many companies have found that their own branches can work together more successfully when they use the Internet to move development projects forward. The ease, reliability, and clarity of communication is a big factor in the success of any partnership requiring regular data exchange. As Marco Iansiti points out in *Harvard Business Review*, "When it comes to jumping the product generation gap, efficiently transferring knowledge is essential" (1993, 144).

Establishing virtual development teams on the Internet can substitute for expensive travel, relocation, and translation of data from one system to another. The network can help to move the development process more quickly toward a completed product by allowing team members to exchange and compare data directly on-line. More and more companies have determined that the Internet offers the best environment for joint development projects.

One such company is Mentor Graphics, which uses its Internet connection to communicate with partners ranging from Hewlett Packard to small, start-up companies. This Oregon-based corporation markets services and products related to automating the electronic design process. It develops software used in designing semiconductors, telecommunications switches, integrated circuits, and other electronic products for customers in the semiconductor, aerospace, computer, consumer electronics, and telecommunications industries. Joint development projects and agreements are an important factor in keeping Mentor Graphics competitive. The Internet has demonstrated its value in this and other aspects of company strategy.

To serve its international market, Mentor Graphics operates fifty-seven sites in twenty-four countries. All these locations need to stay in close communication with one another, and most of the company's 2,300 employees have network access. Mentor supports voice, video, and data on the company's internal network, and also uses the multimedia capabilities of the Internet, including Internet Talk Radio. The Internet serves to link overseas sites with the company's U.S. locations, allowing development staff to work as virtual teams on special projects. To a large extent, the network can substitute for development staff traveling to various sites to undertake projects.

Just at the time the Internet was first installed, Mentor Graphics had planned to send engineers from England to the United States to work as part of a joint development team. Instead, the company decided to test whether such work could be accomplished over the network. The results were so positive that network-based development has become the model for a majority of the projects. The company has also established internal news groups, modeled after the USENET format, to keep everyone up to date on what is happening with various

Mentor products and projects. Each Mentor product now has its own internal newsgroup. These are considered so essential to the development process that all Mentor engineers are expected to access the newsgroups regularly and use them to disseminate work-related information. Mentor administrative groups and development teams use the same internal newsgroups to share information and keep up with the latest developments in different parts of the company.

The external USENET newsgroups also are a standard feature of the company's customer support structure. A majority of Mentor customers already have Internet access, so the external newsgroups reach a large target audience. As the company plans future customer services, using Internet access to communicate with customers is expected.

According to Mark Silbernagle, who manages the technology development group for corporate information systems, the Internet is also essential in development agreements with other companies: "One of the biggest values from an administrative perspective is that the Internet provides a common carrier." Previously, Silbernagle says, "the company had to establish custom connectivity for every development partner that came along." This sometimes required extensive effort and expense. With an Internet connection in place, he notes, "the cost of adding new partners is almost zero. We are able to support a higher level of functionality while spending a lot less resources."

Mentor Graphics has found that working with partners over the Internet reduces the development cycle time and decreases time-to-market, both factors that are worth a lot in a competitive arena like software development. Silbernagle feels the Internet has evolved into a common electronic data interchange medium. It is standard enough for people to understand and implement. But, unlike typical electronic data interchange (EDI) programs that may cost $100,000 or more and require extensive system changes, the Internet is already in place in many companies. Silbernagle calls the Internet "a poor man's

EDI; it may not have everything, but it works now and it works well."

Because of the disadvantages of working on development projects outside this common networked environment, Mentor Graphics is increasingly reluctant to establish partnerships with businesses not connected to the Internet. According to Silbernagle, "No one can do business on a competitive schedule without access to the Internet; it just takes too much time to deal with communication any other way. If other companies say they want to exchange data on tapes, we are more and more likely to say no and look for someone already on the Internet."

When organizations with totally different corporate cultures need to work closely in a development environment, the Internet provides common ground. The CORE Project, a cooperative undertaking of Bellcore, the American Chemical Society, Chemical Abstracts, Cornell University Library, and OCLC premiered at Cornell University in April 1993 (Krumenaker 1993). According to Stuart Weibel, senior research scientist at the OCLC (Online Computer Library Center), the CORE Project would not have been possible without the Internet.

The goal of CORE is to provide desktop access to the full text, including high resolution graphics, of selected chemistry journal titles and reference works. Eventually the CORE database will contain all American Chemical Society journals since 1980, with newly published volumes added as they become available. In addition to serving the immediate information needs of chemists, the project serves to test the optimal interface, database design, storage, and delivery mechanisms for even more extensive libraries of on-line text.

Technical responsibility for the project was divided between Bellcore, OCLC, and Cornell. With a very large and detailed set of data, a lot of effort was needed on the technical level to move the project forward. The Internet allowed the developers to exchange not just ideas but very concrete suggestions for technical solutions; models could be mounted at one site and accessed by all participants for review and comment. Researchers at each location could actually put prototypes through their paces on-line, instead of just looking at static descriptions or limited demonstrations. In addition, holding discussions via the Internet provided a more accurate written record of decisions at every stage of the project than most face-to-face meetings would offer.

ViewLogic, a Boston area high-technology company, has used its Internet connection to carry out long-distance development projects with newly acquired facilities. When the company bought a small development facility in California, the network allowed people there to continue working without disruption on important projects even though they had joined a new organization three thousand miles away. With a regular flow of information over the Internet, there was no need to relocate the staff. In ViewLogic's software development projects with other companies such as Texas Instruments, the Internet has played a key role in speeding up the development process.

After two years of working with the network Steve Caissie, ViewLogic's Unix systems administrator, believes the Internet still has a lot of room to grow before it reaches its full potential. Many people are not aware of the resources that are available on the Internet, and find it too difficult to locate the specific information they need. Caissie looks forward to a better method for developing and sharing standard interfaces that will allow all users to jump into the Internet and find their way—not just system administrators like himself. Until that happens, he sees companies missing out on many of the things they could be accomplishing on the network. "The Internet is still kind of a magical mystery place that not everyone understands completely," says Caissie. "Most people are left to figure it out for themselves as best they can; I still feel there are lots of resources and recent developments that are just too hard to track down. We tend to use what is familiar and forget about the rest."

Caissie is not alone in his sense that something is missing from the Internet information scene. While the network has succeeded in opening up new avenues for cooperative research and development, establishing itself a major component of corporate research and development, the rapid proliferation of its resources has left many users feeling out of date. In some companies, library and information centers are working to help bridge the gap by providing a better level of intellectual control over the electronic universe.

POWER LIBRARIES

Taking the mystery out of Internet resources, sifting through oceans of networked oysters to discover the pearls of essential information, requires a special set of skills and expertise. In many companies, corporate information centers have taken responsibility for exploring the Internet and delivering the most important resources in a more digestible form through the company's local network. In the process, such centers have redefined and expanded the role of the corporate library, making it more of a partner in research and development.

Marian Bremer, manager of the library at Bolt, Beranek and Newman (BBN), is continually seeking new ways to bring the resources of the Internet into the corporate and research environment. Her definition of library services includes monitoring the Internet and disseminating strategic information to individuals and departments where it will be of interest, sometimes even before they are aware it exists. She feels that the library will have an increased role in locating and evaluating networked information when user interfaces improve enough to encourage the casual searcher:

The Internet is changing our job totally; librarians will end up being teachers as well as information specialists. As the Internet becomes easier to use, researchers may think that it provides all the data they need. But because of its distributed organization, Internet data varies a lot in quality and comprehensiveness. Researchers who venture just a little outside of their field can be misled. For example, I've received messages from scientists who have concluded that there may be a market for a new product or service based on a few hours of Internet browsing. Despite its size, the Internet provides just a fraction of the information necessary to make that kind of decision! Librarians must help their organizations to use it, *and* to understand how it fits in with other resources.

BBN has always been active in using the Internet, and its library staff is familiar with its intricacies. The network is regularly used to answer reference questions and locate government information, statistics, and standards. Many items are accessed and downloaded through file transfer. The concept of "just in time delivery of information" was practiced at BBN before it became a widespread idea in the corporate and library world. In addition to locating the information resources needed by other departments in the company, the library accesses commercial search services like Dialog and Dow Jones through the high-speed Internet connection, and follows a number of newsgroups relevant to the research and products at BBN.

Bremer herself is a regular Internet user. She finds it to be helpful in practical support for the management of the library; most of the library's vendors are on the Internet, so routine business and order requests can be handled over it. The network offers a number of library discussion groups oriented to exchanging information about new electronic resources and answering specific questions. At times these can be invaluable in locating materials needed by a researcher.

Looking forward to expanding the value of the Internet for BBN, Bremer believes the kinds of resources available on the network will grow, and internal mechanisms for processing and delivering information will become more sophisticated. In terms of resources, she thinks the most important development for most companies will be the increased availability of federal information. "There is more government data going up on the Internet each month," says Bremer. "Many federal sources have important market research, financial, and technical applications; their distribution on the network will transform many business research departments. Also, information on specific research discoveries and strategic collaborations is being reported more regularly and is essential for companies with research and development programs."

Internally, Bremer is exploring the use of Internet tools like Gopher and WAIS to mount the most valuable Internet resources on the local BBN network. One of the attractions of the Gopher design is that it is so easy to customize the screens and menus to suit the information and research priorities of different areas. This allows the library to develop customized Gophers for certain departments so they can have the tools and resources they would most frequently use right in front of them.

Bremer envisions the library working to combine internal and external information resources and put them into a customized package depending on particular user needs:

> Because of the distributed nature of the Gopher model, you don't have to put all corporate information into one computer. The centralized approach requires a lot more effort and maintenance, that has limited our thinking about providing information services in the past. Now the Internet offers a good model for accessing internal information in combination with outside resources.

The proliferation of external information resources shows no sign of abating, making the role of interpretation and synthesis increasingly crucial for informed decision-making (Osborne 1992). Librarians can help to determine how internal and external information fits together and how to access it most efficiently. As Bremer points out, the distributed nature of the network makes it especially difficult for people to figure out exactly what they are accessing on the Internet or how valid or current the information might be. This skill will be increasingly important as more companies get involved in distributing or posting information that may reflect their own interests and viewpoint; it will be vital to distinguish self-promotion from independent research.

Libraries that play an active role in evaluating and disseminating networked information throughout their companies will be making a strategic contribution to research and development in the future. Bremer is convinced that the Internet resources will prove essential to corporate development, and that libraries must be at the center of a new approach to information access and utilization.

At Intel Corporation, six company libraries connected through an internal corporate network have also found that the Internet changes the way they relate to information. Capturing resources from the Internet and distributing them to the desktop via the internal company network makes library services more visible and more central to the development process. The main library maintains its own bulletin board utility to pull materials and newsgroups off the Internet. Topics like semiconductors, neural networks, artificial intelligence and related newsgroups are downloaded, organized, and posted to the library's utility. Items can be accessed via the bulletin board system or routed directly to the mailbox of a specific individual who has expressed an interest in a particular topic. The Internet information is just one part of the internal bulletin board services, which now have the highest activity in terms of total transactions in Intel's libraries.

Internet-based services have increased the visibility of the libraries at Intel. Because they find the Internet-based updates to be valuable, more departments more often contact the library to obtain information, before going to other sources. From an information management point of view, this integration of internal and external sources is highly desirable, since the next strategic insight may come from any part of the globe. But the flow of information coming from the Internet can be almost overwhelming. To promote effective dissemination of key data, the library strategy has begun to change its focus from text delivery to current awareness and information processing. Librarians are putting the technology in place and building library employee skills to make the staff conversant and comfortable with the Internet. In training sessions, they focus on the bigger picture of the network's impact on the whole company and how the library can make an important contribution. Or, as one Intel librarian sums it up, "If we don't have a role, we'll be history."

For the many corporate librarians who see networked information as the model of the future, there seems little danger of obsolescence. The librarian at a leading metals and materials company uses the Internet to locate resources, download documents, and access electronic publications that can be redistributed over the internal network. A current awareness service delivers e-mail text weekly on the Internet. News of general interest can be posted on the library bulletin board within the corporate e-mail system, while individuals requesting specific subject updates can get customized postings sent directly. Even though the researchers at this corporation are already heavy users of the Internet themselves, often working on collaborative projects, they have come to appreciate the importance of library assistance in tracking down elusive sources and locating the most current information on the network.

Frank Lopez, a librarian at Chevron's Research and Technology Center in California, has found the Internet invaluable for communicating with colleagues, monitoring current research and developments in chemistry and geology, and finding elusive reference sources. He will post difficult questions on the appropriate discussion groups, and has found that he almost always receives a useful answer in response. He sees more and more messages that are relevant to Chevron researchers and uses the internal mail system to distribute particularly useful information.

At SilverPlatter Information, Inc., publishers of CD-ROM information products, librarian Gerry Hurley scans a number of newsgroups and listservs to keep current with changes in the CD-ROM publishing industry, to follow technological developments of interest to the company's managers and engineers, and to track comments and questions posted by customers in universities, hospitals, corporations, and other settings. Important information is routed to decision-makers in the company, up to and including the president. Hurley's use of the Internet as a current awareness tool has definitely had an impact on corporate strategy, and the use of the network within the organization has expanded considerably to include support for product development and use of public domain software, as well as communication between SilverPlatter sites in Boston and London.

In a recent article in *Business Information Review,* Michel Bauwens calls for a total rethinking of the role of the corporate librarian in the age of networked information:

> Books and databases are no longer sufficient to carry out our job well. The new corporate librarians could be seen in the middle of a concentric circle of cyberspace (i.e. the electronic information space or ocean), consisting not only of external databases, but also of E-mail, Bulletin Board, and Computer Conferencing systems (1993, 66).

Bauwens dubs these new librarians "cybrarians," and predicts that they will contribute to the future success of their corporations by creating a new model for information management. Connection to the global network is essential to such a model. Relatively small numbers of corporate librarians have put such concepts into practice, but interest in the Internet is definitely on the rise (Ladner and Tillman 1993). Librarians and information specialists who are active users of the Internet can create a vital link between corporate strategy and the new information services required for research and development.

THE NEW BASICS

Corporations investing millions in research and development have no question that the Internet is essential for collaborative research. High-technology firms are finding the global network a boon in facilitating development projects between remote offices and far-flung business partners. Forward-looking corporate librarians and information centers give the Internet high marks for offering a new level of information services. Clearly, the network already plays a major role in the transformation of research discoveries into product applications for many American companies.

What about the vast majority of business in the United States; the hundreds of thousands of manufacturing and service companies where research and development has never been, and may never be, a priority? Steven Gage, president of the Cleveland Advanced Manufacturing Program (CAMP), thinks that no matter how small and nontechnical the company, wherever competitiveness counts the Internet can make an important contribution. His work on technology transfer for small and medium-sized business has convinced him that even though these companies have not previously used high-speed networks, they can reap tremendous benefits from the Internet and the growth of a more comprehensive national information infrastructure:

> CAMP serves as an intermediary for small companies that don't have direct access to the Internet. It has proved ex-

tremely valuable in tracking down resources, helping them deal with technical problems, and getting them in touch with suppliers and potential partners. Many manufacturing companies have difficulty changing from a 1950s style of operation to the high-technology world of the 1990s. But they have to make that adjustment to survive. The Internet can become a great source of support.

The faster the world of telecommunications advances, the more small companies stand to gain from active participation in networking. Testifying before the U.S. House of Representatives Subcommittee on Technology, Environment, and Aviation in March 1993, Gage provided examples of ways small manufacturers can use the global network. In order to manufacture parts for the international market, companies need assistance understanding and meeting new manufacturing standards. Adopting Computer Aided Design (CAD) capabilities contributes to increased productivity, but also requires frequent software upgrading and communication with vendors to obtain satisfactory performance. Access to experts and advice over the network can help with these and other tasks:

> Companies need help in planning, purchasing, integrating, and trouble-shooting their in-house communications systems as well as the interfaces with other companies and national networks. Small and medium-sized manufacturers also need help in dealing with specific customer product information data (e.g. Computer-Aided Design files) sent to them in a format not compatible with their own system and in achieving compatibility in the future... A network would enable companies to directly access information databases and specialized bulletin boards covering job quote opportunities, available capital equipment, new regulations, new technical support resources, and upcoming workshops (Gage 1993).

Gage points out that regional centers supported by the National Institute of Standards and Technology (NIST) can provide an important link to networked information for the companies in their area. The Northeast Manufacturing Technology Center (NEMTC) works with Tufts University to offer a special information service, TECnet, aimed at bringing the benefits of collaboration and global networking directly to the small and medium size companies. By paying a small annual fee, companies can access TECnet through a personal computer and modem. They are connected to federal information resources, databases of used equipment for sale, and sources of advice for small business. At the same time, they have access to the cooperative power of the network, to exchange information with one another or to tap into the expertise represented in Internet technical discussion groups. Such access gives them a more competitive basis for dealing with technical changes.

TECnet describes its mission as "helping companies work together to cope with the special challenges they face—the high cost of new technologies, the absence of skilled workers to operate them and the lack of management expertise to efficiently implement new technical systems" (Havens 1992). Its success in introducing small manufacturers to the benefits of the Internet provides a model for matching "low-tech" companies with high-impact information resources.

Participation in the Internet's research and development community is becoming a "new basic" for some of the smallest and the largest U.S. corporations. The global network can support high-powered research teams on the cutting edge of discovery, and simultaneously provide a source of practical guidance for low-tech organizations adapting to the requirements of a high-tech future. Over the past decade, the United States' approach to research and development has undergone a profound transformation. The era when the most important basic science often emerged from corporate research centers seems to be ending. Instead, the discoveries of the future are more likely to emerge from cooperative alliances of business, government and universities joined through high-speed networks in long-term consortial agreements or temporary product development efforts. A connection to the Internet has become a basic requirement for productive research in the 1990s.

REFERENCES

Anderson, Roger N. 1993. Recovering dynamic Gulf of Mexico reserves and the U.S. ecology future. *Oil & Gas Journal*: 85–90.

Badaracco, Joseph L. 1991. *The Knowledge Link: How Firms Compete Through Strategic Alliances*. Boston: Harvard Business School Press.

Bauwens, Michel. 1993. The Cybrarians Manifesto. *Business Information Review*: 9(14):65–67, April.

Brandt, Richard, Kathy Rebello, and Peter Burrows. 1993. Three scrappy startups that could help rejuvenate IBM. *Business Week* 3317:138. May 3.

Broad, William J. 1993. Doing Science on the Network: A Long Way from Gutenberg. *The New York Times*. C1, C10. May 18.

Burrows, Peter. 1992. Consortia: Are They Getting Better? *Electronic Business* 18(8):47–50. May 18.

Corcoran, Elizabeth. 1992. Redesigning Research. *Scientific American* 266(6):103–110.

Cozzolino, Thomas J. and Thomas H. Pierce. 1993. Internet User Survey Results. *Internet Business Journal* (1)1:23–24.

Havens, Dorothy J. 1992. TECnet brings collaborative manufacturing to Massachusetts. *AIM Business and Industry Reporter* 4(9):2.

Hughes, David. 1993. New center advances real time computing. *Aviation Week and Space Technology*. 138(16):55–57.

Iansiti, Marco. 1993. Real World R&D: Jumping the Product Generation Gap. *Harvard Business Review* 71(3):138–147.

Intel Corporation. 1992. *Annual Report*. Santa Clara, California.

Krumenaker, Larry. 1993. Virtual libraries, complete with journals, get real. *Science* 260:1066.

Ladner, Sharyn J. and Hope N. Tillman. 1993. *The Internet and Special Librarians: Use, Training and the Future*. Washington: Special Libraries Association.

Levin, Jayne. 1993. Companies Tap Internet's Power. *The Internet Letter*. 1(1):2–5.

Levy, Jonah D. and Richard J. Samuels 1991. Institutions and innovation: Research collaboration as technology strategy in Japan. In *Strategic Partnerships: States, Firms and International Competition*. Edited by Lynn Krieger Mytelka. Rutherford, N.J.: Fairleigh Dickinson University Press.

Motorola. 1992. *Annual Report*. Schaumburg, Illinois.

NIST (National Institute of Standards and Technology). 1993. *NIST UPDATE* electronic version, June 14.

Osborne, Richard L. 1992. Information power in the private company. *Journal of General Management* 17(4):13–24.

Robertson, Jack. 1992. *Electronic News* 38(1922):1(2). July 27.

Rotemberg, Julio J. and Saloner, Garth. 1991. Interfirm competition and collaboration. In *The Corporation of the 1990s: Information Technology and Organizational Transformation*. Edited by Michael S. Scott Morton. New York: Oxford University Press.

Wrubel, Robert. 1992. Down from the Mountain: How IBM Research Woke Up and Reorganized Itself for the Nineties. *FW: Financial World* 161(22) 36–44. November 10.

6

Customer Connections

You can't say it often enough: Don't lose touch with the customer.
—**Stratford Sherman**, *Fortune*

Fortune 500 corporations with billion dol-
lar budgets, small local companies with a handful of employees,
entrepreneurs hoping to turn ideas into enterprises, are all
ultimately dependent on finding enough people who want to
buy what they have to sell. Acknowledgement of this basic
reality has prompted a rising tide of management counsel for
keeping customers loyal, anticipating their future needs, improving service, and responding to their concerns (Stahl and
Bounds 1991). The advice ranges from pithy principles to
weighty volumes. But the basic message is the same: Whatever
the business, customer connections are essential for success.

It is no wonder then that "customer focus" has become a
watchword for companies intent on improving their reputation
for service and increasing market share (Garfield 1992, Schnaars
1991, Deming 1993). Whether that focus takes the form of a
quality-enhancement program, a drive for innovative products,
or a commitment to excellent service, its effectiveness will be
evaluated in terms of the customer. A *Harvard Business Review*
article notes: "The driving force behind world economic growth
has changed from manufacturing volume to improving cus-

tomer value. As a result, the key success factor for many firms is maximizing customer value. Rather than price, quality has become the dominant influence on customers' perception of value" (Carothers and Adams 1991, 32).

Companies that consistently offer the best value from the customer's point of view make it a priority to know their customers and to respond to changes in the marketplace with new, more attractive products. In today's competitive environment, keeping in touch encompasses more than just the occasional sales call or promotional mailing. It requires the ability to keep track of individual customer preferences and overall market trends, to provide a steady stream of new information to potential customers wherever they are, and offer high-level support services tailored to individual needs. "Companies that excel in customer intimacy combine detailed customer knowledge with operational flexibility so they can respond quickly to almost any need, from customizing a product to fulfilling special requests. As a consequence, these companies engender tremendous customer loyalty" (Treacy and Wiersema 1993, 84).

What does it take to create this level of loyalty to a particular product or company? More and more businesses are using technology and networking to achieve the personalized service and flexibility that underpin excellent customer relations. These companies manage to offer their customers all the benefits of advanced technology combined with painstaking attention to individual details. The often-cited success stories like Wal-Mart, Home Depot, and Kraft USA don't just rely on friendly staff and personal service. Behind the scenes they maintain sophisticated in-house information systems to collect and analyze huge amounts of data. Information generated by these systems is used to fine-tune the merchandise stocked in different parts of the country, and even in different neighborhoods. Kraft, for example, maintains an integrated database combining individual store sales, customer preference profiles, and demographic information from around the country. The company's marketing teams can use this data to design customized promotion programs tailored to specific stores and population groupings (Treacy and Wiersema 1993).

Many businesses that cannot afford to maintain such elaborate internal information systems, and even some that can, are taking another path to strengthening connections with their customers. They have discovered that an increasing percentage of the individuals, organizations, and enterprises that comprise their market can be reached through the Internet. These customers are already connected to the network, and their numbers are growing at an unprecedented rate. Today, companies large and small are finding that their customers want, and expect, to communicate with them via the Internet (Collet 1993).

Suzanne M. Johnson, an information technology manager at Intel, recalls that her corporation was initially slow to see the value in connecting to the Internet. Most managers felt that the company's internal networks and customer support systems were meeting all their communication requirements. The turning point came in the mid-1980s at a customer workshop sponsored by Intel's Scientific Computer Division, that makes parallel computers for customers with high-level computational and research needs. One of the messages of the workshop was that Intel was committed to providing excellent support for its computer customers. As one aspect of this service, workshop leaders announced that users were encouraged to send problem and bug reports directly to Intel. Over one third of the participants asked for Intel's Internet address, assuming this was the best way to send their reports. This was a real eye-opener for managers about the network's potential for improving customer service throughout the company.

Yankee Book Peddler, a book dealer in Contoocook, New Hampshire, serves a very different group of clients than Intel, but its customers were sending the same message. Amy Miller, Yankee's chief information officer, says it became clear by 1992 that a direct link to the Internet was essential to keep pace with changing customer expectations:

> The institutions that buy from us wanted more on-line information about our inventory and the status of their orders. Many of our customers were already connected to the Internet and waiting for us to catch up. With an Internet link in place, we are able to meet the immediate demand for enhanced information and explore other value-added services for the future. The Internet will definitely have an impact on the shape of our business over the next several years.

Even in the short term, linking to the Internet has improved Yankee's relations with customers in the United States, and has opened up some new international connections. Now the Internet is the preferred method of communicating with overseas customer.

Norm deCarteret, a manager at the Advantis Corporation, recommends Internet connections to companies interested in improving their customer support programs. He feels that effective use of the network can strengthen customer relations for almost every type of business:

> The use of the Internet, when that's the customer's "natural" medium, is a necessity for companies to keep pace with them. Failure to work with the customer in their preferred medium is just abandoning the market. The Internet bypasses formal processes (which can cause time delays) in favor of direct interaction between user and developer. It creates a tighter bond between customer and company, increasing customer satisfaction and loyalty.

BUILDING THE CUSTOMER CONTINUUM

A strong customer relationship is not created by a single sales transaction. It results from a continuum of interactions taking place over time. At each stage, the quality of communication and perceived responsiveness will have an impact on customer satisfaction and loyalty. Using a variety of Internet resources, it is possible for any size company to create a customer-oriented environment while obtaining valuable information about specific customer interests, responses to new product offerings, and feedback on company performance. The Internet also provides an excellent mechanism for expediting ordering and delivery. On-line customers can continue to receive enhanced support services through the network.

Figure 6.1 illustrates how the Internet can be used to enhance customer connections at three crucial points of interaction on the customer continuum: marketing, sales, and support.

Marketing

The first contact may occur long before a sale takes place, when prospective customers are seeking information about a product or service. Typical questions at this stage include: How does it work? Who else is using it? How much does it cost? The ability to reach millions of potential customers with product information is one of the great advantages of the Internet. Chapter 4 discusses how some companies already maintain an active presence on the network by using information-based marketing to distribute company information, new product announcements, and other items of interest to prospective customers. With additional high-profile Gopher sites like Sun Microsystems' Sunsite at the University of North Carolina, the Electronic Newsstand, and others, the number of businesses establishing a presence on the network is increasing at a rapid pace.

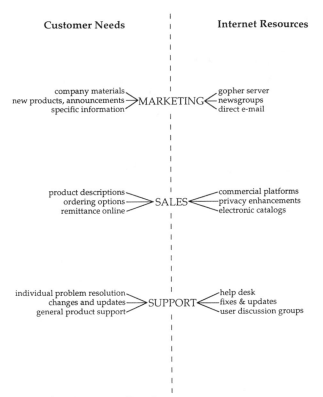

FIGURE 6.1   The Customer Continuum.

Sales

Internet users are already comfortable with on-line transactions and have grown accustomed to the instant flow of information available to them on demand. Most of the companies that have started to offer sales over the network have found that customers respond positively to this option, as long as the customer feels in control of the process. Negative responses are more frequent for unsolicited sales offers, particularly those distributed to serious discussion groups. Internet sales are especially attractive when on-line ordering can accelerate delivery time. Publishers, bookstores and software companies already on the Internet are being joined by organizations that offer electronic "store fronts" to promote the sale of many types of products on-line.

One recent example announced in August 1993, MarketBase Online Catalog of Goods and Services, provides free access for potential purchasers via gopher, telnet, ftp, and dial up modems. Vendors pay a monthly fee to list their product information. In its first month of operation, MarketBase listed around five hundred products and services in more than one hundred and fifty categories and received more than five thousand queries. CIX, the Commercial Internet Exchange, has also announced plans to offer a product listing service for business. Many more such announcements are likely to be made in the coming year.

Support

The third, and perhaps most important, aspect of keeping in touch with the customer is the quality of support and service after the sale has been made. A number of companies have enhanced their customer support programs by intensive use of the Internet. Support mechanisms, including on-line help desks, newsgroups, and bulletin boards, also provide valuable feedback about customer satisfaction.

THE ELECTRONIC MARKETPLACE REVISITED

The model for buying and selling on the Internet is still evolving. In fact, there is a persistent myth that anything resembling sales activity is strictly prohibited on the network. Many companies have contracted for commercial Internet connections and yet are hesitant to consider accepting orders or delivering products, in part because they fear this will be labeled "unacceptable use."

Commercial traffic—including sales and product distribution—is perfectly legal on the Internet, as long as these activities do not take place on the National Science Foundation backbone. Only a few years ago, most network traffic had to use government-subsidized connections, because the commercial alternatives were few and far between. At that time, network providers required their customers to agree to the Acceptable Use Policies of the National Science Foundation that were designed to support research and educational network use and specifically restricted commercial activities. Use policies restricting commercial traffic are still in place—but only for the shrinking percentage of the Internet that is subsidized by the National Science Foundation.

The past several years have witnessed significant growth in commercial networks that do not rely on the backbone subsidized by the federal government. All of the network providers mentioned in Chapter 2, and many others, offer the option of a commercial, unrestricted connection to the Internet. This makes it possible for companies to conduct any business transactions, including sales, over the commercial components of the network.

Bill Yundt, executive director of BARRNet, an Internet provider in the Bay area, and director of Networking and Communication Systems at Stanford University, believes that the lingering confusion about acceptable use stems from the diversity of the network combined with number of unresolved logistical and security questions regarding commercial transactions. He points out to new users that by definition the Internet is a network of networks, with different components operating under somewhat different policies for use. In his opinion, this diversity is no barrier to commerce on the Internet, but misunderstanding about acceptable use still needs to be addressed:

"I believe that any commercial organization that wants to use the Internet for any legal commercial purpose can find a supplier of services that will let them do so. They may elect not to use it for some purposes because of other concerns—fear of compromise of confidential information, security of their corporate network or integrity of data in transactions." According to Yundt, "these concerns are often not separated in discussion from the views about Internet use restrictions or limitations, adding further confusion to the picture."

The lack of a standardized, secure infrastructure to support financial transactions, taking orders and delivering products over the network, presents a more serious limitation on company use of the Internet for sales. Many of the basic issues remain unresolved, including security, authentication of orders, the need to protect confidential information like credit card numbers, and uncertainty about the number of customers interested in using the Internet, as distinct from explicitly commercial networks like America Online, for making purchases. Nevertheless, buying and selling on the Internet is accelerating in anticipation of solutions emerging in the near future. The exponential growth and global reach of Internet connections over the past few years have made the network an attractive and cost-effective option for providing information, service, and support to customers around the world even for companies not ready to embark on sales programs.

As the Internet attracts more business users, new approaches to commercial use are beginning to emerge. A number of corporations are gearing up to take advantage of the security and privacy features available from commercial network providers. The Internet Engineering Task Force has developed an Internet standard for Privacy Enhanced Mail. Even without a perfect solution to every issue, some companies have already demonstrated that the Internet can serve as an innovative delivery channel for their products. This chapter provides a closer look at the experiences of a few of the pioneers in using the Internet for ordering, sales, and product distribution.

Digital Equipment Corporation

When customers ask for a new way to order products, responsive companies listen. So when Digital's program of posting company and product information on the Internet generated a number of requests to use the network for placing orders, Digital developed a plan to sell its products directly on the Internet.

According to Mark Onderko, a Digital marketing consultant, as more and more customers discovered the value of accessing Digital's product information and other information services on the Internet, the number of suggestions for expanding the program mounted. Making it possible for customers to actually obtain quotes and place their orders through the network was the next logical step. The customers were ready. When Digital conducted a preliminary survey of potential sales over the Internet, 40 percent of existing customers requested that pricing information be made available, while 35 percent expressed an interest in using the Internet to order equipment.

Digital's response is an Internet platform designed to provide a fast and easy way for customers to do business via the network. This new program brings together all the features of Digital's on-line product information with the functionality of a virtual equipment store. For the casual customer, a gopher menu provides access to basic product information, news about Digital Equipment Corporation, software and hardware specifications, even demonstrations of some new software.

Customers at the early stages of deciding about an equipment purchase have the flexibility to access files of price information, product descriptions, and discussions of how particular products are performing at other sites. If they need help in determining the best equipment configuration for the application they have in mind, they will be able to use an on-line help system with built-in intelligence about standard configurations.

Customers interested in obtaining price and delivery information for a specific piece of equipment or preselected configuration can access a "quoting template" that automatically factors in information about the customer's organization, the volume of the order, and any special discounts to provide a specific price quote valid for 60 days. When they are ready to place an order, each customer obtains a special identification number giving them authorized access to Digital's electronic ordering service. Authorized customers can request a draft order based on a previous quote, and simply confirm it, or they can move directly into the order menu. When the order is placed, customers receive on-line acknowledgement and a projected delivery date. All stages of the order transaction can take place at the customer's terminal, with questions being answered on-line or in person, depending on the size and complexity of the order.

Onderko envisions the Electronic Store significantly increasing numbers of basic equipment orders coming to Digital on-line. Most will be handled completely on the network. Many customers already know exactly what equipment configuration they need, and using the Internet makes perfect sense to them. In fact, the network saves time for both the customer and Digital by streamlining the entire order process. Instead of being channeled through a sales representative, orders via the Internet can go direct to the manufacturing unit, which triggers an immediate "build process" response. Using the Internet, customers are able to track the status of their orders whenever they wish. The ultimate result will be faster, more predictable delivery—and increased customer satisfaction.

As more basic equipment orders move to the Electronic Store, Digital reaps another bonus. The huge amount of time that sales representatives used to spend processing small, low-volume orders can be refocused to the strategic advantage of the company. Sales and marketing will devote more attention to finding the best computing solutions for customers, participating in systems integration and planning for the largest installations. Instead of answering the same basic questions over and over, representatives will be able to spend more time listening to customers in face-to-face discussions.

Planning for the Internet trading connection presented some challenges; the new approach required significant rethinking of standard practices within the company. Because computer prices tend to be volatile and include a variety of discounts for educational customers, Digital had not included specific equipment prices in its earlier electronic information sources. But that meant customers weren't finding the information they needed to make a purchase decision. Now that pricing is automated and available through the Internet, everyone has a better understanding of the pricing structure—especially when changes occur.

Digital has implemented the program in phases to gauge the reaction of customers and make adjustments as needed. After implementation at a selected group of universities, the Electronic Store will expand to include Internet access for customers throughout the United States. Digital expects to add worldwide participation soon thereafter, and projects a steep growth curve for orders coming in through the Internet over the next three years.

The company will track all the information on who uses the electronic ordering feature and what kinds of systems are ordered, so that it can be enhanced to serve the needs of key users. Says Mark Onderko, "This project is not only good for Digital, it's going to be great for the customers."

When a large segment of your customer base is university and research institutions already connected to the Internet, investing in improving customer services over the network clearly makes sense. What about companies primarily interested in selling their products to other businesses, or to individuals? Is the Internet a good strategic choice for them? McAffee Associates and UnCover, Inc. both based their business plans on electronic product distribution long before other companies believed it was viable. Today each has an impressive record of growth to show for it.

McAffee Associates

Bill McKiernan, president and chief operating officer of McAffee Associates, a California-based software developer, is convinced that delivering certain products over electronic networks will be a normal part of business within the decade, because the advantages are so compelling. "It makes no sense to take a product like software, that starts out in electronic format, download it onto a disk, wrap it up in cardboard and plastic, weigh it down with two or three pounds of paper documentation, then ship it out to the customer," says McKiernan. "Think of all the overhead, waste, and delay in that process, compared to letting customers download software and documentation onto their own computers. Delivery is instantaneous; the software can be up and running as soon as it is needed."

The business plan that emerged from this logic is stunningly simple: First, develop software that a large number of businesses need. Then, post this software on electronic networks and bulletin boards and encourage individuals to download and test it on a free, trial basis. Consistently offer high-quality customer and technical support services to assist users in getting the software up and running as quickly and easily as possible. Finally, collect site license fees from corporations and institutions that decide to load the software on organizational computers.

Understanding the work habits and needs of potential customers was a key factor in the decision to focus the company's initial software products on protection against computer viruses. A variety of well-publicized problems with destructive viruses being spread through networks and electronic bulletin boards had raised concerns about how to protect corporate networks, personal computers, and valuable data files. While individual users were downloading software from electronic bulletin boards in increasing numbers, businesses had become especially sensitive about the potential danger of inadvertently importing a virus that could destroy vital company data. Every time a new virus—like the Michelangelo scare of 1992—was discussed in the press, the interest in anti-virus software grew as well.

Providing a solution through the same mechanism that had caused the original problem—electronic distribution of software—made perfect sense. McAffee Associates had a high-quality product that could detect and disarm viruses before they did any damage. The real question was whether it would be possible to generate a stable source of revenue from a model based on free and open distribution of the software through thousands of electronic bulletin board services, on-line systems, and of course, the Internet.

Setting up the company in 1989, McAffee Associates bet that the advantages of electronic distribution and high-level on-line support for software that met a critical need for business would generate a large and lucrative customer base. That gamble has paid off. Today, the company has well over sixteen thousand paid licenses from corporate customers, reflected by a growth in net revenue from $1.5 million in 1990 to $13.6 million in 1992 (SEC 1993, 20).

According to McKiernan, electronic distribution on the Internet and other networks is the essential ingredient in McAffee Associates' success. The company derives substantial cost savings from this model: there is minimal overhead for the product manufacturing, packaging, shipping and other activities required by traditional distribution mechanisms. Since the software is so widely available on electronic bulletin boards and networks, with individual users encouraged to download it and test it, a good deal of the marketing and advertising is generated by the product itself.

This cost savings is transformed into competitive advantage by investing heavily in the factors that promote customer satisfaction and license renewals—software enhancements, new product development, customer service, and technical support. Because the software is distributed electronically, enhancements and upgrades can be passed on to the customers at much more frequent intervals. New software releases are included in the two-year license fee, and the typical cycle is to issue a new release with enhanced features every six to eight weeks—a schedule that would be prohibitively expensive for both supplier and customer using traditional distribution methods. One important role of the Internet is to facilitate the distribution of upgrades and new releases of software to customers around the world.

Electronic customer support through the Internet and other networks is another value-added feature emphasized by McAffee. The company maintains its own electronic bulletin board and participates actively in a number of discussion groups. Customer support staff are available to answer all queries on-line. They follow discussions of various network interest groups, as do the development and technical staff at McAffee, posting answers and comments whenever appropriate. This pays dividends in reaching a large number of existing and potential customers who participate in the same groups. In McKiernan's experience:

> When someone posts a message on the Internet asking about a specific technical issue related to our software, we can respond to it at once; the answer will remain on the Internet and be available for other users to read. If anyone has follow up questions, they can also get them answered on-line. This is a big advantage over answering that same question five hundred times on the telephone; it represents another way

to realize significant savings in support costs while actually improving our support to customers.

This constant on-line interaction makes the whole company more responsive to customer opinion, and stimulates development of new products and enhancements. "The Internet provides us with a vital feedback loop to our customers and users; we are constantly made aware of the user's evaluation of our software and how it can be improved."

Based on feedback from customers, McAffee Associates expanded its product base to include a comprehensive line of antivirus programs, and has recently introduced software utilities programs for analyzing system memory, programs, and data. Corporations that have already licensed their virus protection software will be the primary market for these new products, also distributed exclusively on-line. The network has given McAffee increased visibility with other software developers; because of its high profile on the Internet, the company frequently receives messages from independent software developers offering products for distribution.

McAffee software has been licensed by a number of international corporations, with licenses outside the United States more than doubling during the past year. McKiernan attributes most of that international growth to the company's Internet connection. "The Internet provides global marketing and distribution for our product," he says. "We can reach customers in Europe or Asia as easily as companies in the United States. It provides us with an electronic channel to reach literally millions of users in minutes at incredible cost savings." The company can then pass on to customers this savings as well as all the advantages of electronic distribution. "That's what enables us to keep growing in a very competitive international market."

McKiernan is quick to point out that a big factor in the company's successful use of the Internet is understanding the network's culture and working with it. The company is selling a product, but it is also providing a solution to the problem of computer viruses, together with important information about avoiding software contamination. By making its software freely available on the network, and asking for payment only after it has been installed on an organizational computer system, McAffee has designed a delivery system that parallels the way in which the Internet itself has developed—with freely shared information gradually evolving into commercial products. The combination of free distribution to individuals and after-the-fact collection of license fees from institutional customers thus fits very well with the prevailing culture of the Internet.

With its entire business built on free downloading of its product, and a more or less unenforceable collection of license fees, McAffee Associates might look like a risky venture to many corporate planners. But its management is convinced that they represent a model many businesses will find attractive in the not-too-distant future. As more companies and individuals link up to the Internet, and want to make the most of the powerful connections available to them, it just seems logical that electronic delivery will become the norm, not the exception. By plunging in early, McAffee has gained invaluable experience upon which it can develop new products and markets. The key lesson, says McKiernan, is understanding the dynamics of the network and offering products designed to take advantage of its capabilities. Often, this means disregarding traditional assumptions about product distribution and customer behavior. "This is the business model of the future," McKiernan maintains. "If you provide a high quality product, with excellent support, companies will pay for it."

UnCover, Inc.

Other companies that have taken the plunge of offering products over the Internet tend to agree. Rebecca Lenzini, president of CARL Systems, Inc., in Denver, Colorado, recalls the initial skepticism expressed by other information providers in 1988 when her company launched UnCover, a database featuring table of contents information for thousands of journal titles:

> People thought we were crazy at the time, putting all this information into a database that existed only on the network with no printed equivalent or even compact disk format. From the beginning, UnCover was a product intended for customers with network connections. Some people simply couldn't believe that was a real market. They predicted UnCover would never become self-supporting.

No one stands by that prediction today. By spring 1993, UnCover was generating enough business to spin off as an independent enterprise. Its parent company, CARL Systems, Inc. started as a consortium of Colorado research libraries and incorporated in the early 1980s to market the software it had developed for automating library catalogs. Working with library clients, CARL management identified a need for current awareness and document delivery services specifically tailored to a networked environment. More and more databases were being mounted on the Internet, ranging from research library catalogs to unique information files on esoteric subjects. But it was difficult to find a fast and cost-effective source for locating just-published journal articles.

Analysis of the information flow within the CARL organization revealed an opportunity to create a new current awareness product, based on information that was already being processed by CARL's existing customers. The value-added component would come from the table of contents of the thousands of journal titles that CARL libraries received daily. By capturing that contents information and entering it into a database, CARL would have the foundation for a new network-based information service.

According to Lenzini, the Internet was an important factor in planning for UnCover very early in the process. Only the Internet could provide access to enough potential customers to make the expense of creating the database worthwhile. "By fall 1988 it became clear that Internet was going to be the primary vehicle for reaching a large number of organizations and individuals," she says, "so we began focusing on how to get UnCover up on the Internet and how to market access to it."

CARL decided not to distribute the table of contents database as a product. The database would reside on the CARL computer in Denver, and customers would be offered access to the data through an Internet gateway for an annual fee based on the number of people who would access it at any one time. With a business plan and network marketing strategy in place, Lenzini faced a step that had deterred many companies from actively distributing their products on the Internet—the government's Acceptable Use Policy. Lenzini knew that she had to ask permission to offer access to the UnCover database over the Internet as a business venture.

She soon discovered that it was extraordinarily difficult to get an answer to her request, not because the response was negative, but because she literally couldn't find anyone who was willing to take responsibility for saying either yes or no. It was a classic example of the nebulous governance structure of the network in that no one was quite ready to speak for the whole Internet:

> Everyone was very positive about the concept of UnCover, especially since our early planning emphasized sales to libraries and research organizations. But no one felt they were in a position to make a decision about whether selling access was appropriate for the Internet. When I finally got to talk with the folks at the National Science Foundation, they recommended that we go ahead, but treat the whole service as a kind of implementation-experiment. We were able to

get a general blessing to proceed on that basis, but never did get any official written authorization in response to our request.

At this point, CARL's small size became an advantage. It might be risky to proceed on an experimental basis with the new service, but it was also clear that without the distribution power of the Internet, UnCover would never get off the ground. While larger corporations might be understandably reluctant to move forward without a definitive authorization, CARL took the initiative to link UnCover to the Internet through the Colorado Supernet and declared itself open for business.

Customers were ready and waiting for this new type of service. UnCover access soon accounted for a significant percentage of Colorado Supernet transactions as more organizations signed up for a connection to the database and use skyrocketed. During the past five years, UnCover has experienced a growth rate parallel to that of the Internet itself. In 1990, the UnCover database was accessed about five hundred times each day; by spring of 1993 the rate of use had increased to more than nine thousand uses daily.

One major growth spurt took place in the spring of 1990, when UnCover added a document delivery service linked to the articles in the contents database. Direct payment for journal articles on-line would make it possible to expand UnCover's customer base from primarily educational institutions and corporations with deposit accounts to a broad base of independent researchers, professionals, consultants, and businesspeople. These were the people behind the growing numbers of individual Internet connections around the world, and CARL wanted a convenient way for them to become UnCover customers. The most straightforward method seemed to be to accept credit card transactions over the Internet, allowing individuals to locate, order, and pay for journal articles as part of a single transaction.

Credit card transactions represented another threshold in defining what constitutes acceptable use of the Internet. UnCover now had its own commercial link to the network, but it seemed likely that some customers would be ordering documents over federally subsidized segments of the Internet. Lenzini did more investigation to determine whether this kind of sales activity would be considered appropriate for the Internet. The results were much the same as in 1988; while there were no clear cut answers, eventually she was told to go ahead as long as this step was also regarded as an experiment.

CARL set up an internal system to handle the large volume of individual traffic and credit card orders it anticipated. UnCover established an onward link to a bank network in order to verify the credit card information while customers were still connected via the Internet, so that their orders could be expedited once the transaction was approved. This new layer of service would require a hefty increase in volume to justify the overhead expense.

At this stage, Lenzini still wondered just how many individuals would be willing to pay for personal document delivery, especially if it involved sending credit card information over the Internet. The UnCover staff took local steps to safeguard the security of confidential credit information, but it quickly became apparent that customers didn't hesitate to submit such data on-line; they thought of it as similar to phoning in an order to a mail order catalog.

Once again, the Internet connection became a major factor in expanding UnCover's customer base. For the millions of people already connected to the network, access to the UnCover data was very straightforward; no additional data connections or services were required for individuals to log on and begin ordering documents. Since beginning the new service, UnCover has delivered about fifty thousand documents, and with a 300 percent increase in the last eighteen months, the pace shows no sign of slowing down.

In fact, the document delivery business has now generated enough revenue for UnCover to make its original product, the table of contents data base, available for free. This decision is expected to attract new customers, so that the volume of use will continue to climb. In spring 1993 UnCover became a separate company, a joint partnership of CARL Systems and the Blackwell Group. This partnership will allow UnCover to enhance its journal title base and expand into the international market; a natural step for an Internet-oriented product. At a recent workshop on document delivery in Budapest, Blackwell demonstrated the ease of connecting to the UnCover host in Denver over the Internet to representatives of over forty countries.

The UnCover Company also uses the Internet to provide regular updates on new services and software enhancements, and well as to orient customers to the use of the system. Users can track the progress of current orders, check their account balance, and obtain a listing of past orders through their Internet connections. Like many companies that have an active presence on the network, UnCover maintains its own listserver to answer questions and to encourage customer suggestions for improving service or adding new products.

Rebecca Lenzini has no regrets about being a pioneer in selling products over the Internet. In addition to generating a new company in UnCover, CARL's success in networked distribution has attracted interest from other businesses looking for a presence on the Internet. One new partner is Journal Graphics, profiled by *Forbes* as the country's leading supplier of television news transcripts (Young 1993). This Denver-based company recently teamed up with CARL to offer on-line access to its Transcript/Video Index on the Internet and to accept credit card orders along the same lines as UnCover.

CARL Systems plans to keep on changing as the Internet changes. Lenzini predicts the next growth opportunities will come from synthesizing information in all formats and expanding the customer base by offering better navigational assistance. Like many other managers using the Internet regularly, Lenzini sees the need for better interfaces in the near future. "The graphical presentation to the user will improve radically over the next few years," she predicts, "and we intend to be part of that development."

Ron Creamer, president of PageWorks, a Boston-area design software firm, looks forward to the day when improved interfaces make using the Internet intuitive enough for staff to jump right in without any training or hesitation. Even though that day hasn't arrived, he feels the benefits have more than justified the cost of network connections for his company. Working from three locations around Boston to provide finished output for computer graphics and design programs, thirty PageWorks employees do a lot of customized software development, to match customer specifications. Creamer was initially attracted to the Internet because of the potential for communicating with programmers and downloading code from the network. Once connected, however, use of the Internet quickly focused on an expanding base of customers who saw the network as a better vehicle to submit their jobs directly to the company.

Creamer put together a series of tutorials for the staff on sending and receiving files using the company Macintoshes. Now, everyone in the company has access to the Internet and uses it daily, mainly to interact with customers. "Because of being on the Internet," he says, "we have received jobs from all over the country. We are so dependent on network access, that it's hard to define where the Internet stops and the company begins." Creamer is convinced that the Internet will eventually become the preferred method for moving information, software, and documents among all types of companies. "It has tremendous commercial applications, once people begin to feel comfortable with it. We are still discovering new benefits."

ELECTRONIC PUBLISHING

When a message posted to a popular Internet discussion group can reach a wider audience than many specialized printed journals, it may be time to redefine what "publishing" means in a networked environment. After years of reserving judgment on the viability of the network as a distribution channel and predicting consumer allegiance to print over computers, traditional publishers are joining a new rush to market on-line products. (Potharst 1993, Pullinger 1993). As Figure 6.2 illustrates, the number of electronic journals and newsletters available over the network has increased significantly over the past two years. A number of publishers have recently announced pilot projects to test the market. Journals ranging from the scientific and scholarly to the simply recreational are beginning to make an appearance on the Internet. An Electronic Newsstand already offers editorials, contents descriptions, and some full articles from magazines like *The New Yorker* and *The New Republic,* with the promise of many additions in the coming year.

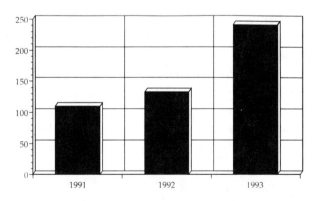

Electronic Journal Titles Published

Source: Directory of Electronic Journals,
           Newsletters, and Academic Discussion Lists
           Association of Research Libraries 1993

FIGURE 6.2   Growth of Electronic Publications.

Daily newspapers, cognizant of the proliferation of on-line current-awareness services, are also beginning to experiment with "electronic editions" (Glaberson 1993). The Internet has influenced the news-gathering process itself. Jayne Levin, editor of the *Internet Letter*, notes that "the Internet has boosted my powers to gather news." On-line via the Internet, she says, "I can communicate with anyone in the world at any time of the day and have information delivered to me via electronic mail—in split seconds. I also don't feel the prejudices I felt as a member of the paper press. In this electronic world, you're only as good as your e-mail."

As video and multimedia capabilities continue to spread through the network, and better-quality graphics become the norm, it is possible to move beyond the confines of print-on-computer-screen to multimedia formats. Subscribers to the Global Network Navigator, dubbed an "Internet-based Information Center," and published quarterly by O'Reilly and Associates, can browse though its contents with the navigational tools compatible with World Wide Web. The Navigator offers network news, an electronic marketplace, and on-line descriptions and connections to a variety of Internet resources. The Navigator is free to subscribers—O'Reilly charges companies wishing to advertise in its electronic "pages."

Publishers like O'Reilly and Associates already use the Internet at every step of book production—for manuscript preparation, editing, production, and distribution. As a result, books can be published on a much shortened time cycle—a crucial advantage for the time-sensitive information in most technical works. The next logical step is to bypass the print version altogether and publish exclusively on-line. For many subject areas, this seems to be a realistic prediction. The *Journal of Online Clinical Trials*, developed jointly by OCLC and the American Academy of Sciences, is now in publication. Offering excellent on-screen graphics, the new format makes use of the hypertext capabilities of the computer by linking documents with graphics and references for a more detailed presentation of a topic. The journal is published continuously, bringing new information to subscribers' desktops as soon as it becomes available.

Outside the academic community, a number of pilot projects are underway to deliver popular titles through the Internet (Strangelove 1993). It remains to be seen whether customers are prepared to substitute electronic access for the familiar aisles of their local bookstore or library, however. Before electronic publishing becomes a mass phenomenon, there are many issues still to be resolved. Authors and publishers are concerned about the ease of unauthorized reproduction over the network, not just of a few pages but of entire volumes in seconds. Scholars worry about verifying the easily altered electronic references when it becomes crucial to establish the original source of an article. Librarians wonder whether and how electronic documents will be preserved for future generations.

Rob Raisch, president of The Internet Company and chief operating officer of the Electronic Newsstand, asserts that despite these questions, the time has come to adopt a new paradigm for publishing that can accommodate the realities of an electronic universe. "Whether or not traditional publishers are ready", he says, "electronic books and journals will soon be a pervasive feature of the Internet."

AFTER THE SALE—ENHANCED CUSTOMER SUPPORT

While actual sales through the network are just beginning to take off, many companies have already discovered that the Internet is an invaluable tool for reaching customers after a sale has been made. Vendors of computer software and hardware components were the first to establish Internet connections as a basic requirement for service and customer support.

Using the Internet, even small companies can stay close to customers in all parts of the world, without establishing expensive networks of service representatives. Over the Internet, customers can ask questions, receive upgrades and fixes for their software programs, and demonstrate performance problems on-line to an engineer at a remote location, all without leaving their computer terminal. Most problems can be resolved quickly, at an enormous cost savings to the vendor. Wingra Technology, for example, with thirty employees headquartered in Minnesota, services a customer base of more than six hundred organizations in thirty-three countries. Almost all its interactions—with customers, development partners, and vendors—take place over the network.

While hundreds of companies now offer customer support via the Internet, not all of them have integrated this service into an overall strategy for gaining competitive advantage through outstanding customer connections. Some companies, however, are mentioned repeatedly by customers as examples of the excellent service and support available through the Internet. One such company is Silicon Graphics, the California manufacturer of high-resolution graphics workstations, where President Clinton first unveiled his National Technology Policy in February 1993. The company's products have also been highlighted for supporting the photorealistic images and special effects for movies like Jurassic Park and Nintendo video games (Fisher 1993).

Customers are more impressed with the consistent support and information available from Silicon Graphics than with the company's visible stints in the presidential and entertainment spotlight. Rick McLeod, the independent hardware vendor technical support manager for Silicon, gives the Internet due credit for making the company's support program a success. A large majority of the technical people at the company follow the

Internet discussions and newsgroups every day, in addition to responding directly to individual queries from customers. One employee who has developed a reputation for being especially active on the network reportedly follows and posts responses in more than twenty newsgroups on a regular basis—and still finds time to do the rest of his work.

McLeod prefers to field questions via the Internet from the third-party developers that are his responsibility, because the e-mail format allows him to gauge the level of the question, find the answer as quickly as possible, and get it back to the customer or ask for clarification without any distractions: "Typically, when someone is developing a product to be compatible with Silicon Graphics, they need very specific and exact information about it," he says. "My role is to try to support them by getting them that information. The questions run the gamut from something requiring an immediate two to three line answer to a six month conversation involving the exchange of extensive data files."

Customers who post questions and comments to the newsgroups with specific reference to Silicon Graphics products (com.sys.sig groups) get a lot of attention, since these groups are followed by most of the engineering staff at the company. In addition to sending back specific answers, the technical and support staff at Silicon will consider whether to make changes based on customer comments. This level of responsiveness is appreciated by customers and aspired to, but not always achieved, by competitors.

McLeod notes that the give and take of information on the Internet is generally quite positive, even when people are asking for problems to be resolved. Often, other users who have helpful advice will post answers even before Silicon staff have a chance to respond. The result is a community of users who are satisfied with the product and happy with the follow-up support they receive whenever they need it.

The Internet also facilitates communication with Silicon Graphics' application developers located around the world. The company has a special e-mail address dedicated to third-party developers in remote locations. When they have questions, messages, or files to send to someone at Silicon, they forward them to the dedicated e-mail address. This "mailbox" is regularly scanned like a switchboard, and the messages are forwarded to the appropriate people within the company for responses. All new developers are expected to obtain an Internet connection for their communications with the company.

Another company making intensive use of the Internet for customer support is Xylogics, a manufacturer of networking and communications equipment headquartered in Burlington, Massachusetts. According to its Annual Report, Xylogics is "dedicated to the highest standards of quality, reliability and customer service" as well as being "an exciting, challenging and rewarding place to work, a growing and profitable company to invest in, and an easy, flexible company to do business with" (Xylogics 1992, 1).

To accomplish this mission:

> Xylogics offers extensive technical and installation support, in order to enable the customer to more easily test and integrate the Company's products. Through this close co-operation, the Company believes that it is able to establish long-term relationships with its customers. The Company also works closely with leading edge end users in government, universities and commercial businesses to stay abreast of the new features and application needs of customers that buy products through the Company's resellers. The Company is also active in several standards organizations to remain on the leading edge of new developments in the technological areas that it serves with its products (Xylogics 1992, 7).

For the past five years, the Internet has played a vital role in Xylogics strategy. Doug Mildram is the network services administrator who ensures that the company's employees have the potential to connect directly with the Internet from their desktop. Mildram is responsible for network security and for managing Internet resources like USENET groups and electronic mail so that they are as available to the documentation writers and the marketing staff as they are to the software engineers. The Internet also provides a direct link to Xylogics International, Ltd., in England, which has established its own network connection through PIPEX, a British Internet provider.

According to Mildram, the most popular use of the network for all employees is e-mail, closely followed by participation in newsgroups and discussion lists. Because the company manufactures controller boards and network connection servers, a large percentage of its customers are already connected to the Internet. Xylogics maintains an ftp area on the network to communicate directly with beta sites during the installation and testing processes. The company can also distribute and upgrade software to beta sites directly over the Internet.

What distinguishes Xylogics is the way it has integrated the network into daily work across departments. A large number of employees are in regular direct contact with competitors, customers, partners, and other networkers in a variety of contexts. The Internet promotes a keener awareness of the external environment and the strategic opportunities available to the company. Unlike some companies, Xylogics staff are free to take part in as many groups as they choose, contributing actively to the on-line discussions, and often responding directly to customers.

Jim Carlson, a Xylogics software engineer, regularly uses telnet to log into customer sites and diagnose what is happening with network performance. The ability to connect to a customer from his desktop via the Internet means that as soon as a problem is reported he can begin working on a solution. "Through telnet," he says, "I can go directly to the customer host and check their set-up. Sometimes that allows me to spot the problem almost instantly, and explain how to solve it. It eliminates a lot of travel for me and delays for the customer. There's really no way to accomplish that without the Internet."

Carlson, like many of his colleagues at Xylogics, keeps up with a variety of newsgroups to see what is happening with customers, competitors, and technology developments. The collective information garnered from these discussion groups helps the company to strengthen customer relations and keep ahead of the competition. The engineers and development staff are especially interested in seeing how customers respond to existing products, and what other needs are waiting to be met.

Customer support teams can use the same information to determine whether a performance problem is coming from the Xylogics product or another part of the customer's system. According to a customer support specialist at Xylogics:

> Newsgroups can be very useful in a development context. Lots of users are asking for help with a specific problem, and that gives us ideas about how to improve our products. We can also find out what other vendors are offering, and whether customers are having problems with certain kinds of equipment connecting to a particular network configuration. If lots of users have complained about one vendor's equipment or software, that gives us a way to identify the problem more quickly.

In fact, if you want a brutally honest evaluation of whether a product works, the Internet is probably the place to find it. Reid Simpson of Xylogics has noticed that people will share much more candid information about products and vendor performance over the network. "You never find a printed evaluation that criticizes vendors the way some users do on the network," he notes. "Maybe people are less worried about liability or something, but if some product is a real dog, you will hear about it through the newsgroups. And you can tell which vendors are paying attention by the way they respond."

Xylogics makes paying attention to customer comments a priority, whether they are requests for more information or suggestions for improvement. When employees spot messages related to the company's products, they make every effort to ensure a positive response, whether or not the comment was addressed to them. Software developers also monitor the network to get ideas about the next generation of products that will be needed, and the evolution of standards. Xylogics maintains an updated database of Internet Request for Comments in house, and staff member Gary Malkin has contributed to developing a number of Internet RFCs. Developing Internet standards involves working closely with people at other companies, devoting time to the development of the Internet as a whole. That activity is also encouraged.

With such pervasive access to the Internet, it is sometimes hard to distinguish where work applications end and employee's recreational interests begin. Along with all the newsgroups on computers and software, employees may be spending their time following travel and hobby discussions, or keeping up contacts with old friends in other companies. Even though Internet use is not monitored by the company, Mildram's experience is that work-related use clearly predominates. Many employees have set up individual Internet connections at home so they can pursue personal network interests on their own time. Often, they will check in on some of the computer and software groups from home as well. Rather than decreasing productivity, the mix of technical and recreational components of the Internet seems to have encouraged more sophisticated business-related use. In the overall strategy, such use can also help to make nonengineering staff more comfortable negotiating the intricacies of the Internet.

One software documentation writer who started by following some of the more recreational newsgroups at home has found that she can get help with the software she uses for creating documentation from a software user group. Now, when she has difficulty with a particular feature of the software, she can get a fast answer on-line. She also finds it helpful to read discussions about the development of standards for the products she describes in her documentation. "The more I can find out on the Internet, the better," she says. "It makes it easier to write the documentation." And, from the customer's point of view, easier to read it.

CONCLUSION

Companies that have not thought about reaching customers through the Internet may have to think again—and soon. Many of the problems of commercial activity on the network are being addressed. Whether it be marketing, sales and distribution, or customer support, the network can offer almost every business an opportunity for improving customer connections. For certain applications, including information, software, and electronic publishing, the Internet can provide an important distribution channel. Even more businesses will find it a place to connect with customers after the sale is made—to offer the support that encourages them to keep coming back.

REFERENCES

Carothers, Harlan G. Jr., and Mel Adams. 1991. Competitive Advantage Through Customer Value: The Role of Value-Based Strategies. In *Competing Globally Through Customer Value: The Management of Strategic Suprasystems*. Edited by Michael J. Stahl and Gregory M. Bounds. New York: Quorum Books.

Collet, Robert D. 1993. The role of public data Internet service providers in corporate information networking. *Telecommunications* 27(1):50–55.

Deming, William Edwards. 1993. *The New Economics for Industry, Government, Education.* Cambridge: MIT Center for Advanced Engineering Study.

Fisher, Lawrence M. 1993. Video game link is seen for Nintendo. *New York Times.* August 21, 1993, 37.

Garfield, Charles A. 1992. *Second to None: How Our Smartest Companies Put People First.* Homewood, Ill.: Business One Irwin.

Glaberson, William. 1993. Creating electronic editions: Newspapers try new roles. *New York Times.* August 16, 1993. p. 49.

Potharst, Jan. 1993. A publisher's view. *Proceedings of the First Annual Conference on Information Networking.* London: Meckler.

Pullinger, David. 1993. At last!—Usable networks for publishing. *Proceedings of the First Annual Conference on Information Networking.* London: Meckler.

Schnaars, Steven P. 1991. *Marketing Strategy: A Customer-driven Approach.* New York: Free Press.

Sherman, Stratford. 1993. The New Computer Revolution. *Fortune* 127(12):56–80.

Stahl, Michael J. and Gregory M. Bounds, eds. 1991. *Competing Globally Through Customer Value: The Management of Strategic Suprasystems.* New York: Quorum Books.

Strangelove, Michael. 1993. An overview of the rise of network-based publishing. Unpublished manuscript.

Treacy, Michael and Fred Wiersema. 1993. Customer Intimacy and Other Value Disciplines. *Harvard Business Review* 71(1):84–93.

Xylogics. 1992. *10K Report.* Securities and Exchange Commission. 1992. Annual Report. Burlington, Massachusetts.

Young, Jeffery S. 1993. Alfred Knopf, eat your heart out. *Forbes* 151(11):186–187.

7

The Entrepreneurial Edge

> *So far, nobody has figured out how to make big money on the Internet, but that day is coming soon.*
> —Thomas G. Donlan, *Barron's*

Put together the following ingredients:

- creation of an electronic "superconnector" with repeated technological breakthroughs in how fast and how much and what kind of traffic can travel electronically from virtually any point on the globe to any other point,

- a 100 percent a year growth rate for the amount of traffic and the number of connections to this electronic superconnector called the Internet, and

- various low-cost entry points for individuals and small businesses to offer superconnector-based goods and services.

What do you get? An ideal breeding ground for an outburst of innovation and entrepreneurial activity. Joseph Schumpeter, early twentieth-century economist and scholar, noted for his analysis of the recurrent "long wave" cycles of economic boom and bust, theorized that major inventions lead to periods, or "outbursts," of intense technical innovation. These periods are followed by the "creative destruction" of old industries as innovation diffuses through the marketplace, transforming products and consumer expectations (Schumpeter 1942). If global connectivity is the technological breakthrough of our decade, then the outburst of innovation is just beginning.

Groping for historical points of reference, we compare the advent of "supercommunication" in the information age to the invention of the printing press, or the first industrial revolution, or the impact of airplanes and interstate highways on life in the twentieth century. These comparisons convey some sense of transformational impact of earlier technologies, but they fail to capture two distinctive aspects of our new revolutionary period. The first is the speed of change. Hundreds of years passed between Gutenberg and the advent of electronic text. The industrial revolution was a half century in the making. Decades elapsed before the highway and the airplane overtook the railroad as the preferred means of moving goods and people. But high-speed electronic networks have already compressed the cycle from invention to innovation and seem poised on the brink of diffusion (Drucker 1993).

The second difference is the unprecedented availability of not just the products, but the means of production and distribution in the electronic age. While the total investment in global network infrastructure is substantial, the structure is such that any individual can replicate the capacity of the whole by purchasing only a small segment. In practical terms, this means that once connected to the Internet, small businesses can produce, market, and distribute their products globally with minimal incremental costs.

If Schumpeter and other economists are right, this mix will spark the "creative destruction" of traditional business, and generate the enterprises of the future. The first wave of innovation is beginning to take shape, as new companies are established to provide the access, the tools, and the services that facilitate participation in the information age. Will these early entrepreneurs be the ones who strike it rich on the Internet? Certainly not all of them. Transitional periods pose great risks as well as great opportunities. The faster the rate of change, the more danger of misjudging the trend and spinning off into a dead end while technology rushes off in a new direction. But the innovations that succeed will help shape the twenty-first century. The small sample of Internet entrepreneurs profiled here are convinced that their vision of a new era will prevail.

It is not just the money that attracts entrepreneurial spirits to the Internet, although the phenomenon of exponential growth certainly factors somewhere in their planning. The network has the lure of the last frontier, the pull of infinite possibility. Becoming an Internet entrepreneur requires risk-taking, frequent course adjustments, and a vision strong enough to stand up to the skeptics. A sense of humor is highly recommended. Internet's pace of change is exhilarating, but it can be a maddening place to make a living.

BREWSTER KAHLE AND WAIS, INC.

Brewster Kahle, founder and President of WAIS, Inc. doesn't mind the madness when the stakes are important enough. In fact, after years of relative stability working at Thinking Machines, the supercomputer company in Cambridge, Massachusetts, he welcomes the bumps and turns of a start-up venture: "We are lucky to be early enough to look adventurous—I love being back at the stage when people are calling us crazy." His vision places WAIS at the center of a whole new network-publishing industry, serving as "the printing press company for an electronic age."

Kahle's decision to establish WAIS, Inc. to market a commercial version of the Wide Area Information Server grew out of a Dow Jones DowQuest information project in the late 1980s.

DowQuest used a powerful Thinking Machines parallel-processing supercomputer to provide a comprehensive search and retrieval system for business information. Brewster Kahle recognized in this system the potential for a distributed server application that would allow users to access any electronically stored information with one search strategy.

KPMG Peat Marwick, interested in a new approach to information management and document retrieval for its two hundred offices around the world, joined a development effort with Thinking Machines, Dow Jones, and Apple to test the concept of a Wide Area Information Server (WAIS). Brewster Kahle organized a working team to design a pilot system that would allow a Macintosh client application to access information from both the supercomputer and Unix servers. The goal was to create an easy to use, single point of entry to any electronic information source the user wanted to access. Since the target group for the pilot project included managers and accountants not familiar with search software or computer terminology, the interface had to be as straightforward as possible.

The WAIS software was designed so that a user could select databases around the world, then enter a question in natural language, like "find information about the common market and interest rates in Germany." WAIS would transmit the query across networks to selected sources and return with headlines from documents matching the relevant terms, displayed on the searcher's work station. The results of a search would be displayed in order of relevancy, offering the opportunity to scan and request more documents based on the closest matches. Information was accessible regardless of format: graphics, video, audio, and spreadsheets were as retrievable as text documents.

The working prototype demonstrated the feasibility of networked information retrieval, even though its bandwidth requirements ultimately proved too costly for the internal Peat Marwick network. Convinced that WAIS was ideally suited to the Internet environment, Thinking Machines released the first incarnation of WAIS—both Unix server code and Macintosh client software—into the public domain in spring 1991. Almost overnight, quake.think.com became one of the hottest telnet addresses on the Internet, as other network sites set about downloading and adapting the prototype to their own local settings. Just six months after the first public release, there were more than a hundred WAIS servers on the Internet.

WAIS has entered the repertoire of virtually every Internet user who has browsed the network for files, documents, or other resources. After eighteen months in the public domain, the number of WAIS server locations had grown to include university campuses, government agencies, information publishers, and organizations large and small. Use of WAIS was doubling every six months, as information-hungry clients and information-rich servers teamed up around the world.

Even with a public domain WAIS freely distributed throughout the world, Brewster Kahle saw a business opportunity in developing a WAIS product for commercial distribution. Why would people pay for a commercial version of software that was already available for free? Corporate and government customers, he reasoned, would be willing to invest in the superior quality and dependable support a company dedicated to developing WAIS could offer. Many of the users familiar with WAIS wanted a more capable version, but didn't have the resources to upgrade and maintain the software themselves. The widespread use of WAIS in the public sector could actually be an asset in marketing a commercial version, since the prototype had proved viable on a global scale.

In summer 1992, Brewster Kahle established WAIS, Inc. as an independent corporation. His founding statement concludes:

> Now WAIS, Inc. is positioned to take the lessons learned from the long history of WAIS and to apply them to the needs of business, education, and government organiza-

tions. Today, most documents are created on computers and networks increasingly tie computing devices together. Wherever there is someone with something to say, there is an appropriate place for WAIS.

One of the first projects for WAIS, Inc. was to provide an information system for the Ross Perot Presidential Campaign organization. Perot supporters used the system to keep campaign offices in all fifty states up to date on internal materials and current publications. They entered news clippings and all press releases into a WAIS-searchable database to ensure that field and headquarters shared the same information. As it turned out, the campaign results didn't hinge on information access, and Perot's withdrawal from the race put an end to this application. However, Perot Systems was sufficiently impressed with WAIS to become a customer in its own right. Other early customers included the Environmental Protection Agency, the Library of Congress, the Department of Energy, Rice University and T.R.A.D.E. Inc.

In general, Kahle expects the market for the new WAIS and other Internet tools to include:

- The U.S. government, the largest publisher in the country and now faced with a mandate to share federal information electronically. WAIS offers a cost-effective, easy to implement solution for many federal agencies. The Environmental Protection Agency has already contracted with WAIS to set up e-mail browsing and a digital library.

- Libraries, which have always collected and distributed information, and have a track record of implementing new technology. With WAIS, libraries can make in-house publications, full text, images, and other media immediately available to their campus and the community.

- Distributed corporations. As companies grow more global

and less hierarchical, they need efficient ways to share information laterally. WAIS combines of internal and external information access to provide maximum flexibility. Sun Microsystems, for example, uses WAIS to disseminate information to users. Their servers are handling more than seven thousand searches each day.

- Traditional publishers, which have the content expertise and the customer base, and must find a way to adjust to the changes in information access. Publishers are looking at wide area networks as a new distribution medium, and WAIS can provide an entry point.

- Information owners who see the opportunities for republishing their data to new audiences on-line; for example, T.R.A.D.E., INC. has all of the import manifests for all shipments arriving in the U.S. before they get into port; using WAIS to package this information in different ways for different markets, they have created a whole new generation of information products.

Kahle is counting on the biggest long-term growth from the commercial sector, and WAIS expects to work successfully with the business market. Businesses are accustomed to paying for products and software support, so he feels the transition from a free product to a for-sale item should not be a barrier to attracting corporate customers.

Customers who purchase WAIS servers may find that is just the beginning of the relationship with WAIS, Inc. Recognizing that many organizations and potential users may not have the technical staff to implement WAIS, Kahle's company offers a range of consulting services to help users get the system up and running. Consultants can also work with customers to capitalize on the new-found information retrieval capabilities WAIS provides within their organization. Kahle believes that it will become so cheap and easy to make large collections of information available either internally or externally, that many organizations will want help in establishing priorities that fit their overall strategies.

WAIS often teams up with a Gopher that allows users to browse through different segments of the Internet to locate resources, then zero in on a particular document or topic. People use Gopher to get to WAIS-enabled databases because a hierarchial information structure works only for small amounts of information. In this configuration, Gopher works as the table of contents, while WAIS provides the detailed index, capable of searching through many documents to retrieve those that provide the best match. Kahle sees this combination, together with e-mail, as the "magic triple" that makes Internet resources available to all types of users.

WAIS can function for the whole Internet as well as for internal organizational databases. As the browsing structures change and improve, WAIS, Inc. will keep updating its product to make it fully compatible with the most advanced tools available. Kahle, who serves on the Internet Engineering Task Force, is concerned with the viability of the Internet from the point of view of network planning as well as of a vendor. He wants to ensure that the resources of the Internet become more accessible to individuals and small businesses. "There is still a tremendous pent-up demand for higher level resources and better information-finding tools on the Internet," he says. "People are looking for mechanisms to upgrade both the information content and the tools used to access it. Unless both needs are met in a way that makes sense to the nontechnical business user, the Internet will become just another novelty and information will flow through other channels."

Kahle's vision of the future includes more and more people turning to their computers to answer questions; where they currently use paper and the phone he believes that soon workers will use their networked machines to find answers. This transformation of information-seeking behavior will make a dramatic difference in the nature of work and leisure. Kahle feels the success of WAIS, Inc. should be measured by the quality and availability of WAIS servers around the world, as well as by the number of customers his company attracts:

> WAIS, Inc. numbers so far have been doubling every seven months. If we can keep up with rate of Internet growth we will be successful—and thousands of customers will be able to access and to publish valuable information over the network. This change is definitely coming, and WAIS is one of the reasons. In 1990 when I said I was going to start a new industry of network publishers, very few people could understand how that would be a viable model for the future. Now everyone sees that by end of the decade, networked publishing will be the standard way of doing business.

One of the early converts was Perot Systems, which purchased a WAIS system to facilitate access to its own information and databases. WAIS provided the flexibility to allow the searching of files from any company location in combination with restricting access to confidential information. Perot Systems is the kind of corporate customer Brewster Kahle was hoping for when he founded WAIS, Inc. Defining itself as a "global information technology and business transformation firm," Perot Systems was founded in 1988 and now has operations in France, England, Germany, and Ireland as well as the United States. Its seventeen hundred employees are distributed around the world and are highly dependent on the latest information to be successful in their assignments. However, the company does not have a large internal systems support staff to design and update an extensive in-house information management system.

With staff expertise in different countries and a number of consulting projects underway at any given time, the challenge of matching existing resources with new projects is considerable. Perot Systems recognized that it needed a better method to share sources and project profiles, reports, resumes, and other information of interest to people throughout the company. After seeing WAIS in action during the presidential campaign, managers decided to implement a pilot WAIS server to test its potential.

The WAIS server rapidly became a focal point for internal company resources. It was easy to scan in documents, project reports, consultant profiles, even databases. The search interface provided an intuitive way for employees everywhere in the company to search and receive information on demand. The systems staff found that it was even possible to download some of the CD-ROM databases into the WAIS server so that everyone could get access to marketing, product, and other types of information. With WAIS, it is also possible to keep track of who is searching what; the system can monitor simultaneous use of certain data where licensing is based on a formula according to number of users.

According to the information support staff at Perot Systems, WAIS offers a significant benefit to the company, facilitating publication of internal research results and reports. A company like Perot has to provide easily accessible information about previous consulting studies, or consultant teams start new projects from scratch, instead of building on what has already been accomplished. The WAIS server also helps project managers at remote locations keep up with new information and new expertise coming into the company. This is crucial when managers need to bring in additional project team members or are working with tight deadlines. Previously, a manager trying to locate someone with a particular skill for a new project team would be unable to search the file of consultants and credentials outside of normal business hours at headquarters. If he worked in a different time zone from the Texas office, that could lead to the lost project time.

WAIS has provided a new level of access to the resume bank that Perot Systems keeps for all the consultants on its staff. This information has strategic value for the company in competing for customers and completing projects as efficiently as possible. When each project requires a different combination of expertise, it is critical to identify the people within the company who have the best combination of skills and experience, no matter where they are working at the moment. There are other commercial tools to keep track of employee skills and areas of expertise, but they are expensive and complicated to use. Even though Perot maintained an inventory skills system, it was not providing enough information throughout the company. WAIS made it possible to create an on-line resume system, offered a front end that was simple enough for everyone to use, and added the advantage of displaying the resumes retrieved in order of how closely they match the particular search terms.

One of the most attractive features of WAIS for Perot Systems staff has been the intuitive interface that allows people to feel comfortable with searching it almost at once. Instead of requiring a lot of additional training and implementation time, WAIS has allowed the systems staff to be more efficient in making resources available. The single interface allows users to search as many diverse resources as they wish, without having to learn new commands for each database. That stimulates the company to put even more resources on-line for internal access. The WAIS server has also led to more exploration of Internet resources, because the same interface can be used to pull in resources from the global network. Often searchers can locate items that they didn't know existed and combine the external information with the resources on the Perot system.

For Perot Systems, WAIS proved to be an easily implemented, simple to use tool that transcends the boundaries between internal and external information. Once in place, its value multiplied as more and more relevant information was opened up to employees. If Brewster Kahle's vision of the future prevails, many other companies will soon have the same experience.

CARL MALAMUD AND INTERNET
TALK RADIO

Internet Talk Radio is a vision born of technical expertise and frustration with conventional print coverage of information issues. Carl Malamud, Talk Radio founder, has been in the computer, network, and information business for the past decade. In his work as a computer consultant, network designer, writer, and all around Internet expert, he looked in vain for a concise, regular source of current news dedicated to the information needs of the Internet and networking community. "I always felt there was a need for a magazine on the specifics of the network tools and analysis of new developments," he says, "but starting a magazine is very expensive. Printing and mailing costs are high, it is hard to grow gracefully, and a print product just isn't a good match for network technology."

The obvious solution, and the first one Malamud considered, was to create an on-line newsletter and distribute it through the network. It seemed like a good idea until he started to contemplate the volume of information that landed in his electronic mailbox already. Suddenly, adding yet another piece of written information—even a useful, relevant piece—didn't make that much sense. He realized that "lots of us who use the Internet intensively may get 200 to 300 messages every day. We already have too much input to deal with. I don't read even important newsletters that come now, so there didn't seem to be any point to creating another one."

The expanding multimedia capacity of the network suggested another model for disseminating information. An audio broadcast on the Internet was technically feasible; it could deliver right to the desktop the kind of in-depth coverage and feature stories associated with National Public Radio—without adding to the mail overload. Malamud theorized the audio could play in the background while listeners attended to their work (after all, one may not need to devote total attention to those hundreds of e-mail messages), or could be stored and replayed at will. Having thought it through, an Internet radio station seemed like such a good idea that by November 1992 Malamud decided he had to make it happen.

In addition to its affinity with National Public Radio and the appeal of listening to information rather than having to read it, the radio model had some practical advantages for Malamud. A radio program is a lot easier and cheaper to produce than its video equivalent, especially at the commercial level. Professional audio equipment and the adjunct network hardware can be purchased for a reasonable amount of money. Malamud estimated that he could get a radio program up and running on the Internet for an initial investment of under $100,000.

The next question was how to turn the concept into a business. Initially, Malamud considered finding venture capitalists who would provide the start-up funds to establish a for-profit corporation. After thinking about the potential for marketing the project, he decided that following the nonprofit route would provide a better opportunity to get more people involved from the beginning. It would allow him to get a critical mass of listeners for Internet Talk Radio and to follow his own sense of priorities. This strategy also offered the maximum opportunity to "do more fun stuff on the program."

With a nonprofit start-up venture in mind, Malamud put together a plan of action. The main feature of the weekly program was to be an interview with a well-known network expert, accompanied by coverage of current news, reviews and comments by listeners. The audience could listen as the program was broadcast, or store the digital audio data file for later access. The technical operations were kept simple so that users would not require special software to convert the file into audio. The idea was that anyone with sound support should be able to handle it.

To raise initial capital, Malamud went to O'Reilly and Associates and Sun Microsystems and obtained their support as sponsors of Internet Talk Radio. By January 1993 he had all the pieces in place to go on the air. The very first broadcast reached an audience in thirty countries. Malamud's best-known program to date is "Geek of the Week," featuring in-depth interviews with the Internet's technical experts. He also offers syndicated programs from national public radio. Although it is hard to tell who is actually listening, Malamud has had feedback from a number of sites that are distributing the show internally. He knows that some companies have spooled it into voice mail systems or file servers for employees to listen at their convenience. He has heard from one listener who puts the show on his Powerbook, then listens in the car on the way home.

Malamud estimates that by June 1993 the regular audience was already near one hundred thousand listeners around the world. In addition to Sun Microsystems, he is aware of a number of companies that organize internal distribution of the show. Some national networks, such as Australia, bring it in for whole country, and there are sites tuned in from Europe to Japan. Internet users who don't receive Talk Radio are looking for ways to get into the loop.

Internet Talk Radio is a business in its own right, as well as a demonstration of the network's potential for combining the features of traditional broadcast tools with the advantages of networked access. Commenting on the introduction of Talk Radio, Paul Saffo, a computer industry analyst, noted, "This is pregnant with possibilities. It's proof that the era of mass media is past" (Markoff 1993, 1).

In addition to creating a successful network radio program, Carl Malamud also has a mission; he wants to push the technology of the Internet to its fullest capabilities. He expects this initial effort to grow into a more comprehensive "multicasting" environment that incorporates live, interactive programs, video, and links between television, radio, and computers. Malamud's "Internet Multicasting Service" already includes an Internet

Town Hall channel devoted to public affairs, and broadcasts from the National Press Club in Washington, D.C.

Seeing this vision become reality is rewarding for its own sake, according to Malamud. "One big benefit is that I get to run my own network, with great equipment and the challenge of planning new programs. It's a lot of fun." But Malamud, the entrepreneur, also expects Internet Talk Radio to prove itself as a business venture. "I took every single asset I own and put it into this business," he says. "We are just getting started, and a lot of exciting new additions will be coming soon. You can believe that I am planning on this being around for a long time."

TERRY BRAINERD CHADWICK
AND INFOQUEST

Terry Brainerd Chadwick has a different outlook on the entrepreneurial value of the Internet. Her company, InfoQuest Information Services, works with businesses and other organizations that need more information or want training in how to find it for themselves. For the past seven years Chadwick has run the company on a part-time basis, but in 1993 she decided it was time to become a full-time entrepreneur. Client calls had skyrocketed because her company was mentioned in an *INC* magazine article describing specialties and services. The Internet was also a major factor in her decision—more and more companies were looking for help in using the resources on the Internet.

InfoQuest business is divided into three major segments. The first is training clients to use networked information resources more effectively. Chadwick offers a two-day program on "Communicating with the World through Networks." One whole day is devoted to using the Internet, with the second divided among the other information providers and services. She will also make site visits to companies to do customized training in using the

Internet for information retrieval. The second component of InfoQuest is information audits for business, which include a full range of analysis of information needs and how to meet them most efficiently. Chadwick's special focus is with working companies engaged in international trade. Finally, InfoQuest contracts for specific information retrieval projects.

The Internet is an essential factor in every part of Chadwick's work. She uses it to start her own information searches, because it is the best means to establish the scope of on-line information available on any topic. There are clear advantages for most of her clients in connecting to the Internet. At minimum, she recommends that companies use the Internet to identify and correspond with other businesses interested in international trade, and to identify new commercial opportunities:

> The most exciting benefit of the Internet is not the information resources per se, but the opportunities in the discussion groups to make contacts and get questions answered. I had a client who had heard that food in Hungary didn't make it through the winter; he asked me if there was a market for food dehydrators. I posted messages on Eastern European listservs and got answers within days directly from Hungary. Through the contacts established on the network, the client got a response within three weeks from people who wanted to buy his product.

Small businesses seeking international trade connections can also use the Internet to get standard of living statistics and other demographic information from Gopher servers in different countries; often this local information is more useful than standard printed resources, and it can be accessed directly from the desktop at no added cost.

Chadwick herself uses the Internet more and more for the lesser known resources that are becoming available there. She has found that economic information, agricultural resources, financial statistics, and other sources are often overlooked, but can be of great value for small companies interested in identifying new markets or evaluating the potential of overseas partners.

According to Chadwick, what makes the Internet valuable to business can be summed up in one word—communications. "You can reach people in any country and keep track of what's going on there," she says. "It's possible to look at the state of technology transfer in many counties and determine the potential for introducing new products. There are mechanisms to contact partners or customers. If a company needs to find out what is happening in the rest of the world, the Internet can deliver that information to your electronic mailbox."

One of the great advantages of the network for commercial and trade transactions is that it provides a direct connection from businessperson to businessperson instead of third-person or indirect communication. The dialogue can be very straightforward: I have a product; is there anyone in your country who might be interested in buying it? This communication between two people with similar goals is not commercial in the same way as broadcast advertising.

Chadwick welcomes the advanced retrieval tools like WAIS, and sees the growth of in-house sophistication about the Internet as a complement, not a threat, to her business services:

> No matter how easy information retrieval gets, there will always be an advantage to getting tips and training and professional assistance from someone who makes it a full-time job to be current with the latest resources and techniques. My mission is to help people to make the best possible use of information, especially small businesses that don't have the tools or background to make the most of what is readily available on the Internet.

Chadwick admits to being "something of an evangelist about the Internet," and that explains the vision behind Infoquest:

to make networked information work for people in business. Small companies are often the best clients, and she enjoys working with them because they quickly see the difference that her services can make in increasing their competitiveness. Chadwick expects to keep doing her business on the Internet for some time to come.

PHILIP WINTERING AND AMERICAN CYBERCASTING

For Philip Wintering, CEO of American Cybercasting, the Internet has the potential to create a powerful bridge between classroom learning and real life—a bridge he feels is a worthwhile business investment. His own experience as an undergraduate political science major convinced him that there had to be a better way to bring primary materials directly to students. "One of the best courses I had in college was also one of the most frustrating," he remembers. "My political science professor wanted to demonstrate how political theory related to the actual electoral process, so during the presidential campaign he structured the class around daily reading assignments in conservative and liberal newspapers. It was a great basis for discussion, but a logistical disaster. All 150 students were fighting over the same newspapers in the library every day."

With the spread of campus networks, Wintering saw the potential for solving the logistical bottleneck and structuring more teaching around current publications, if the right materials could be made available directly to faculty and students. About the same time, Dr. Thomas Grundner, who had already worked on developing the Cleveland Free-net, had arranged rights for on-line access to *USA Today* through the Internet for the Free-net community and realized that there was a market for the same kind of network delivery in education. This was the beginning of American Cybercasting in January 1991.

The combination of ready-made business opportunity and educational mission was irresistible for Wintering. "I had been looking for a company to buy at the start-up level," he says. "American Cybercasting seemed like a perfect way to test a new model for delivering current publications and other full text to schools and colleges. With the rights to just one publication and a few target schools, it was a modest investment financially and it really matched up with my ideas about electronic information."

By the summer of 1992 Wintering was convinced that American Cybercasting was not just an attractive vision, but also a viable business. It was time to put serious money into the program to attract new publications and sign on customers. During his first year as CEO, he discovered that being a pioneer has challenges of its own:

> No matter how much capital you think you need to start a business, get twice as much. It goes fast in the early stages. Remember there will come a point when no matter how much money you have, you will have to adjust and adapt your plan to the unexpected. If you don't adapt, it will drain all your funding, but if you make the right changes, that's the time you will make real progress.

American Cybercasting has been able to change and grow with the Internet. Now the company has rights to distribute more than twenty-five publications, with new agreements being signed every month. By the fall of 1993 the company had more than a hundred customers, and Wintering feels that many more are waiting in the wings. One of the lessons he learned from marketing an innovative information concept is that customer acceptance of advanced products is not linear. He realized that "Our first customers were the pioneers—that small percentage of any group ready to try something brand new. Then there was a period of resistance because most campuses were not ready to jump into a new concept, even if they could see the practical advantages." At that point, it became a struggle to get the next cluster of customers on-line. "Now that we have a critical mass and the Internet is more accepted as a delivery mechanism," however, "suddenly people are calling us and asking for information. They have heard about the Internet and are ready to subscribe."

Wintering is gratified to observe that on-line access to major daily newspapers and journals like *Forbes, Investor's Business Daily*, and *Foreign Policy* really does have an impact on the assignments and the curriculum at colleges using American Cybercasting. Some faculty use the service to have students track stocks and bonds or get corporate and business information, while others work the daily news into class discussions and course work.

The Internet is essential to the American Cybercasting business plan, since it allows schools to receive the distributed information easily, with a low incremental cost. Without the Internet, there would not be a viable product or delivery mechanism. Using the network, Wintering hopes to make his vision a reality:

> We can help make education more dynamic. When I was in school, so many people found history and political science boring because it didn't seem to relate to real life. By using network information delivery, professors can bring the real world into the classroom. That makes a huge difference in getting students to see the relationship between what happened in the past and current events.

BRAD TEMPLETON AND CLARINET

Electronic newspapers don't rival the readership of the major dailies yet, but Brad Templeton, president and publisher of the ClariNet Electronic Publishing Network, is convinced that it's only a matter of time. "It's all a question of timing," he believes. "In the long run, electronic access will be the standard way of getting the news. Delivery is fast, efficient, doesn't eat any trees. ClariNet delivers tomorrow's newspaper stories today, in a form that can be adapted by individual readers. It combines the best of radio and print."

Rather than transmit existing publications electronically, ClariNet has licensed the building blocks of newspapers—wire services like UPI along with news and feature syndicates—and organized the stories into topics in the USENET style of hierarchical newsgroups. Individuals already participating in USENET can use the standard newsreading tools to select topics for regular posting and to filter out irrelevant subjects. According to Templeton, the most popular area for all subscribers is international coverage—apparently most people feel that their daily newspapers don't provide enough. During the Gulf War, ClariNet made the Gulf news available for free. It became one of the busiest sources on the network during that period.

Since ClariNet started operation in 1989, approximately thirty thousand people have signed on through companies ranging from Apple to Xerox and in a number of universities. Templeton is convinced that this is just the tip of the electronic information and publishing iceberg. He founded ClariNet after a long-time involvement with USENET, having decided that the same format would work for transmitting published information. His inspiration, he says, came from trying to find a way to get Dave Barry's columns distributed on the Internet. At that point, network distribution was such a novel suggestion that Barry's syndicate didn't really understand what Templeton was talking about. The wire services were, however, willing to sell rights and ClariNet was born.

Templeton had been in business since 1983, running a software development firm called Looking Glass Software. He didn't start ClariNet with any expectation of an immediate windfall—in fact, if money had been the object, he reflects the best course would have been to accept that job offer from Microsoft and buy lots of stock. Instead, he was motivated by the chance to craft a unique service on the Internet. "I have always wanted to do something that no one has ever done before," he says. "Obviously, I could have made a lot more money if I had taken the Microsoft job I was offered in 1982, but it seemed more important to take a chance on charting a new course. The potential of the Internet was irresistible."

Templeton is still convinced that when it comes to delivering certain services, the Internet is the only way to go. His next venture will be an experiment in electronic book publishing. Clarinet has the electronic rights to publish all the nominees for the prestigious Hugo Book Award; one year's nominations add up to more than 1.4 million words of science fiction. Through the ClariNet service, anyone with an Internet connection can pay for on-line access with a credit card, then use a special password to get access to an ftp server, where the text will be stored. Science fiction seems an especially appropriate medium for electronic distribution, and Templeton is waiting to see the response before deciding whether to expand into more variety of text on-line. Once again, it will all come down to timing:

> If this fails, it means it is still too early for the public to accept. I've watched some other electronic publishing ventures fail and learned from their mistakes, and I can't think of anything obvious that we have done wrong in setting up this new venture. Now we just have to see if customers are going to respond.

If for some reason they do not, it seems very likely that Brad Templeton will have yet another entrepreneurial idea waiting just off line.

MICHAEL STRANGELOVE AND
STRANGELOVE PRESS

Three years ago, Michael Strangelove had not even heard of the Internet. Today, he is the founder and owner of Strangelove Press, a company that specializes in publishing journals and newsletters about the network. In between discovering the Internet and starting his own business, Strangelove created an experimental network-distributed academic journal, wrote a comprehensive guide to Internet-accessible religious studies resources, and compiled the *Directory of Electronic Journals and Newsletters*, now in its third annual edition. Strangelove's transition from academic to entrepreneur, like so many other things on the Internet, took place at something approaching light speed.

Strangelove started using the Internet as a research tool, while completing his master's thesis at the University of Ottawa, to communicate with religious studies scholars around the world. Now a Social Sciences and Humanities Research Council Doctoral Fellow, he sees the Internet as a turning point in his career. "What has happened to my career might never have been accomplished without the network," he reflects. "Because of specializing in the Internet, I have been asked to write regularly for both academic journals and the mass media. Now, Strangelove Press is successful enough to allow me to employ a highly skilled team of individuals. If my experience is at all typical, the Internet will soon be seen as the essential basis for every small business."

Strangelove Press started in 1993 with the launch of the *Internet Business Journal*, a monthly publication designed to inform the international business community about the potential of the network. Within a few months of its first issue the journal attracted more than a thousand readers in two dozen countries. Since the vast majority of subscribers have e-mail addresses, the journal is able to interact with its audience via the network. According to Strangelove:

> One aspect of the *Internet Business Journal's* tremendous success completely surprised us. We knew the journal would be attractive to the computer and telecommunications industries, but we never expected such enormous diversity among our readers. Subscribers come from every imaginable industry, including automotive, legal, pharmaceutical, medical, housing, steel, utilities, and even fiber glass manufacturers. Clearly, sooner rather than later, the Internet will become as ubiquitous to the business world as the asphalt highway, the telephone, and the fax machine.

Building on the success of its initial offering, Strangelove Press has gone on to launch two new publications. The *Best of the Internet*, a magazine that informs readers of new documents and programs available on the network, is designed to keep Internet users up to date on new resources in a digestible format. *Internet Publishing News* aims at the publishing industry, which Strangelove feels has an urgent need to learn about Internet-facilitated publishing and information dissemination:

> Only those publishers that integrate the Internet into the structure of their operations will survive the transition to the network age. The commercial infrastructure is just coming into place to allow publishers to identify and reach vertical markets on an international scale. It will be possible to reach virtual communities with very distinct information needs, and to deliver information tailored to their interests. Success will depend on how well publishers are able to adjust to this new electronic market.

Strangelove doesn't see a contradiction in publishing traditional print versions of his journals as well as electronic formats. He regards the next few years as a transitional stage where people will still depend on paper and print for much of their information. Many of his readers are new to the Internet, and need a printed resource to get them to the next stage of network utilization. At the same time, he expects Strangelove Press to move and adjust to new forms of communication right along with the Internet community.

Like many other Internet entrepreneurs, Strangelove has put his vision for the future ahead of immediate financial gain. He decided against selling his company to a bigger publisher, and is working on an ambitious business plan for the next five years. "I could have become part of a well-established chain of publications," he says, "but that would mean giving up my own unique vision of what the Internet community can become. Maybe entrepreneurs live on dreams, cheap wine, and miracles, but it's not just a living. I'm doing something to help create a new kind of future."

THE NEXT STEP

There seems no doubt that some of the most exciting business opportunities of the decade will emerge from the convergence of connectivity, information, and entertainment represented by electronic networks. Surveying the exhibits at Interop, Thomas Donlan of *Barron's* reflected, "The next Microsoft may have been there, to say nothing of the next Random House, the next National Broadcasting Company . . ." Will today's Internet entrepreneurs become the corporate icons of the next century? Even though the odds are that only a small percentage will be in the same business a few years from now, those who have taken the risk represent a powerful vision. The electronic news service, the enhanced, all-purpose information and retrieval tool, networked media broadcasting for home and office—it seems very likely that some form of all these visions will become a way of life by end of the nineties.

REFERENCES

Donlan, Thomas G. 1993. Editorial Commentary. *Barron's.* 10. March 29.

Drucker, Peter. 1993. *Post-Capitalist Society.* New York: HarperBusiness.

Markoff, John. 1993. Turning the Desktop PC Into a Talk Radio Medium. *The New York Times.* 1 (D18). March 7.

Schumpeter, Joseph. 1942. *Capitalism, Socialism and Democracy.* New York: Harper.

CHAPTER *8*

Putting the Network to Work

> *A network is only as successful as the users say it is.*
> Connecting to the Internet
> Request for Comments 1359

Other people's success stories and hard-won lessons can be instructive, but in the end the value of the Internet for any business depends on matching network capabilities with that company's priorities. As the previous chapters illustrate, there are many ways the Internet can work for business. Internet connections can reduce communications costs and extend the effective reach of large and small corporations. The network has demonstrated its ability to enhance the support services provided by hardware and software vendors to keep vital automated systems operating at peak efficiency. Marketing departments are using the Internet to determine customer response to new products and to provide information to a new base of networked consumers.

Research and development divisions at Fortune 500 corporations depend on the Internet or Internet-compatible networks to share information with research partners in corporate, university, medical, or other settings. Some companies have made an Internet connection a fundamental requirement for new business partners. Others describe the network as an essential ingredient in internal collaboration and teamwork among branch offices in remote locations.

The Internet also serves as a mechanism for sales and product distribution. As more individuals and organizations establish Internet connections, the number of products available over the network is on the rise. Even when direct sales are not desirable, the Internet provides an option for electronic product catalogs as well as enhanced customer communication and support.

The most wide-spread Internet application for business users is access to global electronic mail and data exchange. A large number of corporate users also participate actively in USENET and other network discussion groups, and many technical staff put the availability of public domain software high on their list of Internet benefits. Beyond these top three network applications, the companies surveyed for this book have started using the Internet for the following functions (in descending order of popularity):

- obtaining support from vendors

- participating in joint development

- collaborative research projects

- providing customer support

- marketing

- sales

- product distribution

Each Internet application, from the most basic communications routine to the most sophisticated sales and marketing plan, also requires internal flexibility and some degree of organizational change. The more departments which are involved, the more complex such change may become. A successful strategy for Internet implementation will combine the immediate communication needs of a business with its long-term strategic goals for network participation. No company is too large, or too small, to benefit from a strategic Internet plan. The planning process need not be complex, especially for small businesses.

Whether the question is how to make an existing Internet connection more valuable, or how to connect for the first time, there are some fundamental points to consider in determining how effectively the network can work to meet business needs. These questions may seem very basic, but more than one company has connected to the Internet without articulating specific objectives or even deciding who within the organization would benefit most from using the network.

1. *Why the Internet?*
   - Is there a specific need for global connectivity?
   - What benefits are expected after one year of Internet use?
   - How does the Internet fit company priorities and existing communication systems?

2. *Who is responsible?*
   - Where does Internet management fall within the organizational structure?
   - Who will provide overall administrative coordination, support, training, and departmental or individual connections?
   - Who evaluates the effectiveness of Internet use and decides about expanding or upgrading the connection?

3. *How is it working?*
   - Are there criteria for selecting a service provider (if already connected, how well are the criteria being met)?
   - Have security and privacy issues been addressed?

- Are internal use policies and documentation in place?
- Are use statistics for various applications captured and analyzed regularly?
- Is there an evaluation process to determine how well the Internet is meeting company needs?

Until such basic questions are answered, companies are not likely to benefit as much as they should from participating in the Internet. If all these points have been addressed in your organization, congratulations—it is time to move on to planning for the future, covered in Chapter 9. Otherwise, stop for a moment to consider the generic, but nonetheless representative, experiences of three different types of companies already connected to the Internet.

Case I: Fortress, Inc.

Several research centers in this multinational manufacturing corporation established Internet connections in the 1980s as part of federally funded projects using supercomputer resources. Use of these connections was strictly limited to research applications to ensure adherence to the National Science Foundation's Acceptable Use Policy. A separate, dial-in connection was established in 1990 by the corporate Library and Information Center to access various bibliographic and document delivery resources available over the network. Because there was no internal Internet training and support available, and only limited resources for outside training, this connection was designated primarily for library use and not publicized to the rest of Fortress, Inc.

As part of an overall audit of internal data security, the company determined in 1991 that a more secure Internet gateway was required for all network users. The security design, which assumed primarily research use from specific centers, was in place only a few months when the marketing division became interested in using the Internet to distribute product information. This type of activity was prohibited by the terms of the Acceptable Use Policy for the research connection, and required a new management and security review to determine whether a commercial connection would be justified. While the review was underway, a development group in an overseas office contracted with a local network service provider to establish a direct Internet link to facilitate work with several new development partners.

When the switch to a commercial connection was finally approved, it was discovered that the new security design did not allow for the extensive multimedia applications envisioned by marketing, and coincidentally, required by a new research project. Several overseas offices, some of which were still waiting for full connectivity to the corporate enterprise network, were also requesting direct local connections to the Internet. The corporate enterprise network, which included a variety of different e-mail systems, was laboring under the challenges of internal connectivity and the speed of communication among different divisions in different locations was not satisfactory. The Chief Information Officer determined that this situation required priority attention and declared a moratorium on all new Internet connections until internal connectivity concerns and external security requirements were resolved.

Case II: Laissez Firm

This small electronics company with fewer than a hundred employees connected to the Internet through a commercial service provider in 1991 to link its development groups in two locations. At the time of the connection the network manager, who had used the Internet for years in a university setting, decided to bring in a USENET newsfeed and to offer Internet access to anyone requesting it.

A large percentage of the staff are now regular e-mail users. Though the network manager doesn't tally and compare usage statistics on a regular basis, he knows that the traffic is increasing rapidly for both e-mail and file transfer. Many employees follow a variety of newsgroups and discussion groups not directly related to their jobs. Some make regular use of the career leads and job postings, either for themselves or their friends outside the company. A lot of software for personal computers is being downloaded.

Questions and comments about Laissez Firm's products occasionally appear on Internet discussion groups, but there is no dedicated discussion list just for Laissez Firm customers. Answers to specific questions and general comments are often posted by employees on an informal basis. Sometimes, technical issues raised in network discussions are brought up in the development groups. No one is quite sure if all the relevant discussion groups have been discovered. The network manager intends to get around to producing a more comprehensive guide to important lists and other Internet resources after the next upgrade of the internal system. He has also promised to find out more about navigation tools and graphical interfaces—but in the meantime, people are working out their own navigational solutions.

Some of the public domain software on the Internet has proved useful in speeding up product development. The two development groups, however, disagree about whether it is appropriate to incorporate public domain code into company products, so most of the required software is still written internally. The Internet has proven invaluable for receiving quick responses from system vendors when there is a glitch or a bug in any of the internal technical support systems, and the technical groups are quite pleased with the network's performance. The firm's customer support group would like to experiment with offering a similar Internet-based service for Laissez customers. They are waiting for some direction from management about whether this type of support fits in with the company's plan to market a new product in cooperation with a business partner. Meanwhile, a number of individuals are actively exploring the network for new ideas and creative applications for the variety of resources they are discovering.

Case III: Balanced Business

Balanced Business, a medium-sized service company with branches in seventeen countries, selected a dedicated commercial Internet connection in 1991 with two objectives in mind: saving money on internal communications and travel costs, and providing better technical support to overseas customers. In preparation for the Internet connection, Balanced redesigned its enterprise communication network to utilize TCP/IP architecture. Even though many of the company's computer and technical groups were quite familiar with Unix systems and Internet applications, a small implementation team worked to develop an in-house Internet training program accessible to all employees, including marketing, sales, and customer support divisions. Training materials were distributed to each branch office and an Internet liaison was selected for each site to coordinate the details of connectivity with headquarters. An Internet Advisor bulletin board on the internal network features new Internet resources and training tips, and answers specific questions from anyone in the company.

In addition to USENET newsgroups, Balanced Business subscribes to the ClariNet news service, with a special emphasis on technological developments and international news for employees dealing with overseas locations. The company library also set up a scanning and current awareness service for selected "hot topics" of interest to management, development, and other departments.

The company's MIS department drafted and circulated network use policies as part of the Internet training package. These included security procedures, company policy on use of public domain software and other data, generally acceptable network behavior, and guidelines for personal use of the network for e-mail or nonbusiness discussion groups, among other topics. Security for the Internet gateway was designed to facilitate remote access to the network for traveling employees, and full access to existing and experimental multimedia applications, without compromising the company's internal data.

After one year of operation, a simplified cost-benefit analysis and customer survey showed that Balanced had achieved its original goals—communications costs are down and customer satisfaction is at a high point. Other company divisions have proposed a number of additional applications, and these are regularly reviewed by management to ensure a coordinated strategy.

Balanced employees see the Internet as a useful tool for getting the job done. Many express enthusiasm for the new perspective it offers them on the company's business and the contacts they have made with customers, business partners, and colleagues in distant branches. They like the regular updates on new Internet resources and the availability of navigational tools for locating software or other useful materials on the network. Branch offices are able to exchange data, work more effectively on development projects, and participate in companywide planning sessions. The target for reducing travel and communications costs has been more than met. Based on these results, management has set up a small group to investigate the costs and benefits of using the Internet for marketing and customer support activities.

A surprising number of companies already using the Internet

look a lot more like Fortress, Inc. or Laissez Firm than Balanced Business. Figure 8.1 highlights some of the key elements of these three approaches to the network. The Fortress approach puts security first and foremost. The only problem is that security in the absence of strategy can become an impediment to effective use. Instead of asking what applications are important for the whole company, and how to implement them in a secure fashion, Fortress concentrates on building ever more impervious firewalls between it and the outside world. The result may be missed opportunities and stifled innovation.

Laissez faire, on the other hand, gives free rein to individual innovation. Many ideas and experiments in networked communication are likely to be underway at any given moment. Unfortunately, these activities are not guided by any sense of overall strategy or priority from top management. A good deal of creativity and effort are channeled into directions that are not especially productive for the company.

In the absence of clear policy, there may be frequent internal debates about how to use Internet resources appropriately. A

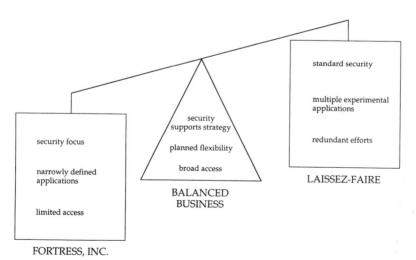

FIGURE 8.1 Implementation Strategies.

number of positive, productive applications do get implemented in this setting, but they are somewhat random rather than concentrated in an area that offers the best opportunity for competitive advantage.

The Balanced approach has obvious advantages, but it will seldom evolve spontaneously. It starts with a plan; not a time-consuming, detail-ridden blueprint for every aspect of Internet use, but a flexible strategy for using the network to achieve priority goals. These priorities are built into every aspect of Internet implementation, policy, and training. Valuable information derived from the network is shared throughout the company. New ideas for Internet applications are presented and evaluated in terms of how they will advance the overall business strategy. If Fortress and Laissez Faire sound all too familiar, but Balanced sounds impossibly utopian, it may be time to take another look at putting the Internet to work for you.

GETTING THERE: FIVE EASY PIECES

It is not impossible to achieve a balanced approach to the Internet; in fact, if one analyzes the requirements one by one, it looks rather easy. Why don't more companies do it? Partly because the Internet is regarded by many managers as a separate, technical application instead of a strategic resource important to the whole business. The very real and immediate security and network configuration issues required by implementation often overshadow the long-term implications and opportunities of global connectivity. The technical details of the Internet can be complex; mastery of them has been the topic of a number of publications (see Appendix A). Management responsibility, however, is more productively focused on managing the implementation process to achieve strategic goals and assure smooth, secure operations.

The road to balanced implementation can be traversed successfully by following a logical progression starting with clearly defined goals; to defining specific network requirements; to selecting a provider and establishing the actual connections; to addressing the security, policy, and training issues; to bringing the process full circle by measuring and evaluating the results at regular intervals. Rather than focusing their attention on the myriad technical details involved in each step, managers need to concentrate on maintaining the balance between network requirements and company priorities at each stage of the process.

A Whole Company Strategy

In *The Whole Internet Guide*, Ed Krol notes that many people already have access to Internet connectivity without being aware of it (1992, 9). This includes a number of companies where the Internet is known only to a select few, and news of its availability spreads primarily by word of mouth from one department to another. Krol advises would-be networkers to make inquiries about whether an Internet connection has already been established for their company and to find out who makes decisions about access. If Internet connectivity within their own organization is new information for many employees, however, it will probably be a long time before a "whole company strategy" becomes the norm.

In fact, many companies do start by connecting just one department to the Internet, focusing on an application of immediate interest, such as research collaboration or improved support from systems vendors. This approach can be the beginning of a balanced, whole-company strategy, or it can be the end of the story until another priority presents itself. Unless management looks at the Internet in the context of overall corporate goals, requests for connectivity within the company are likely to be addressed on a "squeaky wheel" basis. Once the network is in place, many ideas about applications will begin to surface, and more areas will request connectivity. Developing a whole-company strategy at the outset will help to prevent delays, frustrations, and end runs or short-term solutions. Part of the overall plan can be an assessment of the cost and benefits associated with various network applications, to estimate which efforts are likely to yield the most positive results. The process for expanding connections or undertaking new applications can then be staged in a flexible way.

Some applications, like e-mail capability and newsgroup access, will be useful immediately to a large number of people in the organization. For those departments where keeping up with technology, international developments, or other news is a priority, a current awareness service may be a good investment. Once employees are active Internet users, they will locate and access a number of external information sources that are valuable for the whole company. These include discussion groups on new trends, activities and innovations by competitors, groups in which customers participate actively, evaluations of products and vendors the company may be considering, information and contacts from countries of particular strategic interest, and more.

A whole-company approach to information management can encourage sharing and synthesizing such insights internally, so that everyone is well-informed about internal network use and external developments. If a library or corporate information center is in place, it can take responsibility for collecting and distributing the most important external information and sifting through the large number of newly announced sources to avoid redundant effort and to keep departments up to date. Even without such a formal information structure, small companies can develop a plan for sharing the most important data derived from the Internet throughout the organization.

A number of Internet applications—for example marketing over the network—will require support from the whole company to succeed in the long term. Posting and updating company information on the network can be a very effective means of reaching customers. Taking advantage of the dynamic and interactive nature of the Internet, however, means a higher level of commitment to keeping all postings current, responding to comments and suggestions, and improving the "look and feel" of the network interface. Cooperation among several divisions is crucial for success.

Participation by top management, and a broad understanding of the workings and scope of the Internet are also important factors for developing an effective whole-company strategy. Implementation, training, security, and information management will require resources. Management must recognize that an investment in the Internet will promote the long-term success of the company, and must identify the critical areas in which the network can contribute to competitive advantage, so that these can receive priority attention.

Service and Support

The level of support required to set up and maintain an Internet connection varies according to the size of the company and the complexity of any existing internal network. Taylor Walsh, an electronic communications consultant at Washington Information Services Corporation, specializes in advising companies interested in connecting to the Internet. He emphasizes that each company, large or small, initiate the decision process with a thorough needs analysis. "If you expect the Internet to add value to your company," he says, "it's important to begin with a thorough analysis of the strengths and weaknesses of your existing communications and information systems. Look at what is happening with internal connections and with linking to the outside world." Such an analysis should include an estimate of how much additional support the Internet connection will require to operate effectively.

Small organizations interested in trying out the Internet with a limited number of internal computers to be connected may be able to get up and running with only the part-time attention of computer and network-literate employees. Working out the details of linking internal networks, establishing and maintaining security mechanisms, and documenting policy for a larger company will require full-time, dedicated network personnel with Unix experience. The larger the company, the more likely that at least basic expertise and support will already be available in-house—but someone's time will have to be dedicated to overseeing and coordinating the Internet. Since many internal networks don't even communicate very well with one another, establishing a seamless Internet connection with the appropriate level of security for all participants presents a significant challenge. It is not unusual for companies to spend several months on the preliminary work of setting up and testing the configuration. "Connecting to the Internet," is an RFC, or Request for Comment, one of the many helpful background documents prepared by the Internet working groups and freely available to Internet users. Its authors note that appropriate allocation of resources is one of the most important aspects of Internet implementation:

> Perhaps the most challenging task in the initial deployment of the Internet connection is the resulting reorientation of network technical and network information services. There are added responsibilities for network management as well as added network information services to support the connection. Cognizant administrators must recognize, plan and budget for these added tasks (RFC 1359, 1992).

During Internet implementation, it is most important to keep the long-term goals for the network in mind and to build in enough flexibility to expand connectivity to other sites and other applications. At this stage, network managers frequently seek and receive advice from other companies working with similar configurations, in addition to obtaining support from the service provider. The InterNIC now provides another support option, offering both direct answers to specific pre-connection questions and pointers to additional resources and detailed background documentation.

Whatever support services are not available in-house or through the Internet itself can readily be obtained (usually for a fee) from commercial Internet service providers. These include advice on the initial configuration of software and hardware for the network, establishing and registering official network domain names, general recommendations for security, specific privacy and security solutions, training sessions, hardware installation, and ongoing consultation.

Last but never least, decisions about network security must be finalized well before the connection is established. The "Site Security Handbook," RFC 1244 (Holbrook and Reynolds 1989), provides an excellent starting point for understanding security requirements and options. An invaluable source of current security information is the Computer Emergency Response Team/Coordination Center (CERT/CC) housed at the Software Engineering Institute, Carnegie Mellon University. In addition to publishing "Generic Security Information" (CERT 1992), this group issues advisories to inform Internet users about new security problems and distributes information about preventive techniques. CERT advisories are available through USENET in the comp.security.announce newsgroup, as well as through the mailing list available from cert-advisory-request@cert.org. Some of the specific security and privacy issues to be addressed before connecting to the network are discussed later in this chapter.

At the Point of Connection

For some companies, it can be as simple as one phone call to a service provider, followed up by a purchase order. For others it can take months of planning, debating options, reviewing security requirements, ordering equipment, and reconfiguring internal connectivity. No matter how long it takes, at some point the equipment and software is installed, the configuration is ready, addresses and domain names are registered, and the organization officially becomes part of the global matrix. What next?

Gary Malkin, co-author of "Frequently Asked Questions for New Internet Users" (RFC 1325 Malkin and Marine 1992) and a Users Glossary (RFC 1392), tells new users who call him for advice that reading the FYI series on the Internet and consulting the materials on the InfoSource are the best ways to become familiar with network basics. "People really do ask the same questions that are covered in these sources. If you read them thoroughly at the beginning, then check with the InterNIC for any specific concerns, you'll have all the information you need to get started."

Extensive background materials on many network-related questions are available in the Request for Comments series (RFCs), which is continually updated with new material by Internet working groups. It is a good idea to synthesize some of this information into a company-oriented Frequently Asked Questions resource for internal use, both to deal with the questions themselves and to familiarize employees with this common form of information-sharing on the network.

Malkin also recommends becoming familiar with groups like the Internet Engineering Task Force to get the network connection off to a good start. "Any company working in the technology and networking field should consider sending representatives to IETF meetings. It's definitely worth the investment in terms of keeping up with new developments in networking." Even for companies just wanting to keep informed, announcements and summaries of task force meetings, new Internet standards and documents, security updates from CERT, and the newsgroups related to a company's field of business and its internal systems are at the top of Malkin's list of useful resources for a new Internet site.

Once the connection is up and running, each site will need to oversee the flow of incoming and outgoing messages, to maintain the routing tables, and ensure that e-mail reaches its proper destination. Typically, in larger companies, network managers and Internet postmasters are concerned with the optimal performance of the physical network; someone else may be responsible for establishing policy and evaluating how well the connection is meeting company needs. Regular communication among all those responsible for the Internet will contribute to the network's effectiveness.

Policy, Training, and Documentation

A solid foundation of written policy, Internet training, and documentation may not be as exciting as getting the Internet connection up and running, but it's just as important for the smooth operation of the network. This essential step will highlight the company's priorities for network use, and help to avoid confusion about the how and why of the Internet. To get the most from its connection, a company may wish for a pragmatist to promulgate Internet policy, a visionary to design the training program, and a historian to compile and update the documentation required for daily use. Even short of this ideal, management must ensure that each step receives careful attention.

It may not be possible to cover every aspect of network use in a written policy statement, and a pragmatist knows that even the most perfect policy will not be followed to the letter. That is not a rationale to do without any stated policies for Internet use within the company. At a minimum, information about appropriate use of the network and about expectations regarding security practices on the part of users, the posting of company-related messages to discussion groups, and bringing in outside files and data should be familiar to everyone using the network. Policy and documentation on network applications should be kept up to date and accessible on the internal network, and should also be available in written form.

While relatively few companies devote significant resources to training, those that do have a faster and more substantial return on their Internet investment in terms of efficient use of the system throughout the company. Many employees are willing to learn by "trial and error," but this can be time-consuming and frustrating. Pointers to the basic functions and information sources are a basic requirement for new users, and the more that is provided, the more quickly the network connection can begin to make a difference. Ideally, nontechnical corporate users should have an interface available to facilitate functions like following newsgroups, locating and transferring files, and logging on to remote computers. Navigation and retrieval tools like Gopher, WAIS, and World Wide Web should become an integrated part of their access to the network.

There is at least one discussion list (NETTRAIN) devoted to the development of training materials and programs, and a number of sample training programs and packets of materials are shared through the network. Training is frequently overlooked in Internet implementation planning, but the investment companies make in training is paid back in increased staff productivity. The best trainers will combine enthusiasm for the network's resources with a firm grasp of their company's

Internet strategy and an understanding of the needs of different kinds of users.

The Bottom Line

Does the Internet make a measurable difference in terms of cost reduction or performance improvement? Companies that do not ask the question will never know. While overall strategic gains may be difficult to attribute to the Internet or to any other single factor, the impact of global connectivity can be measured in relation to specific applications. An effective evaluation system starts with the articulation of objectives before the Internet is in place. If the short-term objective, for example, is improving international connectivity while lowering telecommunications cost, success can be determined by standard cost analysis. Benchmarks for internal system performance before and after an Internet connection can provide a point of reference for measuring improvement in vendor support. If a faster pace for product development is a goal, the time to complete projects with network support can be quantified. Qualitative improvements in customer satisfaction or the effectiveness of networked marketing can be indicated through interviews or surveys of target groups.

Employee satisfaction and productivity may be more difficult to quantify, but in the end the network can be successful only if those responsible for using it are willing and able to make the Internet work on a daily basis. Policy, documentation, and training provide the foundation for effective use. Well-designed usage surveys can serve to raise internal awareness of the Internet as a resource and increase the level of informed use. Establishing a framework for regular evaluation promotes more sophisticated planning for new Internet applications and makes the expectations for performance improvement a part of the planning process. Putting it all together, from the early planning to the end-of-year evaluation, adds up to the results that companies want to achieve—above *and* below the bottom line.

Management Graphics, a manufacturer of computer graphics hardware and software, watches its bottom line carefully. This Bloomington, Minnesota, company with eighty-five employees has been on the Internet since 1991. The motivation to connect was simple: the convenience of basic e-mail exchanges with vendors and customers. At first, Internet advocates were regarded with skepticism; some departments saw the global network as mostly a perk for the "high tech" people. Rather than invest a lot of capital in setting up the connection, the company bought all the hardware required for the initial Internet configuration at auction for less than $3,000.

Three years later, virtually everyone at Management Graphics, including the CEO, uses the Internet regularly. The company has seen the value of the Internet increase with every new application. E-mail communication with the world was quickly followed by the introduction of USENET newsgroups and other discussion groups. Loren Schoenzeit, observing this progression, notes that the computer and systems groups became a surrogate for the technical advisors that Management Graphics couldn't afford to have in-house. "We just didn't have the technical depth of a big company," he says, "but suddenly it was possible to get high level, workable solutions to any number of technical problems. When an engineer posted a question, he would get several answers back the next day. It made an enormous difference in our ability to get the most out of our systems and move ahead with projects."

Interest in newsgroups wasn't limited to technical support issues. People in accounting discovered groups with valuable information for them. Marketing and sales started to follow the groups dedicated to computer graphics to answer queries about Management Graphics products or generic questions where their product could offer a solution. These leads frequently turned into customers the company otherwise never would have contacted.

Existing customers on the Internet benefitted from the connection, as Management Graphics used the network to enhance its customer support services. In turn, the company also received improved support from its vendors, especially as the major hardware and software companies dedicated more of their resources to networked support.

For a company the size of Management Graphics, every expenditure has to justify itself in real savings and income growth. The investment in the Internet is monitored carefully— the connection charges, the newly upgraded network hardware, and the time of the systems manager who oversees the Internet operations are measured against the gains in technical performance, productivity, sales, and customer satisfaction. The conclusion? According to Schoenzeit, the benefits clearly outweigh the costs, "The Internet has definitely proven its value to the company. We rely on the network now in practically every department." In addition to the specific applications, he says, "the Internet gives our organization much more credibility in our dealings with customers and vendors. On the network we can communicate on equal terms with the largest corporations in the world."

A consistent, whole—company strategy for Internet implementation can help ensure similar results for new business connections.

SECURITY CHECK

It may be the only topic on which the diverse group of corporate Internet users will ever be unanimous—security is an essential component of every company's network connection. Connecting to the world has many advantages and one major drawback;

the exposure to potentially malicious intruders. As the infamous Internet worm and a number of other published incidents have demonstrated (Denning 1990, Stoll 1989), there is ample reason to be concerned. Nonetheless, security and the Internet are by no means incompatible. Appropriate levels of security simply require some corporate investment in terms of time and money, as well as what Bill Cheswick calls "the classic tradeoff between security and convenience" (1990, 1).

Cheswick, a member of the technical staff in the computer science research division and Internet postmaster for this division at AT&T Bell Laboratories in Murray Hill, New Jersey, has worked on three successive Bell Labs Internet gateways. Clearly, security has been a necessity for each one, but with a mandate to serve the research community so were basic Internet functions like telnet and file transfer. According to Cheswick, "Bell Labs has the same mixture of people who can and can't use the system as the typical university. Their major concern is getting on with their research and Internet is an essential tool. Nothing will raise the ire of the researchers faster than finding out the gateways don't work or that e-mail messages won't go through."

The corporate gateway designed for Bell Labs provides the basic Internet services while maintaining a safe distance between the internal network and the rest of the world. In addition to securing AT&T data, the gateway allows detailed monitoring of attempted break-ins. Cheswick and his colleague Steven Bellovin have described this security configuration and its performance under attack in a number of papers available through anonymous file transfer from research.att.com (Bellovin 1989, 1992, Cheswick 1992).

The Bell Labs solution may represent the high end of security consciousness, but the security issue is universal. Fortunately, good advice and solutions are available through the Internet infrastructure. Companies need not come up with a unique local security system from scratch. Straightforward, workable strategies for eliminating common security holes and establishing secure gateways are recommended in the Internet RFCs, by the CERT, and by network service providers. If your company is willing and able to pay a substantial annual fee, turnkey security systems are available from most of the commercial providers, with additional features to safeguard internal network information and monitor remote log-in activity.

Preventing break-ins through a secure network connection meets only half of the security requirements for some corporate Internet users. Privacy of communication while messages are in transit over the network is another important concern, especially for applications involving financial and other sensitive transactions. While some people say the chances of an electronic intruder grabbing anything significant off the tremendous tide of network traffic is no more likely than a phone tap or a safe crack, others argue that encryption of sensitive information to make it accessible only to the receiver is a necessary precaution. Commercial providers also offer privacy and encryption services, and options for privacy-enhanced mail are being actively pursued on the network (Kent 1993, Podesta 1993).

To decide which level of security is appropriate for your company, it may be helpful to compare the choices available to the physical security of your office or headquarters. Companies can secure their premises by simply locking the doors, by installing an alarm system, or by hiring 24-hour security and surveillance. Not every business needs the most intensive security available, but no one wants to be found with their doors wide open in the middle of the night. Following the recommendations for basic Internet security provided on the network will provide the equivalent of a locked door between your company and the outside world. A decision about what else may be needed is part of setting overall company priorities for the Internet.

BEHIND THE CONNECTIONS: POSTMASTER PROFILES

Internet gateways are where it all comes together, putting companies in touch with the rest of the world while offering some level of protection from outside prying. Establishing the best balance between security and ease of use, maintaining directory information files, keeping track of errant e-mail addresses, and maintaining smooth connections between internal communication systems and the Internet all require human judgment and attention. In major corporations, the Internet postmaster function is a full-time job that often includes system security and network planning. Postmasters see the network up close, understand its quirks, and appreciate its potential. Their experiences provide a microcosm of how the Internet really works in the corporate setting.

J.P. Morgan

Like many of his network colleagues, David Spector displays a strong commitment to the value of the Internet. His position as a vice president of technology services at J.P. Morgan evolved from a consulting assignment at the firm, and includes responsibility for Unix services development and state of art technology in the firm's internal systems. One of his first actions was to propose an Internet gateway and oversee its implementation. Now he continues to work to improve the firm's internal mail systems and addressing systems. As head postmaster, he oversees configuration of machines using the mail system, tracks problems, and keeps the messages flowing.

Spector was first introduced to the Internet as a college student, but his enthusiasm for technology extends back to his high school days when he established his own computer consulting business, and even to his first encounter with a computer at the age of five. He describes himself as a "networked kid" and his job at J.P. Morgan strikes him as ideal. "I have always known this is what I wanted to do," he says. "I'm just afraid of waking up and finding out I really have to do something awful for a living."

He is sympathetic to the challenges of setting up Internet connectivity on a variety of platforms ("If I have a hard time doing it, then people with less technical background are going to need help") and makes it a point to deal with connectivity problems personally. Most problems result from trying to route mail along pathways that don't exist, and education is usually the best answer. Aside from the oversight necessary to maintain security, Internet connections are available for the asking; Spector doesn't keep tabs on what J.P. Morgan staff are doing over the network. The company does offer a complete news feed, which is a popular feature, especially with Morgan's thousands of software developers around the world.

Spector thinks the network needs improved standards for security and privacy of information transmitted over the Internet, especially for financial transactions. He still sees problems with the interpretation of the National Science Foundation's Acceptable Use Policy, and looks forward to the day when companies like his can make even fuller use of the network. At the same time, he values the spirit of the Internet today, "I personally hope that greater commercialization and privatization doesn't change the culture and the spontaneity that makes the Internet what it is."

AT&T and Bell Labs

As the Internet postmaster at the Computer Research Division of Bell Labs, Bill Cheswick has made the balance of security and functionality a top priority. In addition to safeguarding Bell's internal network from intruders, he also has worked to devise secure ways to distribute useful information and software to legitimate users, and to allow researchers to access their data when away from the lab. Like many sites, Bell maintains a file transfer service; this anonymous ftp server provides a place for distributing documents and code to the rest of the world, and researchers from many other organizations have contributed to its store of useful information.

For Bell researchers, the secure gateway now allows log-in from the outside through use of a special security token. But it doesn't employ a password, according to Cheswick, because someone could be monitoring the interaction and gain access to the password for future use. Instead authorized users are given a little hand-held device about the size of a calculator (the security token, or "dongle," in Bell Labs parlance), which has an encryption algorithm and key stored in it. The same algorithm is loaded into a file on the home gateway machine. When users log in from a remote location, the home machine gives a random five-digit number as a challenge—they enter that number into the security token and it tells them what to say back. Once this challenge is met successfully, they can log in to their normal network functions.

Cheswick is also working to enhance the multimedia capacity of the gateway. People inside Bell Labs want the broadest possible access to multimedia over the network, which is not possible with some security configurations. The Bell gateway supports programs like Internet Talk Radio (a local favorite) without difficulty. Cheswick himself is interested in the latest weather and solar activity, so he imports the weather maps and photos automatically every hour and uses a program to display the radar track of advancing storms, as well as pictures from NASA of sunspot activity. Like many others, he finds value in a less picturesque, but still vital feature of the network—the rich variety of available software, some of which he uses in his own software development projects.

As a leading research center, Bell Labs is involved in super high-speed networking research and testing applications in cooperation with other organizations. According to Cheswick, a number of research center staff will have the fastest available optical fiber connection installed between work and home so they can test out the potential first hand:

> Management has asked us to go home and talk to our families about what they would like to see in an interactive environment; movies on demand, educational materials and games, to test out what can be done with this kind of bandwidth. There is a new move to put fiber into homes and researchers are looking for the best applications to use this capacity. Our group is joining with others to try to invent the future.

Joe Judge took on a different set of challenges three years ago in his role as Internet postmaster of the gateway that connects corporate AT&T with the Internet. Some of the AT&T internal networks had already established informal Internet connections through their contacts at Bell Labs before he arrived to oversee the official corporate connection. But Judge found that the cultures at Bell Labs and AT&T corporate differed in everything from the philosophy and organization of network support to the kinds of interfaces users might want. One of his priorities became finding the best interface for new, nontechnical users:

> Bell Labs folks don't mind having a fairly basic, technical interface; they're comfortable in that environment. Outside of research, the business users find it weird that anyone could be happy with existing Internet tools. They want Gopher and Archie and something even nicer to use as an interface. I don't see a lot of things out there yet that will be powerful and easy enough for the average nontechnical user, although

the Mosaic servers and the XMosiac information browsers look promising.

Outside of Bell Labs and the special network projects, most people in the corporation were not familiar with the Internet when Judge arrived. He provides the same high-level security as Bell, but combines it with an emphasis on more user education and easier access to the Internet across all departments. This must be accomplished within the strong divisional system at AT&T, which requires that each area recover the costs of its development efforts. Making the Internet connection easily accessible on everyone's desktop, therefore, required an agreement by the other divisions to compensate Bell Labs for the network resources and tools required to make it easier to access and navigate.

Judge surveyed potential users throughout the corporation to determine their level of interest in the Internet, and found that most areas were willing to contribute their share of the cost of resource development. This documentation facilitated corporate approval to publicize the benefits of Internet connectivity. Even before the formal process was completed, more and more people were finding out about the Internet and requesting access. Once everyone has the option of connecting, Judge expects the use of Internet resources to increase rapidly. His personal favorites are the newsgroups on USENET that provide technical tips, and Internet Relay Chat which allows him to keep up with events in countries where he has contacts and language skills.

Speculating about the future, Judge hopes to see significant improvements to enhance the Internet access tools, making them more suitable for nontechnical users. His vision is a one-stop desktop access point, equipped with multimedia; an interface that will pull together all the things a person is particularly interested in and make them directly available. This customized interface would include a variety of powerful search and retrieval tools, to locate new resources and bring them back to the desktop. Combined with a better directory service, this would be his vision of the Internet future:

> I wish we had a way to just point to another company and find out whatever that company is willing to let us know—a compilation of the public kinds of information that are probably scattered around in a lot of different places now; how to contact key departments, information about products, services, and how the company is doing. The information packet could include job openings and applications, press releases and announcements, the annual report, basically anything of interest they are willing to share with the public.

One of Judge's goals is to ensure that everyone at AT&T has the opportunity to be part of the Internet. "In the next few years," he says, "if you don't have an e-mail address you will have great difficulty functioning in the business world. An Internet address belongs on everyone's business card."

Apple

Erik E. Fair has seen, and contributed to, a lot of progress on the Internet since he became Apple's first Internet postmaster in July 1988. His position was created when the pressure to get Internet e-mail working smoothly throughout the company convinced management that the best solution was a full time postmaster. Fair's responsibilities include managing all of Apple's external connectivity and handling engineering security and net news. When he first arrived, a number of employees were unfamiliar with the Internet and unsure what it could contribute to their work. These days, there isn't anybody in the organization who doesn't know about the Internet; in fact, people are clamoring for desktop connectivity to the network as fast as it can be provided. That's fine with Fair—as far as he's concerned, the more people who want to use the Internet, the better it is for Apple.

Apple's primary Internet link to the outside world (apple.com) now has about a hundred people using it at any time of the day. Mail remains the most popular application, with about 120,000 messages moving across the Internet gateway every month. Research and development departments are heavy users of the Internet, and some members of the Advanced Technology Group have desktop connectivity to the network, so they don't need to use the apple.com gateway for research projects. To keep up with developments in technology, customer comments, and the latest trends, many employees participate in the USENET newsgroups and other relevant discussion forums on the network; the ClariNet news service is available to follow daily world news.

Fair himself receives between two hundred and five hundred messages every day, and even for a postmaster, that's a lot of mail. He uses a mail handler interface to keep track of it all and sort the incoming mail into the folders he has established. That way, he can go into the folders with high priority mail even when time is short—which it usually is. He wishes there were more hours in the day, so that he could continue to contribute his time to overall network development. "I just don't have the time to contribute personally to the Internet as much as I have in the past," he says. "I never thought any job could take so much of the available time, but this one does."

Fair's work on the Internet over the past twelve years has helped to facilitate everyone's use of the network. He was a co-developer of the network news protocol, a combined protocol that lets the enormous volume of communications contained in thousands of newsgroups move efficiently over the Internet. This protocol made it possible to have Macs and PCs and work stations access the subset of news a particular user wants, without everyone having to run a full netnews system. The huge number of topical newsgroups and the volume of participation had threatened to grind host computers to a halt with the sheer volume of information flow. Even now, Apple has to have a gigabit disk to hold netnews, and only keeps a few weeks at a time because the file requires so much space. The protocol lets news move efficiently between servers so that users can fetch articles and topics in real time—without it, the sheer size of the news flow would interfere with other Internet applications. Like so many other Internet resources, this protocol is distributed for free to any site operating a news feed.

At Apple, Fair is doing everything he can to remove technical and policy barriers to desktop Internet access for individual staff, including promoting even better interfaces for the Macintosh environment. With his Unix programming background, he doesn't regularly use the new navigational tools, but he supports the effort to make the network more accessible to new users, and wants Apple to make this a real priority.

From his perspective as postmaster, the two things that most need changing on the Internet are the remaining limits of the acceptable use policy ("a big pain in the rear and fundamentally unenforceable"), and tamper-proof authentication of e-mail messages. Fair routes traffic through Apple's commercial connections whenever possible, but communications with research and university customers often travel over government-sponsored networks. The company endeavors to be diligent in observing the research community standards for the Internet, and Apple supports educational use by sharing software and information on its servers, as well as by contributing time to organizations like the Internet Engineering Task Force. But even with the most massive effort to educate all Apple employees about acceptable use and the differences between the thousands of separate networks that make up the Internet, there is no way to control actual individual behavior. Fair looks forward to the day when the government changes its focus from restricting types of use to ensuring that all parts of the network can be used for any purpose.

Resolution of the second point may finally usher in the paperless office, which has been discussed for so many years. As Fair points out:

> E-mail as we know it on the Internet is not authenticated at all. Basically, we are working on trust that the message on our screen comes from the person whose signature we see and has not been tampered with somewhere along the way. That means that Internet transactions have no legal standing. For the future, business will have to use systems that make e-mail as valid as a signed paper document. Deployment of that technology means that the paperless office could actually show up in our lifetimes.

Looking to the future, Fair believes the Internet will become an essential business tool, "It hasn't gotten to be quite as ubiquitous as the phone, but it will get there eventually," he predicts. "Once those two pieces are in place, I don't think there will be a company in the U.S. that won't want to have an Internet connection."

IBM Research

For Nick Trio, being postmaster at IBM Research, Watson Center in New York, "is such a great job, I can't imagine anything else I'd rather be doing." With that as a starting point, it's no wonder that Trio finds a lot to be enthusiastic about in the way Internet use has grown since he started working as postmaster two years ago. He also has a good basis for measuring progress. "When I first joined IBM in a different position, I asked about Internet access. The research division had the only connection, and there was very little access in the rest of the company. People thought it was a strange request."

Trio didn't find much support for expanding Internet connections from other divisions at the time. He points out that this attitude, like many other things at IBM, has changed a lot in the past few years. Now there are many Internet connections available to IBMers in addition to the one at the Watson Research Center, and research use of the network has climbed significantly. Many of the new researchers have come from a university environment where the Internet has been essential to their work, and they want to be on-line as soon as they arrive. Trio expects to see even more reliance on the network as the focus of research at IBM broadens to include more emphasis on collaboration and understanding customer needs—both areas where the Internet provides crucial support. He already credits the Watson Research Center with making OS/2 a player on the Internet through its support of an anonymous ftp server to distribute OS/2 fixes as well as various software packages developed at Watson like the Hermes Compiler. At last check, the Internet server was handling forty thousand connections a month.

The Internet has had an interesting impact on the internal organization of IBM networking. With the increasing number of connections, network groups needed a way to coordinate all the links. Rather than going through a long and tortuous process to establish a formal oversight committee, Trio and others formed an ad hoc Internet coordination council. Everyone at IBM who runs an Internet connection participates in this group, which communicates through an internal on-line conference and mailing list and a few annual meetings. The new level of contact and coordination encourages joint planning for a number of networking issues in addition to the Internet.

The Internet has also facilitated collaboration with counterparts in other companies. Nick Trio and Erik Fair have discussed cooperative efforts to improve management for their respective parts of the Internet domain name system, by providing redundant name servers for each company at the other location. This kind of cooperation makes even more sense as companies that were former competitors establish a variety of collaborative projects via the network.

At IBM, Trio is working to make network access a lot more open by using things like packet filters instead of a firewall solution for security purposes. He wants to eliminate as many impediments as possible to encourage use. "Security is very important, in fact it's essential," he acknowledges, "but it shouldn't be a barrier to functionality or new applications." In the near future, Trio expects to see lots more multimedia, voice, and video applications involving higher bandwidth taking place on the Internet. The spread of multimedia will require rethinking the kinds of security systems that many companies have established.

To remind himself of how the network looks to the average researcher, Trio regularly puts tools like WAIS, Gopher, and World Wide Web through their paces. He likes using the XMosaic front end and exploring new resources. "It encourages me to make sure that things are working well," he says. As a ten-year veteran of the Internet, he enjoys recreational groups like amateur radio (rec.radio.amateur.misc) and alt.fan.howard stern in his free time, as well as the more work-related comp.protocols.tcp-ip and comp.security.misc. And right now, Trio is happy to say, he can't imagine a better time and place to be the Internet postmaster.

WORKING TOGETHER

The Internet is rich in innovation, expertise, and optimism about the future. Some of the most knowledgeable experts in the world of high-speed networking, security, navigation, and system design are working together to make the global network more valuable to the whole Internet community. In addition to being technically advanced, these experts are incredibly generous about advising new Internet users.

Companies just connecting to the network can become a part of this on-line community where sharing of information and expertise is the norm. If a problem arises during implementation, there will be sources on the Internet that can provide an answer. When it comes time to consider a network upgrade or a new application, a company can count on people in other organizations being willing to share their solutions and ideas. The power of this collective expertise is one of the greatest assets of the global network. The Internet is already working for millions of users and thousands of companies around the world. Learning from their experience is one of the best ways to ensure that it will work for you.

REFERENCES

ACM SIGUCCS, 1992. Connecting to the Internet: What connecting institutions should anticipate. FYI 16, RFC 1359. August.

Bellovin, Steven M. 1989. Security problems in the TCP/IP protocol suite. *Computer Communications Review* 19(2):32–48. 992. There be dragons. Unpublished manuscript available from: research.att.com. August 15.

Cheswick, W.R. 1992. An evening with Berferd: In which a cracker is lured, endured, and studied. Unpublished manuscript available from research.att.comm. January. 1990. The Design of a Secure Internet Gateway. Unpublished manuscript available from research.att.com. June.

Denning, Peter J. ed. 1990. *Computers under attack: Intruders, worms, and viruses.* Reading, Mass.: ACM Press.

Holbrook, P., and J. Reynolds, eds. 1991. Site security handbook. FYI 8, RFC 1244. CICnet, USC Information Sciences Institute.

Kent, Stephen T. 1993. Internet Privacy Enhanced Mail. *Communications of the ACM* 36(8):48–60.

Krol, Ed. 1992. *The Whole Internet User's Guide & Catalog.* Sebastopol, Calif.: O'Reilly & Associates.

Malkin, G., and A. Marine. 1992. FYI on questions and answers: Answers to commonly asked 'new Internet users' questions. FYI 4, RFC 1325.

Malkin, G., and T. LaQuey Parker, eds. 1993. Internet users' glossary FYI 19, RFC 1392.

Podesta, John D. 1993. Answers to Clipper Questions. *EFFector Online.* August 5.

Stoll, Clifford. 1989. *The Cuckoo's Egg: Tracking a Spy through the Maze of Computer Espionage.* New York: Doubleday.

9

Looking Forward

> *If we could look back on this period of history in a few decades when the information technology revolution has matured, we would probably be struck by the sharp contrast between the world we left behind and the world we have created.*
> —William E. Halal, *Technological Forecasting and Social Change*

Looking back, of course, is notoriously easier than looking forward. Predicting the future is perhaps the most precarious of all intellectual pursuits. The Internet as a business resource is a very recent phenomenon, evolving rapidly at a pace and in directions that even its founders did not anticipate. Business on the Internet is itself just one aspect of the largest electronic network in the world. With the sum of its parts so literally universal, neither aggregate statistics nor individual case studies can do justice to the impact of the Internet on society as a whole. This network of networks cannot be summed up simply by analyzing traffic patterns and protocols, or even by describing particular applications. These are just part of the picture. The Internet is shaped by the people behind the statistics— the managers and engineers, researchers and developers who debate its future, and the millions of users who turn to it daily.

The Internet offers connectivity at a level not previously available to business, nor to education, government, or individuals. The cultural changes brought about by instant global communication are just beginning to penetrate organizations. For business, the networked environment may eventually outstrip the impact of shifting from mainframe to distributed computing, or from local to multinational markets. The Internet itself seems certain to become an essential corporate resource within the next three years. How will it happen? In stages that are difficult to notice until they have already been completed and we find ourselves looking back on them. Looking forward, the best we can hope is to discern the general shape of things to come. This chapter will venture some modest predictions about the next phase of Internet development, consider the network enhancements most important to business, and briefly touch upon the unresolved issues that are likely to be debated for some time to come.

THE NEXT PHASE: WILL THERE ALWAYS BE AN INTERNET?

Global networks are here to stay. High-speed electronic connectivity is fundamental to business, research, and daily life in the 1990s and beyond. The Internet's component parts may change dramatically, its technical base will certainly evolve, and the look and feel of interacting on the network should be markedly different in the future. But one thing will not change: the Internet function of interconnecting a growing number of networks, computers, organizations, and individuals around the world. The global network, regardless of its governance, no matter what its name, will become even more central to business in the decades to come.

A continuing theme for the Internet will be growth: more networks every month, more registered hosts and domain names; more individuals linking up through work, school, or at home. Tony Rutkowski, who has observed and analyzed this growth as vice president of the Internet Society, believes it will certainly continue: "The Internet is still growing at an unprecedented rate. Commercial participation shows no sign of slowing down; in fact, it's one of the largest growth areas."

The international composition of the network will begin to make an impact. A growing percentage of the networks that make up the Internet are outside the United States. Even though this book has focused on American companies, the number of business users in other countries is growing just as rapidly. The spread of commercial Internet services throughout the world will have an influence over the future culture of the network, as a more diverse community debates the standards for international communication and commerce. Dan Lynch, the founder of Interop, the Interoperability Conference and Exhibition, points out that the Internet is growing rapidly overseas for the same reason it is flourishing in the United States: "It grows because it doesn't need anyone's permission to grow. Anyone can be an information publisher as well as a user," he says, "It's unlike any commercial network in this level of openness to all comers." In recognition of the increasing international composition of the Internet, Interop met outside the United States for the first time this year.

For those who wonder whether business use will change the Internet, the answer is that it already has. The majority of the Internet's component networks are now open to commercial traffic. Business needs are reflected in the patterns of use, the development of new resources, the growth of security and privacy services, and the increasing number of publications and services geared to the commercial sector. The ability to pay for services means that the business Internet community will have a greater influence on shaping those services to meet their needs, but it does not necessarily follow that this will be negative for the rest of the global community. Business use of the Internet is not incompatible with research, education, or community-based applications. In fact, the tools and interfaces required by business will be an asset to all network users. Peter Deutsch of Bunyip Information Systems (and Archie fame) speculated in an Internet discussion group that the growth of commercial providers and increased nonacademic use of the network would lead to improved information systems. "It's my firm belief that we'll be better served by allowing commercial entities to compete in an open market to provide users with information services across the Internet," he writes. "I believe the U.S. has been well served by the growth of a commercial connectivity market over the past few years and am glad to see this trend starting up elsewhere. Information services seems the next obvious growth area in sight."

Change will also be driven by the convergence of telecommunications and electronic networking on both a technical and corporate level. New business partnerships are emerging to invest aggressively in the information highway, and the cycle between experimental technology and production-level services is growing shorter. Richard Mandelbaum, director of the Center for Advanced Technology in Telecommunications at Polytechnic University in Brooklyn and president of NYSERNet, notes that the cycle for new generations of telecommunications technology has shrunk to just about one year. In this environment, the research component of the Internet has an important role as a test bed for cutting-edge technology, while business and educational users will work to perfect navigational tools and resources with popular appeal.

Mandelbaum believes that, "the short-term challenge is to get more information providers, full text, and multimedia on the network. As the large corporate players get more involved and users begin to demand better interfaces this is already beginning." In the future, he expects to see more for-profit ventures devising tools for the Internet, "so you won't have to be a guru to navigate it. At the same time, the wheel is turning in terms of government support to re-emphasize the research function of a new 'high performance' Internet, while the regular users get absorbed into the National Information Infrastructure. The process of absorbing research advances into common network use can and should happen over and over again as the Internet evolves."

As the network continues to grow, incorporate new technical developments, and evolve to meet the needs of its users, it may come to look very different from the Internet we know today. During the past several years, the research-oriented segment of the Internet supported by the National Science Foundation to connect the higher education and research community to supercomputer resources has evolved to include a number of new commercial service providers maintaining their own network backbones, a surge of participation by community Free-nets, a growth spurt of educational networks geared to kindergarten through high school, and inexpensive Internet access routes for individual users. Now more than ever, it is impossible to speak of *the* Internet as a single, homogeneous entity. In the immediate future, it seems likely that some of the network's newly identifiable constituent parts will focus on establishing the network support structures, services, and resources most important for them, while government funding will be channeled back to advanced research efforts. This cycle of growth, expansion, and specialization may become a characteristic pattern of future Internet development. But no matter what its future incarnations may be labeled, yes, there will always be an Internet.

MOST WANTED LIST

For many business users, the first three items on a list of "most wanted" network enhancements might well be security, security, and security. Striking the best balance between protecting corporate data and connecting to the world is still one of the greatest challenges posed by the Internet. It may never be possible (or desirable) to chose one solution and then forget about security issues on the network. But solutions are being devised, tested, and implemented at an increasing rate. The largest corporations, with names that make tempting targets for would-be intruders, have a stake in developing state-of-the-art Internet security systems, and many commercial service providers now offer a range of security options as part of the connection package.

On the positive side, the need to pay attention to security on the Internet has spurred many companies to improve the overall design and security of their own internal networks. In fact, as network consultant and writer John Quarterman observes, at least some of the business concern with security on the Internet is based on a lack of familiarity with the details of network operation and a tendency by the press to highlight security problems because they make news. In many cases, he believes that "companies tend to devote more attention to security on the Internet than to other parts of their communication systems which may be even more vulnerable to break-in. The same businesses that insist on secure Internet gateways may have set up dial-in modems and internal network accounts with little or no password protection, so in fact they are not consistent in addressing security issues."

Like other network experts, Quarterman expects the increase of business users on the Internet will ultimately lead to better solutions for security. Even now, he feels the advantages of an Internet connection far outweigh the potential for security problems.

Next on the corporate want-list comes a nonintrusive, standardized method to ensure the privacy of network transmissions and authentication of mail messages. Until privacy and authentication become widespread, most businesses will be reluctant to conduct certain types of transactions over the network, including financial reports, and charging and paying for services. As with security, different types of solutions do exist, and are available from service providers as well as in the public domain. Cliff Neuman is a scientist at the Information Sciences Institute at the University of Southern California who works on a variety of network research projects. He is convinced that privacy, authentication, and security are issues that will be addressed successfully on the Internet. He points out that the demand for business-level solutions is a fairly recent development that requires a different approach from university-based networks. "A lot of people are working now on developing the infrastructure for different uses of the Internet," he says. "Within the next two years there will be a number of viable commercial products."

Businesses are still looking for Internet directory services that are comprehensive, easy to use, and up-to-date. The services at InterNIC are a beginning, but the chances of finding any individual's e-mail address quickly and easily are still slim. Les Shroyer, vice president and chief information officer at Motorola, sees the need for more directory and navigation tools to open up the power of the network to those outside the world of high technology. But right now, he observes, "It's a little bit like having an international telephone system where most people have unlisted numbers. These challenges have to be addressed before the Internet will be accessible to the average user." To Shroyer, the Internet is a very powerful indicator of what can be accomplished through networking, but he believes there is still more to be done. "Now it only works for those with the expertise to use it. We have to extend its benefits to the other people; navigation is the most important next step to make that happen."

Multimedia applications on the Internet will open the doors for many new commercial services, and multimedia demonstration projects are popping up on the horizon with increasing frequency. Transmission of voice and video over the network is already technically possible, and has been incorporated into some of the products mentioned in earlier chapters. Widespread use of multimedia will put more demands on the network infrastructure, and companies will need higher-speed connections to deliver voice and video effectively.

Today's Internet navigational tools are a good beginning, but corporate users require more graphical, easy-to-understand connections to the network and an even more transparent link to resources. The one, integrated tool that does it all is still an elusive goal. At the same time, regular users recognize that improvements are needed in the organization and verification of resources on the network. Given the highly distributed and often volunteer nature of networked information, distinguishing the true gems from yesterday's outdated files still takes the skills of an information professional.

Most of these and other developments on the business "most wanted" list are already on the agenda of Internet working groups. New network standards for privacy enhanced mail, multimedia, and simplified naming systems are now available, and more developments are in the wings. Network service providers are expanding their security offerings. A number of options for accepting credit card payments and invoicing over the Internet have already been implemented. Solutions are evolving, and even though they may not be perfect, the climate for business on the Internet is more favorable than ever before.

WHAT NEXT?

Other, more controversial issues about the future direction of the network are unlikely to be resolved so easily. Millions of homes and thousands of businesses in the United States have yet to be connected to the electronic highway. New information services, and mechanisms for pricing them, have yet to be designed. Cable companies and the telecommunications industry are both contending for dominance of this expanding market, and the outcome is still uncertain. In a major step for the cable industry, Continental Cablevision announced an agreement with PSI network services in August 1993 to offer Internet access via cable to Continental customers. The same week, AT&T was reportedly "holding talks with the nation's biggest cable-television companies about linking their customers into one big interactive multimedia network" (Cook 1993). New contenders for a leadership role in national networking are also beginning to appear. The latest entrant, according to the *New York Times*, is the electric power company. An experiment in Arkansas that links utility customers to a computer and telecommunications network promises to reduce energy consumption *and* provide households with a state-of-the-art interactive network (Rivkin 1993).

The release of a vision statement entitled *National Information Infrastructure: Agenda for Action* by the White House in fall 1993 reaffirmed the Clinton administration's commitment to building a national information highway. This document calls for communications legislation to "increase competition in communications markets by explicitly promoting private sector infrastructure investments—both by companies already in the market and those seeking entry" (Department of Commerce 1993). However, the statement leaves major policy questions regarding the respective roles of telecommunications and cable companies unanswered (Andrews 1993, Pearl 1993). The debates about federal policy, and the investment of all players in the communications sector, seems set to continue for the next year, since the *Agenda for Action* projects a legislative initiative on the information highway by the end of 1994.

Corporate interest in the growth and development of a national network infrastructure, and in the Internet, has never been stronger. In September 1993, for the first time ever, feature coverage of the Internet reached the front page of the *Wall Street Journal*, with a discussion about the impact of commercial users on the "soul of the Internet" (Stecklow 1993). In the same month, *InfoWorld* editorialized that "Internet must go commer-

cial—and do it right," espousing a controversial position of
billing customers for Internet access by measuring their usage
(Metcalfe 1993). Other analysts predict that new technology
will soon render current approaches to networking obsolete, and
dramatically reduce the costs of connecting to the information
highway (Gilder 1992).

The Internet has become a common ground for debating and
shaping the role of technology in our collective future. As
technology moves toward new combinations of network, cable,
and telephone systems, there will be even more connectivity and
ownership options to debate in the years to come. While there
may never be complete agreement on questions of private versus
public interests on the network, if the Internet can keep all sides
of an issue talking in the same global room, there is some reason
for optimism about shaping the electronic highway in ways that
will benefit everyone.

In the meantime, it does not require a crystal ball to predict
that business use of the Internet will expand significantly over
the next few years. As the resources for commercial transactions
become increasingly sophisticated and reliable, more and more
companies are making the connection between competitive
advantage and Internet access. The electronic highway is not
merely open for business; it is relocating, restructuring, and
literally redefining business in America.

REFERENCES

Andrews, Edmund L. 1993. Policy blueprint ready for data
superhighway. *The New York Times.* D7. September 15.
Cook, Gordon. 1993. Cable tv or the telcos? Who will build
and control the national information infrastructure? *The
Cook Report on Internet—NREN* 2(5):1–13.
Gilder, George. 1992. Into the fibersphere. *Forbes ASAP* no vol.
December 7, 1992.

Halal, William E. 1993. The information technology revolution: Computer hardware, software, and services into the 21st century. *Technological Forecasting and Social Change* 44(1):69–86.

Metcalfe, Bob. 1993. Internet must go commercial—and do it right. *InfoWorld*(15)36:52.

National Telecommunications and Information Administration (NTIA). 1993. *The National Information Infrastructure: Agenda for Action.* Washington, D.C.: Department of Commerce.

Pearl, Daniel. 1993. White House is backing superhighways for data but says it needs more time. *The Wall Street Journal* B11. September 16.

Rivkin, Steven R. 1993. Look who's wiring the home now. *The New York Times Magazine* 46–47. September 26.

Stecklow, Steve. 1993. Computer users battle high-tech marketers over soul of Internet. *The Wall Street Journal.* 1, A15. September 23.

APPENDIX *A*

Selected Internet Publications

BOOKS

Dern, Daniel P. 1993. *The New User's Guide to the Internet.* New York: McGraw- Hill.

Kehoe, Brendan P. 1992. *Zen and the Art of the Internet: A Beginners Guide.* Engelwood Cliffs, N.J.: Prentice Hall.

Krol, Ed. 1992. *The Whole Internet:User's Guide and Catalog.* Sebastopol, Calif.: O'Reilly and Associates, Inc.

Lane, Elizabeth S., and Craig A. Summerhill. 1992. *An Internet Primer for Information Professionals: A Basic Guide to Networking Technology.* Westport, Conn.: Meckler.

LaQuey, Tracy, and Jeanne C. Rose. 1992. *The Internet Companion: A Beginner's Guide to Global Networking. Reading,* Mass.: Addison-Wesley.

Lynch, Daniel C., and Marshall T. Rose. 1993. *Internet System Handbook.* Greenwich, Conn.: Manning Publications Co.

Malamud, Carl. 1992. *Exploring the Internet: A Technical Travelogue.* Englewood Cliffs, N. J.: Prentice Hall.

Marine, April ed. 1992. *Internet: Getting Started.* Englewood Cliffs, N. J.: Prentice Hall.

Strangelove, Michael, and Diane Kovacs. 1993. *Directory of Electronic Journals, Newsletters and Academic Discussion Lists.* Washington, D.C.: Association of Research Libraries, Office of Scientific and Academic Publishing.

Tennant, Roy, John Ober, and Anne G. Lipow. 1993. *Crossing the Internet Threshold: An Instructional Handbook.* 1993. Berkeley, Calif.: Library Solutions Institute and Press.

Veljkov, Mark, and George Hartnell. 1993. *Pocket Guides to the Internet.* Westport, Conn.: Meckler

Vol. 1: *Telneting;* V. 2: *Transferring Files with File Transfer Protocol;* Vol. 3: *Using and Navigating News Nets;* Vol. 4: *The Internet E-Mail System;* Vol. 5: *Accessing Internet Front Ends and General Utilities;* Vol. 6: *Physical Connections.*

PERIODICALS

The Cook Report on Internet—NREN. Cook Network Consultants: Ewing, N.J. cook@path.net.

The Internet Business Journal. Strangelove Press: Ottawa, Ontario, Canada K1M- 1C7. 72302.3062@CompuServe.Com.

Internet Business Report. CMP Publications: Manhasset, N.Y. locke@cmp.com

The Internet Letter. NetWeek: Washington, D.C. 20045. helen@access.digex.com.

Internet World. Meckler: Westport, Conn. 06880. meckler@jvnc.net.

INTERNET REQUEST FOR COMMENTS (RFCS)

This series of documents produced by the Internet Engineering Task Force ranges from technical standards to basic network information and Frequently Asked Questions (FAQ) for new or advanced users. RFCs are recommended reading for any Internet site. There are several ways to obtain copies; access through the InterNIC is explained here.

The following section is adapted from the document '/infosource/internet-info-for-everybody/rfc/paper-rfc,' updated July 23, 1993. It is reproduced with permission from InterNIC Information Services.

Paper Copies of the RFCs

InterNIC Information Services will provide hard copies of any of the more than 1,300 Request for Comment (RFC) documents produced by the Internet Engineering Task Force (IETF). An index to the RFCs is available in the InfoSource. In addition, an overview of the more commonly referred to RFCs is available in the document "Internet Technology Handbook," also available in this directory.

To request an RFC in hard copy format, send mail to info@internic.net or call the referral desk at (800)444-4345. For faster service, know the number of the RFC you are requesting.

On-line Copies of RFCs

RFCs may be obtained from DS.INTERNIC.NET, InterNIC Directory and Database Services, via FTP, WAIS, and electronic mail. Through FTP, RFCs are stored as rfc/rfcnnnn.txt or rfc/rfcnnnn.ps, where 'nnnn' is the RFC number. Log-in as "anonymous" and provide your e-mail address as the password. Through WAIS, you may use either your local WAIS client or telnet to DS.INTERNIC.NET and log-in as "wais" (no password required) to access a WAIS client. Help information and a tutorial for using WAIS are available on-line. The WAIS database to search is "rfcs."

Directory and Database Services also provides a mail server interface. Send a mail message to mailserv@ds.internic.net and include any of the following commands in the message body:

- document-by-name rfcnnnn

  where 'nnnn' is the RFC number The text version is sent.

- file/ftp/rfc/rfcnnn.yyy

  where 'nnn' is the RFC number. and 'yyy' is 'txt' or 'ps'.

- help

  to get information on how to use the mailserver

The InterNIC Directory and Database Services collection of resource listings, Internet documents such as RFCs, FYIs, STDs, and Internet Drafts, and Publicly Accessible Databases are also now available via Gopher. All collections are wais indexed and can be searched from the Gopher menu.

To access the InterNIC Gopher Servers, please connect to "internic.net" port 70. Contact: admin@ds.internic.net.

APPENDIX *B*

How To Contact
The InterNIC

The InterNIC is a collaborative project of three organizations and is partially supported by the National Science Foundation. The three organizations and the services they provide are: General Atomics, Information Services; AT&T, Directory and Database Services; and Network Solutions Inc., Registration Services. Information about all three InterNIC services is available through its toll-free hot line (800-444-4345) and its Gopher service, which both branch to all three organizations. You may also contact each of the organizations as described below.

For general questions about any of the services provided, call the hot line. If you have a touch-tone telephone, you will be able to connect to the provider of your choice.

The InterNIC also has several direct telephone lines and fax numbers:

- Information Services: (619)455-4600;
  Fax   (619)455-4640.

- Registration Services: (703)742-4777;
  Fax   (703)742-4811.

- Directory Services: (800)862-0677 or
                          (908)668-6587;
  Fax   (908)668-3763.

ELECTRONIC MAILING LISTS

You can send your questions via e-mail to the following addresses:

- Information Services: info@internic.net

- Registration Services: postmaster@rs.internic.net

- Directory Services: admin@ds.internic.net

To subscribe to any of the following e-mail lists, send e-mail to: listserv@internic.net and in the body of the message, type: subscribe listname firstname lastname.

In your message, substitute the actual mailing list name for *listname* and your first and last names for *firstname* and *lastname*, respectively:.

- net-resources: Internet resources

- net-happenings: Internet news (5–10/day)

- nics: Info for NIC personnel

To subscribe to the InterNIC newsletter, NSF Network News, send e-mail to: newsletter-request@internic.net.

ON-LINE SERVICES

Each provider runs several servers to provide access to on-line documents, directories, and databases. You can search, view, or retrieve information using the following tools:

Gopher. The on-line documents of all three organizations are available through Gopher. Use the command: gopher gopher.internic.net, or telnet gopher.internic.net, login: gopher.

FTP. Connecting to these addresses gives access to individual document databases. Log-in as anonymous, and follow the instructions on your screen:

- information services: is.internic.net

- registration services: rs.internic.net

- directory services: ds.internic.net

E-mail. Documents can be retrieved via e-mail by sending commands to our mail servers. To learn how to use the mail servers, send a message as follows:

- information services: mailserv@is.internic.net.
  Put "send help" in message body.

- registration services: mailserv@rs.internic.net.
  Put "send help" in subject field.

- directory services: mailserv@ds.internic.net.
  Put "help" in message body.

WAIS

- information services: source name, internic-infosource;
  server name, is.internic.net.

- registration services: telnet rs.internic.net, log-in: wais.

- directory services: telnet ds.internic.net, log-in: wais.

Telnet. By telnetting to the following addresses, you can access a variety of services, depending on how you log in.

- information services: is.internic.net; log-in as gopher.

- registration services: rs.internic.net; log-in as gopher, wais, whois, x500, whois, or status.

- directory services: ds.internic.net; log-in as archie, gopher, netfind, wais, or x500 for application-specific access. Login as newuser or guest for a help tutorial.

Archie. Use any Archie client to make searches, or use the InterNIC client: telnet ds.internic.net.

Log-in as archie.

Or send an e-mail request to: archie@ds.internic.net

WHOIS Protocol

- registration services: rs.internic.net, Provides access to network and domain Point of Contact (POC) records.

- directory services: ds.internic.net, Provides access to POC, non- POC, and military contact records stored on ds.internic.net, rs.internic.net, and nic.ddn.mil.

Send your suggestions or complaints about InterNIC services to: suggestions@internic.net, or complaint@internic.net.

U.S. POSTAL ADDRESSES

InterNIC Information Services
General Atomics
P.O. Box 85608
San Diego, CA 92186-9784

Network Solutions
Attn: InterNIC Registration Services
505 Huntmar Park Drive
Herndon, VA 22070

InterNIC Directory and Database Administrator
AT&T
5000 Hadley Road; Room 1B13
South Plainfield, NJ 07080

The InterNic project is sponsored by the National Science Foundation under Cooperative Agreement No. NCR-9218749. Reproduced with permission from InterNIC Information Services.

APPENDIX *C*

North American Internet Access Provider List

Network	Service Area	Contact Name	Phone Number
* Alternet alternet-info@uunet.uu.net	US & International	UUNET	(800)4UUNET3
ANS info@ans.net	US & International	Joel Maloff	(313)663-7610
*+BARRNet info@nic.barrnet.net	Northern/Central California	Paul Baer	(415)723-7520
* CERFnet help@cerf.net	Western US & International		(800)876-2373 (619)455-3900
+ CICnet hankins@cic.net	Midwest US: MN-WI-IA-IN-IL-MI -OH	John Hankins	(313)998-6102
CO Supernet kharmon@csn.org	Colorado	Ken Harmon	(303)273-3471
CONCERT jrr@concert.net	North Carolina	Joe Ragland	(919)248-1404

Network	Service Area	Contact Name	Phone Number
INet ellis@ucs.indiana,edu	Indiana	Dick Ellis	(812)855-4240
* JVNCnet market@jvnc.net	US & International	Sergio Heker Allison Pihl	(800)35TIGER
Los Nettos los-nettos-request@isi.edu	Los Angeles Area	Ann Westine Cooper	(310)822-1511
MichNet/ Merit jogden@merit.edu	Michigan	Jeff Ogden	(313)764-9430
+ MIDnet dmf@westie.unl.edu	Mid US: NE-OK- AR-MO-IA-KS-SD	Dale Finkelson	(402)472-5032
MRnet dfazio@mr.net	Minnesota	Dennis Fazio	(612)342-2570
MSEN info@msen.com	Michigan	Owen Medd	(313)998-4562
*+NEARnet nearnet-join@nic.near.net	Northeastern US	John Curran	(617)873-8730
NETCOM des@netcom.com	California	Desirree Madison-Biggs	(408)-554-8649
netILLINOIS joel@bradley.bradley.edu	Illinois	Joel L. Hartman	(309)677-3100
NevadaNET zitter@nevada.edu	Nevada	Don Zitter	(702)784-6133
*+Northwest Net ehood@nwnet.net	Northwestern US	Eric Hood	(206)562-3000

Network	Service Area	Contact Name	Phone Number
+NYSERnet info@nysernet.org	New York	Jim Luckett	(315)443-4120
OARnet alison@oar.net	Ohio	Alison Brown	(614)292-8100
PACCOM torben@hawaii.edu	Hawaii,Australia, Japan,Korea , New Zealand,Hong Kong	Torben Nielsen	(808)956-3499
PREPnet twb+@andrew.cmu.edu	Pennsylvania	Thomas Bajzek	(412)268-7870
PSCNET pscnet-admin@psc.edu	Eastern US: PA-OH-WV	Eugene Hastings	(412)268-4960
*PSINet info@psi.com (703)620-6651	US & International	PSI, Inc.	(800)82PSI82
SDSCnet loveep@sds.sdsc.edu	San Diego Area	Paul Love	(619)534-5043
Sesquinet farrell@rice.edu	Texas	Farrell Gerbode	(713)527-4988
*SprintLink bdoyle@icm1.icp.net	US & International	Bob Doyle	(703)904-2230
+SURAnet marketing@sura.net	Southeastern US:	Deborah J. Nunn	(301)982-4600
*THEnet green@utexas.edu	Texas	William Green	(512)471-3241
VERnet jaj@virginia.edu	Virginia	James Jokl	(804)924-0616

Network	Service Area	Contact Name	Phone Number
Westnet	Western US: pburns@yuma.acns.colostate.edu	Pat Burns	(303)491-7260
WiscNet	Wisconsin tad@cs.wisc.edu	Tad Pinkerton	(608)262-8874
*World dot Net	Pacific NW: OR-WA-ID info@world.net	Internetworks,Inc.	(206)576-7147
WVNET	West Virginia cc011041@wvnvms.wvnet.edu	Harper Grimm	(304)293-5192

*CIX (Commercial Internet Exchange) Member

+COREN (Corporations for Regional and Enterprise Networking) Member

This section is from the document '/infosource/about-information-services/'background,updated 7/23/93 and reproduced with permission from InterNIC Information Services.

Index